The Creative

Jewish Wedding Book

is written for you if—

- You are knowledgeable about Jewish wedding traditions but are seeking ways to make your wedding more personal;
- You are just learning about Jewish wedding traditions and want to use your creative talents in designing your wedding;
- You and your partner are both Jewish but have different opinions about Jewish ritual and are seeking ways to honor creatively each other's beliefs;
- You are new to Judaism and want to have a meaningful Jewish wedding;
- You are Jewish, but your partner comes from a non-Jewish background, and you both want to create a meaningful Jewish wedding;
- You are not Jewish, but you want to learn about Judaism and creative approaches to Jewish wedding customs;
- You and your partner are gay or lesbian and want to learn about options for creative Jewish commitment ceremonies or weddings;
- You are Jewish, have been married before, and want to create a wedding that honors the blending of both your families;
- You are Jewish but also find spiritual resonance in Buddhist, Native American, or other traditions and want to incorporate them into your wedding;
- You are the mother, father, sibling, friend, cousin, or other relative of someone who is getting married, and you want to be able to help the couple create some of the rituals and ritual objects that will be used in their wedding;
- You are a rabbi, cantor, or Jewish teacher seeking creative ways to enhance the wedding ritual.

The Creative Jewish Wedding Book, 2nd Edition:
A Hands-On Guide to New & Old Traditions, Ceremonies & Celebrations

2009 Quality Paperback Second Edition, First Printing
2004 Quality Paperback First Edition, First Printing
© 2004 and 2009 Gabrielle Kaplan-Mayer

For information regarding permission to reprint material from this book, please mail or fax your request in writing to Jewish Lights Publishing, Permissions Department, at the address / fax number listed below, or send an e-mail to permissions@jewishlights.com.

Library of Congress Cataloging-in-Publication Data
Kaplan-Mayer, Gabrielle, 1971–
The creative Jewish wedding book : a hands-on guide to new & old traditions, ceremonies & celebrations / by Gabrielle Kaplan-Mayer.
p. cm.
Includes index.
ISBN-13: 978-1-58023-194-7 (quality pbk.)
ISBN-10: 1-58023-194-2 (quality pbk.)
1. Marriage customs and rites, Jewish. 2. Marriage—Religious aspects—Judaism. I. Title: Hands-on guide to new and old traditions, ceremonies and celebrations. II. Title.
BM713.K36 2004
296.4'44—dc22   2004004589

Second Edition

ISBN-13: 978-1-58023-398-9
ISBN-10: 1-58023-398-8

Grateful acknowledgment is given to the following sources for permission to use material: portions of *Engendering Judaism: An Inclusive Theology and Ethics* by Rachel Adler. Reprinted from *Engendering Judaism*, © 1998, by Rachel Adler, The Jewish Publication Society with the permission of the publisher, The Jewish Publication Society. Gender-neutral *ketubah* text, © 1996, by Betsy Platkin Teutsch. Used by permission. Humanistic *ketubah* text, © 2000, by the Association for Humanistic Rabbis and the Leadership Conference of Secular Humanistic Jews. Used by permission. Interfaith *ketubah* text, A Good Company, © 1993. Used by permission. *Contemporary Birkat Hamazon*, © 1987, by Rabbi Shefa Gold (www.rabbishefagold.com). Used by permission. *Contemporary Sheva Brachot* by Rabbi Marcia Prager, © Marcia Prager. Used by permission. *Contemporary Sheva Brachot* by Arthur Ocean Waskow and Phyllis Ocean Berman. Used by permission.

Pages 260–261 constitute a continuation of this copyright page.

Cover design: Stacey Hood

10   9   8   7   6   5   4   3   2   1

Manufactured in Canada

Published by Jewish Lights Publishing
A Division of LongHill Partners, Inc.
Sunset Farm Offices, Route 4, P.O. Box 237
Woodstock, VT 05091
Tel: (802) 457-4000 Fax: (802) 457-4004
www.jewishlights.com

THE CREATIVE

Jewish Wedding Book

2nd Edition

A Hands-On Guide to New & Old
Traditions, Ceremonies & Celebrations

GABRIELLE KAPLAN-MAYER

FOREWORD BY RABBI KERRY M. OLITZKY

PREFACE BY RABBI SUE LEVI ELWELL

JEWISH LIGHTS Publishing

Woodstock, Vermont

For Fred,
my beloved companion
and partner in crime.
With gratitude to the Divine Presence
who brought us together, sustains us,
and allows us to grow each day in love,
friendship, and understanding.

Contents

2 Hear Ye, Hear Ye: Setting the Stage with Unique Invitations 41

3 Let's Make A Deal: Crafting Your *Ketubah* 59

4 *Chuppah* Hooplah: Creative Possibilities for Your Wedding Canopy 93

Foreword

Some couples make their relationship look easy, but the best marriages require hard work. These are the relationships to emulate. Love is not something that should ever be taken for granted; it constantly has to be nurtured and expressed. When I work with couples who are anticipating marriage, I remind them that while most partnerships are a fifty/fifty arrangement with lots of give and take, marriage demands that each partner be prepared to give much more than he or she expects to receive in return. It is in that giving of love, in placing the needs of one's partner—rather than one's own needs—in the forefront, that a person receives the gifts of a marriage in return.

Marriage is a sacred trust held by two people as they together navigate their individual lives and mold them into a shared life shaped by the celebrations and pleasures, as well as bumps and bruises, that are part of every marriage. At its best, a marriage reflects the covenant established between the individual and God many years ago at Sinai, what the philosopher Martin Buber idealized as the "I-Thou" relationship. As a result, it can be said that marriage is divine in origin and that God plays a distinctive role in the relationship between two partners. In its most physical enactment, one loses the self in the other, if only momentarily, as a way of approximating the mystical notion that these two souls were once equal parts of the same soul separated at birth into two individuals. Through the marital relationship, these souls recombine to become two halves of one whole.

Such sentiments and more come together in the myriad rituals and symbols known best as the Jewish wedding ceremony. While the ceremony may differ somewhat even in the traditional Jewish community depending on the background of the participants (this is especially true between Ashkenazim and Sephardim), what really makes the ceremony all the more challenging—whether for the officiant or the couple getting married—is that all these competing and complementary ideas are collapsed into a ritual that is only twenty to thirty minutes long.

In order to construct a ceremony that would be the pivotal event in the life of any couple, the Rabbis determined that the wedding ceremony should be more than an acknowledgment of marriage as the physical joining together of two individuals. They took an inchoate group of customs from folk religion, customs that people were reluctant to give up, and elevated these elemental practices to a sacred level, leaving much—but not all—of their superstitious explanations behind. The challenge now, as is evidenced in the numerous options included in this volume, is to take the meaningful aspects of contemporary culture and weave them into the sacred tapestry of a wedding ceremony, one that reflects all the values that we hold precious today.

It is not an easy task, creating a wedding ceremony, but one that is made much simpler by the helpful chapters and gentle guidance of the author of this book. Regardless of your ethnic background, the level of your religious education, or the structure of your partnership, this book provides you with easy access to the riches of Jewish tradition and guides you in the process of selecting in or out of those elements that will deepen and enrich the ceremony for both partners and their families. It also indicates which parts of the ceremony are indispensable or expected by those who may come from a specific place on the Jewish religious spectrum.

Just as the classic wedding ceremony has evolved with its specific formulas of blessings and the step-by-step procedures developed throughout many generations, your ceremony should encapsulate your evolution as a couple and contain the deep-seated dreams and desires that you have for each other and for your future together. Woven into the ceremony as well may be values from the past that you have claimed as your own, that contributed to who you have become, as well as seeds that you want to plant for the future.

As you plan your wedding and strive to understand the various aspects of the ceremony and the ideas they represent, you may also want to creatively share such explanations with the guests attending the ceremony. In doing so, you will be teaching all those who have gathered to witness your commitment to your partner a great deal about the life you will be leading together. While the ceremony should focus on your consecration as a couple through your public promise to each other and emphasize your separation from other individuals as you become a couple, it should also be as encompassing as possible so that everyone in attendance can be included in the celebration. The wedding ceremony provides you with an opportunity to lower barriers and welcome your guests into your new life together. This is especially beneficial for couples whose backgrounds differ from each other, and when there have been hurdles to overcome in relationships with others, especially family members, along the road to the wedding canopy.

There will be plenty of people offering their opinions as you plan your wedding. Some will share their experiences from their own weddings. Others will tell you what "has to be included in a Jewish ceremony." And parents from both sides will want to see the dreams that they have carried with them of their child's wedding realized in the ceremony. As difficult as it might be at times, the important thing to remember is that it is your wedding, and you can create the ceremony and reception that is right for you and your partner. Your wedding is the opportunity to say to all those gathered what you want everyone to know about your love and your life together as a couple.

Rabbi Kerry M. Olitzky, Executive Director, Jewish Outreach Institute
coeditor, *The Rituals & Practices of a Jewish Life:
A Handbook for Personal Spiritual Renewal*

Preface

More than thirty years ago, as a graduate student in Jewish history, I wrote a paper on the wedding customs of Eastern European Jews. My discoveries led to my decision to create a *tallit* (prayer shawl) for my beloved, and I chose a rainbow of ribbons to distinguish my gift. At the end of the semester, we tied the *tzitzit* (fringes) of the *tallit* to four poles and I stood under the *chuppah* for the first time.

I have stood under the *chuppah* many times since then, under delicate lace tablecloths, blankets of flowers and vines, and beautifully crafted quilts with every square an individually sewn gift for the wedding couple. As a rabbi, I have been privileged to share the sacred space of *kiddushin* (betrothal) with many men and women, a rich range of combinations of ages, life stages, and genders. In the months before each wedding, I have worked with each couple to discover how we can, together, create a ritual of integrity, a ceremony that would truly reflect the values, commitments, and aspirations of two individuals who are becoming a family.

When, five years ago, I once again planned a wedding of my own, I realized how enriched I have been by the wedding journeys of the couples with whom I have worked over the years. Many of the wedding decisions that my partner Nurit and I made were informed by the experiences and innovations of others.

Over the years, I have recommended a variety of resources to the couples with whom I have worked as a complement to the work we do together. I am always delighted when couples have deepened their wedding preparation by taking on the responsibility of co-creating various aspects of the wedding experience.

This guide brings together a range of insights, reflections, and suggestions that will enable you to fashion a wedding that can incorporate and honor tradition while reflecting your own unique commitments and concerns. Gabrielle Kaplan-Mayer's insights and research will serve you as my professional experiences served me while I planned my own wedding. This book is an excellent companion to the work that you will do with your rabbi to prepare for a meaningful and expressive wedding. Kaplan-Mayer writes with sensitivity about the rich range of families in which we live: families of origin, of choice, and of chance. She supplements her own creative suggestions with the experiences of a range of other couples, expanding and extending a conversation she welcomes you to join.

May your wedding journey be enriched and deepened by following the lead of this innovative guide. And may the intentionality that you bring to your wedding be a sign of the clarity and commitment that will bless your days and years together as your partnership extends into a future of love and service.

To partnerships of creativity and mutuality, and weddings of joy!

Rabbi Sue Levi Elwell,
director, Pennsylvania Council
Union for Reform Judaism

A Special Note to the Second Edition

I began writing *The Creative Jewish Wedding Book* the year after I got married. Planning our wedding had been an important part of my life in the year leading up to it and I wanted to capture both the practical details and also the spiritual growth that I had discovered while being engaged and planning our unique celebration with my husband, Fred. Now it is with great delight that I am revisiting my work to update *The Creative Jewish Wedding Book* for the new edition, with new resources, tips and ideas for couples planning a Jewish wedding. I have now been married for seven years. I have had the joyful experience of growing to know Fred even better, through good times and quite challenging times, and to truly appreciate and love him more each day. We have two beautiful children now, George, age 5 and June, age 3. Looking back, I am grateful that Fred and I spent our engagement not only thinking about how to create a beautiful wedding day but also how to use the process of planning our wedding to create a strong foundation for our marriage.

It has been especially enjoyable for me to see friends, relatives and congregants from Mishkan Shalom in Philadelphia, Pennsylvania, where I work, use *The Creative Jewish Wedding Book* and share how the book has influenced their wedding planning. These couples are quite diverse in their Jewish background, practice, and observance—from couples who belong to a synagogue and worship regularly to couples who are finding their way back to their Jewish roots through planning their wedding. A few years ago I heard from an old, dear friend from college whom I had been out of touch with for over ten years when she picked up a copy of *The Creative Jewish Wedding Book* to plan a commitment ceremony with her partner. She impressed upon me how much it meant to her to have a Jewish wedding book that was fully inclusive of gay and lesbian couples and I was so happy that she had found her way to my book (and reconnected with me).

One of the special couples that I've had the blessing to work with recently is my brother Jon Kaplan and his wonderful wife, Stephanie Martin. Jon and Steph were married in a gorgeous, unique ceremony in the outdoor sculpture garden of the Museum of Visionary Art in Baltimore, Maryland. Steph is not Jewish but both Jon and Steph were committed to having a Jewish ceremony, while also honoring Steph's family. One of the ideas that they adapted from *The Creative Jewish Wedding Book* was to create a *chuppah* made with heirloom fabric from Steph's family. They used a beautiful white tablecloth that Steph's grandmother had made years ago as their canopy. Standing under their *chuppah* as one of the four *chuppah* holders, I experienced the depth, commitment, and beauty of their relationship come through in the creative ceremony and celebration that they brought to life together.

I still write about weddings for a variety of web sites and publications. One of the really awesome trends that I have been following is the move toward "green" weddings. Many couples who are conscious of living in a way that promotes sustainability want to bring their eco-awareness to their wedding celebrations. Fortunately, there are many ways to make this possible—from choosing wedding dresses made of organic fabric to using locally grown, organic food for your celebration. In the first edition of *The Creative Jewish Wedding Book*, I wrote about eco-*kashrut* and how couples could bring eco-*kashrut* principles to their weddings. In this edition, you will find an expanded section about greening your wedding. This information comes at a time when many Jewish communities are turning to the wisdom in Jewish texts about humanity's relationship to the environment and applying it to make homes and synagogues into more sustainable places.

Since *The Creative Jewish Wedding Book* was first published, more states have legalized gay marriages or civil unions. While my book addresses the spiritual side rather than the legal side of gay and lesbian partnerships, this is important news and hopefully shows a trend moving toward the legalization of gay marriage throughout our country.

I would love to hear about how you have used or are using *The Creative Jewish Wedding Book* in your wedding planning. Please feel free to write to me in care of Jewish Lights and share your unique wedding stories. It is my hope that *The Creative Jewish Wedding Book* will be a helpful resource for couples, clergy, and families for years to come.

Gabrielle Kaplan-Mayer

Acknowledgments

I am grateful to so many wonderful people who helped in my efforts to put together *The Creative Jewish Wedding Book*. It is truly a compendium of hours of interviews with some extremely bright, innovative folks experienced in creating magnificent weddings. I am grateful to everyone who gave of his or her time and energy to help me write this book.

In particular, some spiritual leaders have been especially generous in sharing their thoughts with me: Rabbi Marcia Prager, Phyllis Ocean Berman, Rabbi Arthur Waskow, Rabbi David Ackerman, and Rabbi Julie Greenberg. My dear friend Rabbi Shai Gluskin helped my husband Fred and me enter a creative process as we thought about our own wedding, and I am most grateful for his wisdom at that time and his ongoing presence in our life. My friend Rabbi Laurie Zimmerman helped me think about issues of concern to gay and lesbian couples, and I am indebted to her for her valuable insights. Rabbi Sue Levi Elwell was also a great source of support and insight, and I am so appreciative that she wrote the Preface to this book.

My most magnificent friend, Dr. Joellyn Wallen Zollman, encouraged me throughout the research and writing process and gave generously of her time to edit the first draft of my manuscript. Her keen eye, perceptive feedback, sharp wit, and loving guidance helped me enormously in my efforts. Thank you, Jo.

In addition to talking with spiritual leaders, I had great fun meeting so many Judaica artists, all of whom bring their unique talents and abilities to their art. Talking with these artists inspired me to spread the word about their work and the possibility of expanding the realm of creative Jewish expression. To each one of you—thank you.

So many friends, friends of friends, cousins of friends of friends, and so on, took time out of their busy lives to answer an extensive survey about their wedding experience and to follow up with me in meetings, phone calls, or via e-mail to discuss their weddings in great detail. Although I do not write about everyone's experience in the book, all of your insights and wisdom guided me as I wrote, and I am grateful for your sharing.

I want to extend a special thank you to Henry Rasof, whose dedication to my manuscript helped connect me to Jewish Lights Publishing. My deepest thanks goes to Stuart M. Matlins, founder and publisher of Jewish Lights, for understanding my vision and helping me bring this book to life, and to Emily Wichland, managing editor at Jewish Lights, for all her guidance and energy. It has been a true delight to work with you both and the entire staff at Jewish Lights. Also, editor Donna Zerner's critical eye and insightful feedback helped me focus and organize my thoughts and put together the best book possible.

I want to give a special thank you to my darling baby boy, George Chaim, who is 7 months old as I write this now. Georgie had just been born when I received word from Stuart that Jewish Lights would like to publish my book. Baby George came with me on countless interviews with artists, rabbis, and friends; he nestled in his Baby Bjorn carrier as I pored through books. What an angel!

My wonderful parents, Steve and Lynn Kaplan, helped watch George for a week when I finally settled down to start some serious writing. I could not have produced this book without their loving support.

And finally—last but not least—my fantastic husband, Fred Kaplan-Mayer, encouraged me throughout this project and put in countless hours babysitting and doing household chores so that I could write. Fred, you amaze me with the way your love continually expands to meet the new challenges that we face together.

Introduction

Mazel tov! If you've picked up this book, I imagine you've most recently gotten engaged, or are at least seriously thinking about it. My hope is that *The Creative Jewish Wedding Book*, 2nd Edition, will speak to you—two partners planning to join lives in the Jewish tradition. I plan to address "you" in the singular, acknowledging that each one of you, as individuals, brings a unique Jewish background and life experience to the process of creating your wedding. While honoring each partner's individual experience, this book also seeks to deepen your connection as a couple.

Unfortunately, planning a wedding or a commitment ceremony has the potential to be one of the most stressful events of your life. Each of you have your own expectations, along with those of your family and its own dynamics. Throw in party planning, money issues, and the prospect of bringing together everyone who has ever been important to you from the various corners of your life for a few brief, highly intense hours, and it's no wonder that taking the first plane to Vegas looks like the sanest option out there!

Take a deep breath. And one more. *The Creative Jewish Wedding Book*, 2nd Edition, will help you step back, take your time, and visualize the Jewish wedding that you want to create. I have included envisioning exercises, for just that, sprinkled throughout the book. These are also listed in the Contents, if you want to skip ahead. Instead of sending you off the deep end, the process of planning your wedding can actually be a great opportunity for spiritual growth. If you don't consider yourself particularly spiritual, or if you express your spirituality in a way that is not necessarily connected to being Jewish, that's okay. This book is designed to meet you and honor you wherever you are, however you connect to your Jewish heritage.

Perhaps at no other time in history has there ever been so much diversity in the Jewish community in terms of customs of worship, types of rituals, and ways of being Jewish in the world. Planning a wedding is an incredibly rich, creative experience, an opportunity to connect to Jewish heritage and tradition, and this book aims to make that legacy accessible to you in myriad ways. There is no one way to describe a contemporary Jewish couple and no one right way for that couple to create a meaningful wedding. Whether you connect to Judaism through poetry or music, through fighting for the rights of the poor and oppressed, or through experiencing traditional or innovative ritual and prayer, there is a way to design your wedding to express and honor those connections.

What's more, each one of you, as part of a couple, may connect to being Jewish in a unique and different way. You may each come from vastly separate Jewish experiences; this book will take you through processes necessary to connect and better understand each other's backgrounds and perspectives. You will not agree on everything as you create your wedding, and you don't have to. Through the process of planning your wedding, you will be on the path to negotiating ways to establish your mode of being Jewish in your home. And hopefully, you will enter your marriage with a new sense of appreciation for your partner's spiritual expressions and practices.

Creativity as Jewish Spiritual Expression

The Creative Jewish Wedding Book, 2nd Edition, is meant to address every reader, whether you consider yourself to be a creative person or not. Creativity takes many forms, from raw artistic abilities to expressing your unique way of looking at the world. This book addresses those of you with special artistic abilities who are trying to figure out how to use your talents in designing your wedding, as well as those of you who do not consider yourselves especially "artsy" or "craftsy." The ideas in this book may simply help you look at and think about the various parts of your wedding in new or innovative ways. You may get excited about an idea and find someone close to you who can help you carry it off. You may even discover some creative abilities that you didn't know you had. When we talk about being creative, we're referring to bringing your unique self—your insights, ideas, abilities, history, and perspectives—to the process of planning a Jewish wedding. By bringing your whole self to the experience of the wedding ritual, you will participate in it in a most authentic and meaningful way.

Many people think of Judaism as an intellectual culture, and rightly so. Jewish teachers have always placed a great emphasis on literary scholarship: Not only are we the people of the "Book," but we are also the people of many books—*Mishnah* and *Midrash*, Talmud and countless other commentaries. The intellectual contributions of our ancestors are an invaluable legacy.

But look closer. Beyond the pages of the texts is a place for those who thrive on experiential rather than book learning. Throughout our history, creative Jewish expression has always taken on many forms, including the creation of magnificent ritual objects that beautify the *mitzvot* (commandments)—from designing *etrog* containers used in the festival of Sukkot to breastplates adorning the Torah. *Hiddur mitzvah*—literally, "to beautify a *mitzvah*"—is a sacred part of our heritage. A wedding offers countless ways to honor the idea of *hiddur mitzvah* and, in doing so, to stimulate and inspire your creative impulses.

Traditionally, Jewish creativity has not been limited to only literary and ritual art; it has also been expressed in an entire cultural tradition of unique food, music, clothing, language, and customs. Unfortunately, many modern Western Jews know only a watered-down version of Jewish civilization. Jewish food—we think bagels and matzoh balls. Jewish music—"Hava Nagila." Jewish art? Maybe Chagall prints.

There is nothing wrong with these associations and connections, but they are only the beginning of what Jewish culture has to offer. As you plan your wedding, this book will lead you through Jewish culture in a way that may surprise you—from discovering the sophisticated voices of contemporary Jewish poets to hearing the wide-ranging sounds of Jewish world music. Each encounter may touch and deepen your connections to Jewish life and may, in turn, affect the way you want to bring Judaism into your wedding and, ultimately, into your life.

We live in a time of Jewish renewal, when new voices are expressing what it means to be a Jew in the world. There is so much collective creative energy in the Jewish world right now: Just browse through a Judaica shop and look at the many forms and styles that traditional ritual objects have taken on. Take a Passover Seder plate, for example. The different artists who create Seder plates maintain the integrity of the object, making sure that its function remains that of holding the ritual items of food that are part of the Passover Seder. But the form, material, style, and expression of the plate is completely open for interpretation. Some Seder plates are made of translucent glass, others of porcelain or copper. Some are flat plates, others have dimensional attachments. Some look bright and festive, others take on a more somber appearance. This kind of creative Jewish diversity can be translated into your wedding planning.

You have the opportunity and the blessing to incorporate your own unique insights into Jewish wedding rituals and traditions. We are living in a particularly innovative time, when more and more Jews are bringing creativity and meaning to Jewish spiritual practices and traditions. By infusing rituals, blessings, and ceremonies with creative energy, Jews are renewing and enriching religion, rather than accepting it as ossified tradition.

A Word of Warning about the Wedding "Industry"

Pick up a bridal magazine. Interview a wedding photographer. Price a catering venue for a Saturday night in June. Can you smell the scam? Today's high-pressure, multibillion-dollar wedding industry makes it seem as if planning a wedding should be more like staging a Broadway show or a major corporate event than creating a meaningful and memorable celebration. Couples feel that their wedding must have all the elements that their friends, families, and business associates have come to expect. Planning a wedding today is all too often a game of "keeping up with the Joneses or Goldbergs" on a large, expensive scale. Yet where does the perfect champagne toast and precise seating arrangement leave the just-married couple when the confetti has been thrown and the limousine has driven off into the sunset? The divorce statistics in America continue to rise; couples with graduate degrees and promising careers are entering marriage with greater debt loads than ever, and many people in post-9/11 America are still seeking ways to find basic meaning in the rat race myth that we've all been force-fed throughout our lives.

The wedding industry spins its high-priced message for those who buy into it, and my simple message is this: You do not have to buy into it. An authentic Jewish wedding flies in the face of all that is garish and superficial; instead, it emphasizes holiness, sacredness, deep love, and honor. Unfortunately, many couples rush through the ceremonial or "Jewish" part of the wedding because of their discomfort with or lack of knowledge about ritual or tradition. It may be easier to plan a party than to determine what you want your *ketubah* to say. But when you embrace the challenge of creating a Jewish wedding, you take a bold stand against an industry that says the entry to your marriage is about wearing the right dress, serving the fanciest food, and spending as much money as possible on all of it.

This book will help you recognize the ways in which you connect to being Jewish, and it will give you the tools necessary to embrace the Jewish part of your wedding and make it your own. As you become more familiar with the spiritual/ cultural/communal aspect of Judaism, you will become empowered to make choices about your wedding that express your ideals, not those of the wedding spin-doctors. Creativity is a powerful tool in fighting commercialism, and each human being is born with tremendous creative potential. Even if you do not consider yourself particularly imaginative, or you don't spend your leisure time engaged in découpage craft projects, you are probably creative in many ways. Just thinking in an original way sets you on a path of personal expression.

An Opportunity for Transformation

When do Jews turn to their Judaism? Often, it is major life-cycle events—births, weddings, and burials—that bring nonaffiliated Jews back to the synagogue. This should not be surprising: Even the cynic or nonbeliever seeks spiritual comfort and community during these highly charged times.

You may be among the many Jews who feel disconnected from Judaism. Suddenly, you're getting married and the force of tradition, ritual, and prayer is weighing and preying on you. The wedding ceremony demands affirmation from a rabbi and a community. All this religious "stuff" may be calling up feelings of ambivalence or even negativity. You are not alone in that feeling. Many Jewish Americans connect more strongly to the secular than to the religious/cultural aspects of their lives.

You may be new to Judaism, or you may not be Jewish at all, but are seeking to learn more about your partner's religion and background. You may be experiencing a range of emotions connected to the Jewish "piece" of your wedding and may be struggling to come to terms with the role your own religious background plays in your life.

The Creative Jewish Wedding Book, 2nd Edition, offers ways for you to become Jewishly connected during your planning process, which may or may not include Jewish ritual observance. Becoming Jewishly connected—in whatever forms that may take—allows you to enter this life-cycle event with a sense of openness and possibility. When you open your mind and heart to the power of Jewish connection, real spiritual healing and growth can occur. Many couples who were feeling disconnected from the ceremonial aspect of their wedding beforehand have reported that a profound, connected moment occurred under the *chuppah*. These moments not only allowed them to experience a Divine Presence at their wedding but also affected their lives from that time forward.

Jewish wedding customs, traditions, and rituals can evoke a powerful transformation. Something will happen to you when you stand under the *chuppah* before your community. The work that you put into creating the ceremony leading up to that sacred moment will affect the ultimate power of your wedding experience. It will be work—negotiations, debates, struggles. But these negotiations and wrestling, if approached consciously, are healthy for you as a couple and are indeed very Jewish in nature.

It is hard to capture what a moment of ritual transformation feels like: Such moments elude description. In researching this book, I spoke to many couples from across the spectrum of Jewish observance about their wedding experience and its transformative effects on their relationships, their spirituality, their connection to Judaism, and, ultimately, their personal growth. Although the responses were as individual as the couples, all of them felt that they emerged from under the *chuppah* changed in some profound way. Here are a few reflections that I want to share, in hopes that you can imagine yourself someday, like these folks, looking back and remembering positively the power of your Jewish wedding.

Jen and I put a lot of time and energy into planning our wedding . . . not because we wanted it to be some kind of performance—like a perfectly staged event—but because we knew how awesome it would be to have so many people from so many different parts of our life coming together. It might never happen again. We wanted to create an atmosphere that would be welcoming and fun, but also honor how serious we felt about making this commitment to each other. The week before the wedding, we became kind of exhausted . . . and so we just stopped. We stopped worrying about the details and just focused on being present for each other, ourselves, and our guests. We took time at some point each day to meditate together. By the time we came to stand under the *chuppah*, I felt like, "Oh my God, it is really happening. I am marrying the woman of my dreams, and everyone I love is here." I don't think I have ever felt quite "present" in that way before . . . so thankful and alive.
—Jess Cohen

A lot of people actually tried to discourage me from . . . making our *chuppah*, but I felt it was just something I had to do. Hours went into it. I used fabric from my grandmother's wedding gown and my mother-in-law gave me some old scarves and handkerchiefs that belonged to her mother to represent my husband's side. I did run out of time at the end, so I took what I had made of the *chuppah* to a professional seamstress, and she finished the last touches. I hadn't seen it for over a month (my Mom had picked it up from her and brought it to the synagogue) until our wedding day, when my parents walked me up to David, standing under the *chuppah*. I looked at him, and then I looked up at the *chuppah*. It was unreal. I felt like my grandmother was right there, watching me. It was so intense. I started to cry and it felt like she was comforting me. I looked at David, and felt so connected to him. I knew, in that moment, why I had decided to make our *chuppah*. When I think about that moment now, six years later, I still get tears in my eyes.
—Allison Cutler

I felt very alive during the ceremony (as opposed, I guess, to being numb or anxious as I had heard so many friends describe, feeling as if the ceremony was just a "big blur") and I felt very connected to Michael and friends, family, and to God—to being a part of the universe. We were outdoors, which was important to me spiritually, and I felt a part of everything and everyone around me and in my consciousness. I felt connected to everything alive, and grateful for all the blessings I have. Something sort of strengthening and cohesive-making happened in that time under the *chuppah*. I felt really grounded and present in a wonderful and real way that I guess I couldn't have anticipated.
—Sheila Nissim

I began planning our commitment ceremony with my partner; it was so important to him, that I wanted it to be special. I had been estranged from anything Jewish for such a long time that I really wasn't interested in the Jewish part. Looking back, I was blown away by how strong it felt to drink from a *kiddush* cup and hear the Hebrew blessings. I am still amazed by how the ceremony made me . . . open up to being Jewish. That it was possible to be Jewish, and to get meaning from it again.
—David Gross

The "Inter-Jewish" Marriage

With all the talk about interfaith issues, it always surprises me that Jewish leaders do not talk more about how to blend "inter-Jewish" couples—those who come from different worlds of Jewish religious and cultural experience. Take my husband Fred and me. When we met, our secular connections couldn't have been stronger. Both of us are products of the '80s: We found out on our first date that we both grew up loving The Smiths and Elvis Costello (and still do), eating all kinds of ethnic food, and taking in art museums. We love documentaries and Christopher Guest/Eugene Levy movies. We're both pretty laid-back people and like to laugh a lot. As we got to know each other more deeply, we discovered that we shared many of the same core values and beliefs, and each of us, individually, began to imagine what it might be like to spend our lives together. We had both been through a number of romantic relationships and had come to a place in our lives where we were both clear about what we were seeking in a relationship. We could communicate with each other in a very open, honest way, which was a healing experience for both of us. We gave each other support and encouragement as we dreamed about and took steps to pursue our career goals. When, after just three months of dating, Fred took a job in another city, two hours away from where we both were living at the time, we decided that both of us would make necessary sacrifices so that we could be together on every possible weekend. It became clearer and clearer to us both that our relationship was becoming one of the most significant parts of our lives.

But despite our feelings of intimacy and connection, we could not have been in more different places when it came to how we experienced being Jewish, even though we had both grown up in homes with two Jewish parents. Although Fred identifies with Judaism strongly on a cultural level, as he grew spiritually, he found a deep comfort and faith in practicing Buddhism. He has been a committed Buddhist for more than eleven years, and I knew this part of his identity when we met. Fred chants from Buddhist scripture daily and deeply believes in the laws of cause and effect—that we can change our lives through our very thoughts and the actions that we take.

Although I connected to and appreciated Fred's Buddhist beliefs, my own very strong Jewish identity was both cultural and spiritual. In my twenties, I became interested in exploring my Jewish heritage in greater depth and was particularly drawn to the power of ritual, prayer, and Torah study. As an aspiring playwright, I found myself delving more and more into work with Jewish themes and wanted to learn all that I could about my heritage. I was finding spiritual depth and connection in the music and rhythm of Jewish prayer and in performing Shabbat rituals, such as lighting candles and taking time out from doing work as part of my weekly routine.

Deeply in love and becoming best friends, Fred and I wondered about how we might have to compromise our individual spiritual practices if we married. We realized that creating a "Jewish home" brought different baggage and expectations for both of us. Fred and I began a dialogue about how we could work out these kinds of issues, and we began to realize that we both needed to expand our vision of what a Jewish home might look like. There was no question that we wanted to marry and that being Jewish was of great importance for us both; we just needed to start imagining what our Jewish life together would be like and start taking steps to build it.

Fortunately, with the help of a wise and creative rabbi, Shai Gluskin, we set out to create a wedding that would honor both of our Jewish backgrounds and spiritual expressions. Almost by accident, our wedding planning turned out to be a highly creative and fun process. When we encountered a tradition or text that didn't feel right to me in terms of women's equality, we explored it. When we struggled with ways to make language honor Fred's interpretation of God, we rewrote it. Rabbi Gluskin gave us the support and encouragement that we needed, and, in the end, the process of creating our wedding helped us connect to each other's spiritual beliefs and embrace the mystery of what drew us together in the first place. It started us on the path for everything that was to come after our wedding day, including the daily way we connect to each other and negotiate issues as a couple. Planning our unique wedding also helped us deepen our respect for each other. We worked hard, we disagreed at times, we made major breakthroughs in our understanding of each other, and we had a lot of fun along the way.

Ultimately, the process of planning our wedding, combined with the actual experience of standing under the *chuppah*—one of the most awe-inspiring moments of my life—encouraged me to write this book. I wrote this book in hopes of encouraging other couples to look at their connections to and issues surrounding being Jewish and to approach their Jewish wedding with an open mind and a creative spirit. Finally, I want other couples to know that the process of planning your wedding, rather than causing you anxiety and distress, can actually help you grow spiritually and become even more deeply connected as a couple. This process will help you long after your wedding day comes and goes and will keep you focused on what really counts: all the days of your life together after the wedding.

Considerations for Interfaith Couples

Although this is a Jewish wedding book, I hope that it will prove to be a helpful guide for interfaith couples as well. Exploring the elements of a Jewish wedding in a creative way can benefit both the Jewish and the non-Jewish partner. It will promote dialogue not only about what kind of wedding experience you want but also about the place of both your backgrounds and cultures in the home you are creating. You have probably already encountered the Jewish community's ambivalence toward interfaith couples, and you may have already had some painful personal encounters with family, friends, or clergy. This reaction stems from a range of issues, and it's not my intention to explore those issues or their consequences in this book. Instead, by sharing some of the creative options and resources that other interfaith couples have found helpful, I hope to help you make the Jewish connection to your wedding—and your life—as meaningful as possible.

A Special Note for Gay and Lesbian Couples

In the course of thousands of years of Jewish history, it is only very recently that gay and lesbian couples have been acknowledged in parts of the Jewish community and have had the opportunity to engage in religious wedding ceremonies. Now, both the Reform and Reconstructionist movements, along with the Jewish Renewal movement, formally acknowledge the rights of gay and lesbian couples. Many of their clergy officiate at gay and lesbian weddings and commitment ceremonies. While not all gay and lesbian couples embrace the need for a formal ceremony to mark their commitment, many couples want to take ownership of this part of their Jewish heritage and are integrating their gay and Jewish identities in a variety of commitment rituals.

The Creative Jewish Wedding Book, 2nd Edition, seeks to embrace all couples, including same-gender couples. Wherever possible, I make notes and references that may be helpful to gay and lesbian couples. In planning the commitment ceremony for a same-sex couple, you may experience special issues, such as how you as a couple are addressed. Hopefully, the experiences and ideas of the other couples mentioned in the book will inspire same-sex couples to create a meaningful, affirmative Jewish ceremony.

Kavannah—Sacred Intention

Frequently, I use the word *kavannah*, which loosely translates as "sacred intention." Forming a clear *kavannah* for why you are taking on a creative project will help you maintain a sacred state of mind, even when much of what you are doing may seem mundane. For example, if you decide to sew your own *chuppah* (wedding canopy), you may want to remind yourself that a *chuppah*, in Jewish tradition, is a sacred tent and that when a bride and groom stand underneath it, they are passing through a special gateway to God's presence. That way, when you are standing in line at the fabric store, spending hours with a needle and thread, and trying to figure out the best way to attach your *chuppah* to four poles, you can stop and remind yourself of your *kavannah*, which may be for you and your partner to be fully open to the Divine Presence during your ceremony. Your *kavannah* is an affirmation of why you are taking on your project; it is an active expression of your spirituality. In some cases, you and your partner may form a *kavannah* together; in other cases, you may each take on your own sacred intention for a project. A *kavannah* is a fluid thing, and yours may evolve even as you are in the midst of a creative project. The hope is that your *kavannah* will help support your hard work and efforts and give you abundant energy and encouragement.

How to Use This Book

The Creative Jewish Wedding Book, 2nd Edition, is organized as follows: One overview chapter is followed by seven chapters that guide you through the specific parts of your Jewish wedding. Each of those chapters includes a brief explanation of the ritual or object; experiences and insights from other couples; craft projects with simple instructions; creative visualization exercises; a section on the influence of family dynamics; and a host of creative ideas connected to the object or ritual that is designed to inspire you. The resources section will help you find the information and products you need to further the process.

You may be reading this book with your partner or on your own. Either way is just fine. As a resource book, I have tried to include many ideas and examples to inspire you, but I am also aware that the book could potentially overwhelm you! Read it slowly, and take your time. You may have specific project ideas in mind and may want to go right to the chapters that address your needs. If a creative Jewish wedding is a totally new idea to you, you may want to skim through the entire book first, then go back to the chapters that interested you most to read again more thoroughly.

Please note: This book is intended to be a secondary resource, designed to help readers think about creative options for their Jewish wedding or commitment ceremony. There are other books available (see Appendix I) that provide more thorough explanations of the history and meaning of Jewish wedding customs and traditions.

Creative Visualization

Each chapter offers an opportunity for creative visualization. If you are not familiar with visualization, the exercises may seem strange to you at first. Creative visualization is an increasingly popular technique that helps people connect to the unconscious part of their brains. It is used by psychologists and psychiatrists for relaxation, by medical doctors for healing purposes, and by athletes and corporate managers because of its proven effectiveness in promoting success.

Visualization begins with relaxing, with connecting to one's breath and trying to empty the mind of all the busy thoughts that preoccupy us so much of the time. Just breathing and sitting still are helpful tools when dealing with anxiety. Visualization moves us from a mentally calm state to actively imagining pictures in our mind's eye. It allows our intuition to surface and speak to us. Visualization can awaken ideas that we might have otherwise ignored. I recommend that you buy a notebook so that you can write down all the pictures and ideas that come to you during these exercises.

While planning a wedding, it is easy to be caught up in the voices of those around us. We want to please our parents, our friends, our colleagues; we may believe that our wedding needs to look like other weddings we've attended. Visualization allows you to become quiet and to let your own unique vision emerge. Some of what surfaces may surprise you; some may inspire you.

Don't feel pressured while you're doing the visualization exercises. Nothing may surface for you. Sometimes, the mood just isn't right. You may feel too wound up to sit quietly. Let it go, and try again another time, if you like. However, if the process just doesn't work for you, it's no big deal.

After doing the visualization exercises, you and your partner may want to sit and listen to each other's "pictures." Your visions don't need to mesh perfectly; you are engaging in a process that seeks to honor both your visions.

As with all parts of this book, it's also fine if one of you gets into the visualization and the other partner does not. Relationships are all about balance, and as you go along you will figure out the best way for each of you to be involved with the wedding-planning process. As an alternative to doing the exercises with a partner, you could sit quietly with your journal and/or ask a friend to help you by reading out loud.

The Creative Jewish Wedding Book, 2nd Edition, offers a range of creative learning experiences. It is brimming with options and ideas, so read through, relax, and choose the projects that speak to you. How many creative projects you take on depends on how much time, energy, and support you have. There is no one way to create the most meaningful wedding for you.

May designing your wedding be an opportunity to engage your curiosity and imagination. May you balance each other's strengths and weaknesses, and further build ties to your family, friends, community, and heritage along the way. May the planning of your wedding inspire the creation of a Jewish home full of love, harmony, innovation, and connection.

chapter one

Getting Started

Creating the Wedding of Your Dreams

Creating your Jewish wedding requires preparation on many levels: emotionally, spiritually, physically, mentally, and, of course, financially. You need to determine how much time and energy to put into wedding planning and how to best distribute your energy to handle all the different tasks. You will be balancing your visions and dreams with practical realities, including setting a budget and dealing with your own family's unique dynamics. The wedding-designing process calls for the most sacred imaginings as well as the most mundane details. But each step along the way can be exciting and fulfilling when you open your mind to the creative possibilities.

First of all, look honestly at what resources and challenges you and your partner may be facing. When you know what kind of budget you have for your wedding, you can work more creatively within your limits. When you acknowledge what kind of issues you face in terms of family dynamics, you will be better prepared to address them, should those issues surface. Stand back and consider the big picture of your wedding; once you've done that, you can bring your creative energy to the more detailed tasks that will help make your wedding unique.

Jewish Connections—Figuring Them Out

As you plan your wedding, one of the many decisions you will face is "how Jewish" you want your wedding to be. Should you have kosher food? Hebrew as well as English on your invitations? Jewish or secular music during your wedding and reception? And how traditionally Jewish your ceremony should be? You may have clear ideas about many of these matters, or you may feel that you need more information before making a decision.

Before you start thinking about the specifics—food, invitations, music, and the like—I suggest that you spend some time considering your own Jewish connections. What elements of Jewish culture interest you? Which family traditions have you carried on in your adult life? What Jewish connections do you and your partner share? In what ways do your observances and interests differ?

Again, even if you and your partner are both Jewish, you may have practiced Judaism in very different ways in your homes of origin. If one set of parents emphasized home ritual and synagogue involvement while the other partner's parents identified as secular, cultural Jews, you may find yourselves speaking different languages when you think of creating a Jewish home. It's important to gain a clear understanding of where each of you came from and where you connect to Judaism as you enter this commitment to each other.

Do the following exercise when you have time to relax and have a long conversation; you may find that the questions prompt a lot of thoughts and feelings. This exercise, which calls for you to write answers to all these questions, concerns your Jewish background and connections. If you or your partner is not Jewish, the non-Jewish partner may want to write about what interests him or her about Judaism, which of the customs and traditions he or she enjoys, and any questions he or she has about Jewish culture and religion.

Judaism in Your Life

1. What is your earliest significant memory of knowing that you were Jewish? What feelings do you associate with that memory?

2. What was a defining Jewish moment in your life? (Examples include a family event, a conversation about God/religion, an experience during prayer, or a trip to Israel.)

3. What do you like about being Jewish?

4. What do you dislike about being Jewish?

5. What are your expectations for creating a Jewish home?

6. In your marriage, how do you hope to honor the differences in religious practices and feelings that characterize each of your extended families?

7. Can you identify any Jewish wounds that you feel you are carrying?

8. How do you connect most strongly with your Judaism? (Examples include food, prayer/ritual, family, study, Jewish friends/community, art, music, or memories.)

Once you have taken time to answer the questions, sit together and listen to each other's responses. Some of what comes up may be old news, but some answers may surprise you. Try to listen to each other without judgment, noting the ways in which you responded differently to the questions.

Use the positive connections that come up in your wedding planning. For example, if one of you really connects to Judaism through food (and many of us do), that partner may want to start researching menus. If one of you really enjoys Jewish music, that partner might want to start exploring CDs and sheet music to find just the right music for your ceremony. If there are areas that interest you both, such as studying Jewish texts, you might choose to work together, researching Jewish poetry to find a quote for your wedding invitation. The more you can incorporate the elements of Judaism that excite you as you plan your wedding, the more connected you will feel to the Jewish wedding ceremony itself.

Of course, these questions are also designed to bring to the surface any issues or old baggage you're carrying with regard to being Jewish. It is much better to face these issues head on—and any pain or discomfort they engender—rather than keeping them suppressed only to surface later. If you had a miserable time in Hebrew school and think of rabbis as stern authority figures, for example, you are probably hesitant about sitting with a rabbi for premarital counseling. Better to get it out there, so that you and your partner are aware of any red flags when it comes to the Jewish aspects of your wedding.

Identifying issues is only the first step. You need to keep a dialogue going with each other, continuing to note what feelings being Jewish evokes. Ideally, the rabbi, cantor, or other Jewish teacher you choose will be open to hearing about your concerns and will help you resolve or at least work on them.

There are few moments in our contemporary lives that force us to think about our heritage, our connection to God, and the power of ritual. Your wedding is one of them, and the time and energy that you put into creating it can ultimately affect the way you live Jewishly once you get married.

Listen to Your Heart, Listen to Each Other

Besides dealing with issues of Jewish identity, you and your partner are confronting a host of other issues connected to your wedding: money, family dynamics, and time management. Being engaged can be an exciting time, but also a scary one. You may each have very different unspoken ideas and expectations about what you want from your wedding. It is not always easy to create an honest dialogue about something that is so emotionally charged, but making the effort to listen to each other's visions and concerns now will help tremendously as you move forward in your wedding planning.

When I first got engaged, the best piece of advice that I received was from a friend who said, "Remember that your wedding is one day, and your marriage is the rest of your life." It is ironic that the stress people put on each other when planning a wedding can actually cause some couples to split up before the event itself. Other couples get so caught up in the details of planning a perfect wedding that they ignore other important issues and needs in the relationship, and they wind up feeling as if they don't really know the person they married so well after all.

When you are planning a wedding, the two of you are going to be talking about it a lot. That's a given. But the nature of your conversations will have a tremendous impact on the quality of your relationship. The projects in this book—from choosing the right rabbi to writing your own *ketubah*—can keep you grounded in why you are getting married, as opposed to focusing on how perfect your wedding can be.

You may want to take a few moments to respond to the following questions, and then use your responses to open a dialogue with your partner:

Addressing Anxiety

1. What aspect(s) of the wedding cause the most anxiety for you? Family? Money? Religion? Being the focus of everyone's attention?

2. What practical steps can you take to manage the anxiety?

3. In what ways can your partner help support you in addressing the anxiety?

The more you listen to each other's concerns and offer genuine support, the less anxiety you will feel as the wedding approaches. Any big life event—even happy ones—are stressful. Sometimes you may even notice yourself feeling ambivalent toward the wedding as a way of ignoring issues and calming fears. As you go through the process of designing your wedding, it's natural to feel all those emotions—excitement, fear, stress, ambivalence—at different moments. If you have been married before, the process of creating this wedding may bring to the surface issues from your other wedding experience. Let your partner know what's going on. It's really challenging when one of you is in the excited phase and the other partner is hit with ambivalence, but it's worse when one of you is holding back what you are really feeling.

Try to accept where each of you stands, and be reasonable with your expectations. As you start planning, you'll figure out the best way to support each other and work together. It may just be that one of you loves the detail stuff, and the other one is more of a big-picture person. One of you may be stressed out by family issues, while the other one is more than happy to talk with difficult family members in a straightforward way. Use each other's strengths. The bottom line is to remember you are a team, you are in the process together, and both of you will go through a healthy amount of anxiety before the wedding takes place.

As you are planning your wedding, it is also critical to spend time together doing things you both enjoy that have absolutely nothing to do with your wedding. Don't let your wedding planning consume you. Go to movies, see friends, take trips—whatever helps you connect, unwind, and just appreciate being together. If your whole life becomes "the wedding," you run the risk of feeling a tremendous emptiness when the wedding is over. Instead, stay grounded in pursuits you will continue to enjoy once you come back from your honeymoon. Keep things in perspective. Your wedding is one day; your marriage will hopefully be what happens all the days that come after.

Managing Family Dynamics

As you will hear time and again, when you fall in love and marry your beloved, you are marrying his or her family, too. Life-cycle moments, for all their potential joy, also bring up lots of anxiety. Death, divorce, remarriage, blended families, old feuds, and decades-old disappointments—all the feelings associated with these come to the surface when planning a wedding. The process of introducing and intermingling two families that may both be Jewish but may be polar opposites when it comes to observance, values, and expectations is a huge challenge and a huge cause of stress for both bride and groom.

One way to ease anxiety and help make the families' blending go a bit more smoothly is to get everyone involved in projects that will help them share in the couple's happiness. Getting *machatunim* (in-laws) to work together on designing a *chuppah* or practicing to sing harmony for pre-processional music can channel the energy of anxiety in a positive direction. Creative projects have a wonderful way of honoring everyone's gifts, and they bring out the best, most giving parts in the people we love. Consider the many talents running through your family. The following list can help you think about your family members' creative abilities. Then match them with the many creative ideas in the following chapters, recruiting them to make your wedding something special. Jot down the names of as many people in your family as you can think of who enjoy and are skilled at the following arts:

- Culinary/Arts of the Home—Gardening, Cooking, Baking, Decorating/Interior Design, Flower Arranging

- Technical Arts—Web Design, Sound Design, Lighting, Slide Shows, PowerPoint Presentations

- Literary/Dramatic Arts—Writing, Puppetry, Acting, Storytelling, Directing

- Music/Dance—Singing, Playing an Instrument, Arranging Music, Conducting, Dance, Choreography

- Visual Arts—Drawing, Photography, Calligraphy, Painting, Pottery, Jewelry Making, Sculpture

- Needlecraft—Quilting, Embroidery, Sewing, Dress Design, Dressmaking

- Fiber Arts—Origami, Paper Cutting, Paper Making

- Other Crafts—Découpage, Stenciling, Scrapbooking, Collage

Even if your mother and mother-in-law live on opposite coasts, it's still possible to get them working together on a creative project. If you and/or your spouse have children from a previous marriage, it is critical to get them involved so that they feel a sense of ownership and inclusion in your wedding. Consider their creative abilities—you might ask a musically gifted son or daughter to play your processional music or ask a talented young artist to come up with a design for your invitations. Asking people to share their creative abilities in designing your wedding opens up the web of energy that allows you to create the wedding that you desire.

Choosing a Date—Factors to Consider

There are many factors to take into account when setting the date for your wedding, from working with a rabbi's busy schedule to making sure the date you want is permissible under Jewish law. As you plan your Jewish wedding, keep in mind that there are certain days when weddings are prohibited under Jewish law, while other days by custom are seen as particularly auspicious. Traditionally, Jewish weddings are prohibited from being held on certain festivals, fast days, and holidays, including Shabbat, and most rabbis today continue to honor this aspect of Jewish law.

Look on the bright side: During most weeks of the year, Jewish weddings can be held any day of the week except Shabbat (sundown Friday to sundown Saturday). This prohibition came about because of all the ritual commandments connected to the Sabbath—not working or carrying, for example. A wedding would, of course, require work on the part of the rabbi and others involved in the reception and also plenty of transporting of goods. It would require that people sign a contract—also a form of work. Another reason that weddings aren't held on Shabbat is because of the injunction "not to mix one occasion of rejoicing with another." Shabbat is meant to be a weekly celebration of the highest order.

What is important for the task at hand is knowing that any Shabbat is out for your wedding. Because of this, most Jewish couples hold a Saturday night (post-Shabbat) or Sunday afternoon or evening wedding. You don't have to stick to a weekend date, although most people inviting out-of-town guests will want to do so. Some couples choose to have their wedding on a Tuesday, because in the biblical story of Creation (Genesis 1), God says, *"ki tov"* (it is good) twice on the third day.

Besides Shabbat, weddings aren't held on major holidays and festivals, including Rosh Hashanah, Yom Kippur, Passover, Shavuot, and the first and last day of Sukkot. Traditionally, weddings also aren't held during the time between Passover and Shavuot (with the exception of Lag B'Omer) or during the three weeks between the Jewish dates of the seventeenth of Tammuz and the ninth of Av (Tisha B'Av), which commemorate the destruction of the Temple. Some Reform and Reconstructionist rabbis perform weddings during those interim dates, while others abide by tradition. What can be tricky is that these dates generally fall during the secular calendar months of April/May and July/August, often desirable wedding dates. But don't despair: In the grand scope of the calendar, Jewish time still allows you plenty of dates to choose from. If you are curious now about when the holidays fall during the current or upcoming Jewish year, go to an online Jewish calendar at www.hebcal.com to find out.

Rabbi Mordechai Kaplan, whose influential writings inspired the creation of the Reconstructionist movement, taught about the notion of living simultaneously in "two civilizations," one Jewish and one American. Selecting your wedding date involves some dancing in the amorphous space between those civilizations. But giving yourself a chance to consider Jewish time as an existing reality does not have to be limiting or negative. Just as Shabbat offers a way for contemporary Jews to set aside time to relax and unwind, other calendar dates offer a chance for spiritual pause and reflection as well. As annoying as it may initially feel to discover that your preferred wedding date falls during the counting of the Omer, it can be an opportunity to discover the spiritual significance of the date.

Besides, there are lots of *positive* Jewish calendar dates when you could hold your wedding, such as on the monthly festival of Rosh Hodesh, which marks the New Moon. It is said that Rosh Hodesh is a particularly auspicious day for weddings—though your love for each other may wax and wane, it will be sure to be renewed each month, just like the moon. The minor holiday of Tu B'Av, the fifteenth day of Av, unlike Tisha B'Av, is another great date connected to fertility and passion: Historically, in Israel, it was a date when young women dressed in white and went out to seek a mate among the young men of marrying age.

Many couples pick a Jewish holiday when weddings are allowed—such as Hanukkah or Purim—and use themes connected to the holiday in their wedding invitations, décor, and even ceremony.

Selecting an Officiant

One of the most critical steps for couples to take is choosing the person who will conduct the ceremony. This is most often a rabbi, but not necessarily so. The careful

Finding an Officiant for Interfaith Couples

Many interfaith couples face extreme challenges in finding a rabbi to conduct their wedding. Orthodox and Conservative rabbis are not permitted to lead interfaith weddings. Although Reform and Reconstructionist rabbis are permitted by their movements to conduct interfaith weddings, few do so. Nonaffiliated rabbis may choose to lead them. As a result, many Jews planning to marry a non-Jew are shocked when they discover that the rabbi they have loved and admired all their lives cannot or declines to officiate at their interfaith wedding. The hurt of this experience can propel the interfaith couple away from Judaism. In some cases, people go through their entire lives without healing from what they experience as rejection at this special moment in their lives. And the issues become even more complex if the interfaith couple wants the rabbi to co-officiate with clergy of another faith.

If you are part of an interfaith couple, hopefully you have already talked about issues concerning how you hope to balance your religions and traditions before getting engaged. These conversations will certainly continue as you plan your wedding, and finding clergy who can work with and support your plans and beliefs may lead you to greater clarity.

choice of officiant may affect the outcome of your wedding ceremony more than any other decision. You want to find a person who will listen to and support you, who will inspire you and connect with your ideas. Your officiant may challenge you at times—and may not always come up with the perfect solutions to your concerns. But if your wedding officiant is someone you feel comfortable confiding in, someone you can place your trust in to support you in the creation of your wedding, you will feel all the more nurtured when the time for the ceremony arrives. Make your choice carefully well in advance and give yourself the wedding gift of peace of mind!

For some couples, selecting an officiant is easy. One partner may have a childhood rabbi she loves dearly and with whom she is still in touch, and it may feel natural to select that person. Or the couple may belong to a congregation and will want to choose the rabbi from their current place of worship. Others may have met in college a favorite rabbi from the Hillel.

But if you didn't have a strong relationship with your childhood rabbi, weren't active in Hillel, don't belong to a synagogue, and don't really know your parents' rabbi, there are still plenty of ways to find an officiant with whom you can connect and get to know well in advance of the ceremony. In finding a rabbi to lead their wedding, many couples end up discovering a new Jewish community.

The person who leads your wedding ceremony doesn't need to be a rabbi—the officiant can be a cantor or another professional serving the Jewish community. However, to meet state legal requirements, the person who signs your wedding license does need to be a recognized member of the clergy or a justice of the peace. If you choose someone who is not a rabbi or cantor, you will need to find out whether the officiant works with a rabbi who can sign the marriage license. Some couples decide to have a secular wedding at city hall and a Jewish wedding conducted by a knowledgeable friend. That compromise avoids any legal complications. It is important to check the legal requirements in the state in which your wedding will take place.

There are also certain states that allow for Quaker weddings—and some couples today hold Jewish weddings in the Quaker style. A Quaker wedding does not require the use of an officiant at all; usually an emcee leads people in sharing readings, thoughts, and blessings for the couple, and the entire community in attendance serves as a witness to the union (more on Quaker-style weddings later in this chapter).

As you see, there are many possibilities for who might conduct your wedding ceremony. If you don't have a person who comes to mind right away, you might start by asking friends about officiants who have led their ceremonies. Find out what they liked (or did not like) about them. Also, think about all the Jewish weddings you've been to: Was there a particular rabbi who really moved you, who you could imagine leading your ceremony? Even if that rabbi lives in another part of the country, you might consider contacting her; some rabbis, especially those who do not have congregational responsibilities, will travel to officiate at a wedding.

If you definitely want to find a local rabbi (which makes the most practical sense because you'll want to schedule personal meetings) but don't know any of the clergy in your community, explore some local synagogues and Jewish events. Anyone is welcome to drop in on a Shabbat service. Look up synagogues in your local Yellow Pages and find out some basic information. Check out other cultural activities led by rabbis, such as lectures and panel discussions. If you find a rabbi who feels right to you, give him a call and find out whether he leads weddings.

Another place to find a great wedding officiant is through one of the several rabbinical colleges (listed in Appendix I). Rabbinical students welcome the opportunity to hone their skills by leading a wedding. While you might feel concerned, on the one hand, that a student is not as qualified as an experienced rabbi, you can feel comforted knowing that for a student rabbi, leading a wedding is a new opportunity to learn and grow, so you may be getting more than your money's worth when you choose one. Student rabbis are supervised by experienced faculty, so if you hit any snag, they will always have someone more practiced who is easily accessible for them to turn to for help and guidance.

It may be tempting to hire a rabbi simply based on convenience. Say you are planning to get married in one of your hometowns, and you choose the rabbi from your parents' congregation. This solution can work splendidly, or it can lead

I suggest that you start by consulting two organizations that can help you find a rabbi who leads interfaith weddings:

The Rabbinic Center for Research and Counseling
www.rcronline.org
(908) 233–0419

Jewish Outreach Institute
www.joi.org
(212) 760-1440

Both organizations can provide you with a list of rabbis and their conditions for leading interfaith weddings. Some rabbis, for example, will lead interfaith weddings if the couple makes a sincere pledge to raise their children in the Jewish tradition, join a synagogue, and the like. A very small number of rabbis will co-officiate with clergy of another religion. Most will not do so.

You might see advertisements in some Jewish newspapers and magazines for what's commonly referred to as "rent-a-rabbis." These rabbis will lead your interfaith wedding. They may also charge you an arm and leg, and probably won't be willing to spend much time with you in premarital counseling. Some of these rabbis are considered in religious circles to be pariahs, making large sums of money by preying on the vulnerability of interfaith couples.

If you get a fast-talking rabbi on the phone whose fee sounds unreasonable, hang up and keep looking.

And remember, you can also look for a judge or a justice of the peace to lead the ceremony that you create, or have a Quaker-style wedding. Read through the experiences of interfaith couples later in this book for inspiration and successful examples of two different solutions to couples blending their faiths. Also, Anita Diamant's *The New Jewish Wedding* features a ceremony created in the early 1980s called "The Children of Noah" that officiants may use for interfaith couples. Other good resources for the interfaith couple are *The Guide to Jewish Interfaith Family Life: An InterfaithFamily.com Handbook*, edited by Ronnie Friedland and Edmund Case, and, by Rabbi Kerry M. Olitzky, *Introducing My Faith and My Community: The Jewish Outreach Institute Guide for the Christian in a Jewish Interfaith Relationship* and *Making a Successful Jewish Interfaith Marriage: The Jewish Outreach Institute Guide to Opportunities, Challenges and Resources* (all Jewish Lights).

to immense frustration. Although it might feel like the easiest solution, if you don't see eye to eye on basic issues, such as egalitarian language, you will be in for some real challenges ahead. Schedule a time to talk with that rabbi before you make any commitment to use her or him.

Most rabbis require the couple they are marrying to attend a number of pre-wedding counseling sessions to discuss not just ceremony details but also larger issues surrounding the marriage. They want to feel sure that the couple has talked through any major issues relating to value systems, religious commitment, money, career, family, and so on. They can see whether the couple is really ready to be married. When you enter this kind of counseling with someone whom you trust, it can have a positive impact on your wedding and on the rest of your life.

I can't emphasize enough that you should try to find your officiant early on. Congregational rabbis and cantors may have packed schedules, with bar and bat mitzvahs planned years in advance. Your childhood rabbi might want more than anything else to conduct your wedding, but if you don't consult him ahead of time about a date that could work for him, you may be setting yourself up for a big disappointment.

When you're choosing the person who will lead your wedding ceremony—and who will hopefully offer you premarital counseling and help with your wedding-creating process—you want to make sure that you and your partner agree that this is the right person for you. You don't have to hold the exact same political beliefs or spiritual interpretations, but you should agree on a few key issues, which can be determined by asking the potential officiant some questions. Don't be shy about asking questions; remember, you are ultimately asking this person to guide you through one of the most important moments of your life.

Checklist of Questions for Officiants

1. Describe one of the most memorable weddings you have led. What made it special?

2. What is your overall philosophy about wedding ceremonies?

3. Are you available for occasional consultation for questions that might arise in the process of creating ritual objects, such as our *chuppah*?

4. Do you like to sing or should we ask a musical friend to sing?

5. How many sessions of premarital counseling do you recommend?

6. How do you feel about updating prayer language to make it egalitarian in nature, such as using a feminine name for God in some places during the ceremony?

7. What types of *ketubah* text do you prefer couples to use? Why?

8. If we write an original text or additions to a traditional text, can you help us translate it into Hebrew? If not, can you help us find someone who can?

9. What dates are you available to lead our wedding?

10. On the day of the wedding, will you make sure that everything under the *chuppah* is set correctly, or do you prefer us to ask someone else to do that job?

11. Are you comfortable sharing leadership duties with another rabbi?

12. What is your fee?

13. Are there any other important factors regarding you and your style of ritual leadership that we should know about?

Although it may feel a bit intimidating to seek out the right wedding officiant, the time and energy you put into careful selection may help you find a spiritual teacher, and a friend, for life.

Setting a Budget

For some couples, talking about money can be by far the single most stressful part of planning a wedding. Unfortunately, more and more couples are starting out their marriage with a tremendous amount of credit card debt, the result of elaborately planned weddings they really couldn't afford. I recommend that you and your partner look realistically at what money you have and what you are

More Than One Officiant

Sometimes both partners have rabbis who they want to officiate. Some rabbis will delight in the opportunity to collaborate with a colleague, while others prefer not to step into such a situation.

Fees

If you already belong to a congregation and are planning to use its rabbi, you may not be expected to pay an additional fee. Many couples make a donation to the synagogue as a way of expressing their gratitude for the rabbi's time and/or give the rabbi a special personal gift or donate to the rabbi's discretionary fund. If you are getting married by one of your parents' rabbis, most likely the above scenerio applies as well. There is nothing wrong with asking about a fee, though, just to make sure that everyone is on the same page. If you are uncomfortable asking the rabbi directly, you could ask his personal secretary instead.

If you are not a member of the congregation, you probably will be asked to pay the rabbi a fee for this professional service. This fee can vary considerably based on the rabbi and the geographic area. (The fee can range from $500 to $1,000, even up to $2,500 if extensive travel is involved.) Although several hundred dollars may seem like a lot of money, remember that this amount is minimal compared to what a band or photographer will charge. Rabbis often spend a great deal of time counseling and working with the couple to create a meaningful ceremony. Also, if money is a problem, you should ask the rabbi whether she has a sliding-fee scale.

willing to spend before you begin planning your wedding. Weddings can be expensive affairs. Before you start planning, it is critical to create a realistic budget that you can stick to. If you don't have a sense beforehand of how much money you can reasonably spend, it's easy to end up choosing food, flowers, and bands that exceed the money you actually have.

In addition to the cost of invitations and the party, the Jewish parts of your wedding also come with a price tag. You may be hosting a *kiddush* at your synagogue in addition to your wedding reception, renting a synagogue, paying for a rabbi's services, and so on. Purchasing beautiful Judaica items can contribute to the expense of your wedding as well. Custom-made *ketubot* and *chuppot*, for example, are not cheap; artists work extremely hard at their handcrafted endeavors. If you are on a limited budget, though, you should not forgo beautiful Judaica items as part of your wedding; these cherished items will later be part of your home. Making your own takes more time and energy than hiring someone to create something for you, but it is one sure way to save a fair amount of money.

Perhaps you want to be married under an original *chuppah*. Commissioning one from a professional fabric artist starts at about $2,500. Purchasing your own fabric and fabric paint may cost about $100. Again, if you are concerned that you are not artsy enough to do such things on your own, please suspend judgment until you read through this book. You may be surprised by how easy and accessible many of the project ideas are.

Depending on your stage of life and personal circumstances, you may have parents who will contribute financially to your wedding. Although this gift can be a tremendous blessing, you must find out what their expectations are. Some parents give freely and allow the couple to plan as they wish; others expect to have a say in decision making.

Years ago, the bride's family was expected to host the wedding. Today, that is no longer necessarily the case. Many families set aside money for their daughters' weddings, but other families are not able to do so. When parents have divorced, determining who pays for the wedding can become even more complicated. One parent of the bride may have money to contribute, while the other does not.

As couples marry later in life, they may also feel awkward about asking parents to pay for their wedding. Statistics show that Jews are marrying later than other Americans and that both Jewish men and women tend to place an emphasis on establishing a career before settling down. Sometimes the engaged couple has been financially independent for years, and their parents are retired and living on a fixed income.

Money is one of the most difficult, emotionally laden topics in our society. Feelings and expectations about money can easily cause friction between parent and child, husband and wife, and future in-laws. The added pressure of trying to create a wedding of your dreams only heightens the emotional tensions.

Before determining who will pay for your wedding, you and your partner should sit down and have an open, realistic conversation.

Financial Considerations

1. Who is going to pay for the wedding? Are expenses going to be split between your families?

2. Will each of you talk to your own parents or will you approach them together? What approach would make each set of parents feel most at ease?

3. If you and your partner are going to pay for your own wedding, what is your budget?

4. Which items are you willing to do without or scale back on? Which parts of the wedding do you feel are most important to pay full price for?

5. In what areas might you be able to save money by tapping the creative talents of your friends, families, and yourselves, rather than employing professionals?

6. What resources do you have to help out with finances? Family help? Savings? Gifts? Credit cards?

7. How much will you pay for up-front and how much are you comfortable charging?

8. What are your financial goals as a couple, both short term and long term? How does your wedding fit into your overall plans?

This conversation may not be easy, but it is an important first step to take. Fighting over finances won't solve any problems or address any concerns. Talking openly—and planning wisely—is the only productive thing to do.

Unfortunately, when one family is contributing more money to the wedding than the other family (or one parent as opposed to another parent), the one paying the bills may feel entitled to have more of a say in planning the wedding. Try to explain that while you appreciate the input, you want to make sure that everyone feels included. Keep in mind that your families are going to be connected to each other from this point on: Even if they don't live near each other and won't be seeing each other on a regular basis, they will be together (God willing) at all of your future milestones, and maybe even for an occasional holiday meal. So encourage parents to treat each other decently and make their best efforts to get along.

Although it can be a financial burden, some couples choose to pay for their own wedding just to avoid family politics and power struggles. The choices you make should be based on family dynamics and what will give you the most pleasant, peaceful kind of wedding celebration possible.

Style, Approach, and Location

There are so many different ways to create a beautiful Jewish wedding. Your wedding should reflect your own personal style—the way you carry yourself in the world. What is critical is to figure out a style and approach that naturally resonate with you. If you are a "nature guy," don't feel pressured to put yourself into black-tie mode. If you are a gal who appreciates theatricality and spectacle, it doesn't make sense to plan an ultra-casual affair.

Of course, you and your beloved may have different visions of your ideal wedding. That's natural and okay: Your divergent approaches, if given thoughtful consideration, can blend together and complement each other. When James Goldberg and Marsha Blume were engaged, for example, they each had strong opinions about the kind of wedding they wanted. James is a fun-loving person who wanted to make sure that all the wedding festivities were full of rocking music, open bars, and great food. Marsha is a much more reserved person and wanted to spend quality time with their guests.

James and Marsha worked together to create a wedding weekend that responded to both their needs. It began on Friday night with a Shabbat dinner for their parents, their siblings, and their siblings' partners and children at Marsha's sister's home. On Saturday morning, the couple had an *aufruf* (special blessing for being called up to the Torah) at their synagogue, followed by a simple luncheon. Many of their out-of-town friends and family were there, and Marsha and James had a good amount of time to take it easy and be with them. During the afternoon, James took some time out to relax and Marsha spent the afternoon hanging out with her three closest friends. The couple decided not to do a big rehearsal dinner; instead, Marsha spent time with her sister while James and a group of his friends went to a ball game and out dancing. Their wedding reception had all the elements that James had hoped for—a great band, ample drinks and food, and great energy from people having fun. Marsha was fine with it because they had figured out a way for her to have quality time throughout the weekend to connect with the people she really wanted to be with. There are many ways to think about how to bring your unique styles together.

If you aren't quite sure what style of wedding you want, it might be helpful to think location first. The right location can help inspire your choice of style and approach. The good thing about a Jewish wedding is that if you have your *chuppah*, you can travel anywhere. Your *chuppah* could be in a synagogue, but it could also be in an art museum, on a mountainside, in a bed and breakfast, or in an old movie theater. One couple I spoke with got married—under a *chuppah*—in a bowling alley. Your Jewish wedding could be a Victorian picnic lunch, a rigorous trek up a hillside, or a formal black-tie bash at a fancy hotel. Rabbi Jamie Korngold has become known as the "adventure rabbi" because she specializes in leading weddings and other life-cycle events in the wilderness (see Appendix I for her contact information). If you have a vision, there is a way to make it happen. What's critical is that you and your partner decide on the right style and approach for you, rather than listening to anyone else's expectations for you.

1. Of anywhere in the world, where are your favorite places to spend time?

2. Where have you spent your most meaningful times together?

3. How would an acquaintance describe your personal style? What about your partner's?

4. What are some of the activities that connect you to each other?

5. When your guests leave your wedding, which three words do you want them to use to describe it?

Use your responses to help you focus on the ideal place and style for your wedding. For example, if you both love spending time with books, you might want to think about getting married in a beautiful library (many universities have such spaces available). If one of your favorite activities as a couple is fishing, consider having your wedding at a restaurant overlooking the bay where you fish. If one of your most memorable dates took place in a certain restaurant, find out whether that restaurant hosts private receptions. Question number five can help you think in reverse: Once you pinpoint the feeling you want your guests to leave with, you can figure out how to create a wedding that exudes that feeling.

The task can seem daunting, but once you start to imagine the right style and approach for your wedding, the other choices will be that much easier. The rituals and ceremonial objects in a Jewish wedding can reflect and illuminate your personal style. One couple I know, who were married on a tall ship, stood under a *chuppah* that mirrored one of the ship's sails. A simple detail, but one that enhanced their ceremony and made the religious aspect of their wedding resonate with everything else.

The Professional Wedding Planner—Yes or No?

Some couples retain a professional consultant to handle most of the party planning so they can focus more intensely on the spiritual aspects of their wedding, such as writing their own vows or fashioning an original *chuppah*. Many couples are overwhelmed by the myriad details associated with arranging a big event; they lose sight of the sacred occasion the event is celebrating. If you feel comfortable handing over some of the party-planning work to a professional, a consultant might work well for you.

To make a calculated decision, take an honest look at your lives. What demands, outside of your relationship, must you attend to? Is this a particularly stressful time at work? Are you enrolled in a rigorous academic program? People getting married for a second or third time may be juggling the demands of aging parents as well as their children. With everything that's on your plate, do you have time to work with caterers, photographers, florists, and a host of other vendors? If you are facing a big list of other demands in your life, it may be wise to look into hiring a wedding coordinator who can take over many of the more mundane but critical aspects of planning your wedding.

Of course, before hiring a professional, it's crucial to look honestly at your wedding budget and see whether you can afford to do so. If retaining a wedding planner is above your means, don't despair. First of all, many venues for weddings offer an in-house wedding coordinator who comes with the package when you reserve the site for your ceremony and/or reception. For example, a reception site might have a team, including a florist, a photographer, and a videographer, whose work will be coordinated through one of the venue's employees. Oftentimes, these sites offer discount packages when you use the in-house team.

Another alternative, if you feel overwhelmed by details but can't afford to hire a professional, is to assemble a team of friends who can act as your wedding *havurah* (group of friends). Your team can handle some of the detail work for you (see checklist of tasks in Appendix II). Make sure not to ask any one person to take on too much, and be understanding if a friend declines to help out in this way.

As a corollary of that idea, Rabbi Arthur Ocean Waskow and Phyllis Ocean Berman suggest to the couples whom they marry that they pick a close friend (or two) to serve as "lieutenant general" for the day. This person will deal with any last-minute catering concerns, make sure the band is set up and ready to go, and so on. Waskow and Berman stress that it is really difficult to be present for your ceremony and party if you have to handle details and straighten out any glitches that come up. "Let go of that before the day of the wedding," Berman recommends. "Put it into the hands of someone whom you trust and know that everything will work out just fine."

Finally, if you are considering hiring a professional consultant, make sure you hire the right one. If you are thinking outside the box and want to create an original wedding that expresses your style, your consultant should be on the same page. Too often wedding consultants know what has worked for couples in the past and will pressure you to make the same choices. Feeling vulnerable and overwhelmed, you may be persuaded to listen to the professional. Before hiring a consultant, write out a clear vision of what you hope your wedding will be like, and ask her how she could help you make that vision a reality. If she starts trying to talk you out of anything, say thank you and good-bye. Even if you do need to make some compromises along the way, you want to work with people—from your rabbi to your caterer to your wedding planner—who are excited and enthusiastic about your particular wedding ideas.

You also want to find a wedding planner who is already familiar with Jewish wedding customs or is willing to learn all about them. Make sure that he understands and respects your sense of how Jewish you want your wedding to be.

Honorary Roles

You and your partner will need to talk over who will play honorary roles in your wedding. There are many ways to involve your closest friends and your families in your wedding—from having them design and create your *chuppah* to performing a reading or song as part of your ceremony. Honorary roles include:

- Best Man and Maid/Matron of Honor
- Bridesmaids and Groomsmen
- *Chuppah* Holders
- Greeters and Guest Book Attendant
- *Aydim* (witnesses) for signing your *ketubah*
- Ushers

How many attendants you choose for your wedding is up to you. Unfortunately, many people feel obligated to include certain people as attendants, whether or not they really want them in this special role. Talk honestly with your partner and imagine your ideal wedding: Who would you each like to include most with an honorary role? Make a list of those people and start from there.

The people who are holding your *chuppah* play a very special role—they will be very close to you during your ceremony. Think about who among your family and friends will generate a great sense of love and support for you. Your maid/matron of honor and best man also will be there with you under the *chuppah* and should be supportive presences, too. Some couples create a very large *chuppah* so that bridesmaids and groomsmen can also stand under it, while other couples have bridesmaids and groomsmen create a circle or semicircle just outside the *chuppah*.

If you and your partner disagree about how many attendants to have, put the issue aside for some time. One of you may be extremely extroverted, with twenty best friends, while the other might be more introverted, with two or three best friends. Neither of you is right or wrong—just different. Talk about a way to strike a balance between your styles: Maybe you can each have two attendants, then find another way to honor the extrovert's other good friends.

Be sure to speak to the people you'd like as attendants well in advance of your wedding. While you hope they will gratefully accept this honor, they will need to clear their calendars and make the necessary arrangements. If you are going to ask your bridesmaids to purchase certain dresses you've already chosen, let them know approximately how much money they will need to spend. It can be awkward for a friend to accept the role of a bridesmaid, only to find out that she and the bride have very different ideas of how much money is acceptable to spend on a dress. Keep in mind that there are a lot of lovely ways to have your attendants look nice without purchasing the exact same dress. For example, you could choose a color that you think would suit all of them and send them a swatch of fabric. Then let them find a dress in a similar color that looks flattering on them. You can give them guidelines regarding length and style if you have specifics in mind.

If your attendants aren't Jewish, fill them in ahead of time about what your ceremony will be like so they will feel comfortable with what is going on.

Because they won't have the opportunity to sit and look at your wedding program, a short explanation can help them follow along and add to the *kavannah* of the rituals and blessings that are taking place.

If you have children from a previous marriage, you can help involve them in your wedding by honoring them with a special role. Whether as bridesmaids or *chuppah* holders, witnesses to your *ketubah* or ring bearers, they will be participating in your ceremony rather than watching from the sidelines. Depending on their ages and your family circumstances, it is natural for them to feel some ambivalence about your wedding. If they refuse to participate in this way, don't pressure or force them; just let them know that you would love to include them. Talk to them and find out what role they imagine playing. Keep the door open, so that if they decide to participate at the last minute they know that you will cherish their being part of your wedding ceremony.

What about the Guest List?

Deciding whom to invite to your wedding can cause all kinds of family commotion. Your parents may be so excited about your wedding that they want to invite their two hundred best friends; all of their second, third, and fourth cousins; and the entire synagogue sisterhood! Will there be any room left for your friends?

It is critical to talk honestly with your parents about how many guests you would like to have and about the balance you imagine between family and friends—and their friends and yours. For example, if you are really set on having a more intimate wedding—say sixty to seventy guests—and your parents want to invite all your uncles, aunts, and cousins, which comes to sixty to seventy guests, you have a dilemma. And if your parents are paying for the wedding, they may feel entitled to invite whomever they want.

Before anyone starts screaming, take a few deep breaths and try to listen to one another. In today's society, in which extended families are often spread out over great geographic distances, life-cycle events provide some of the few opportunities for reconnection. Sometimes, as people get older, they crave the chance to renew ties with their cousins and old friends, the people they knew best in their childhood or early adulthood. They are proud of you and excited about your wedding and they want these folks to be there, to share in the joy of the moment.

On the other hand, you and your partner may feel strongly that part of creating a meaningful wedding is having guests you know well—or at least have seen more than once since your bar mitzvah! Your ideal wedding may be an event shared by your closest friends and colleagues, with only the family members and friends of your parents you know well.

Rather than thinking "either/or," try to create a guest list that is most meaningful to you and your partner but that also honors your parents' wishes. You might give them a number of guests they can invite, for example, and then let them decide who to invite within that number. If you are really worried about the guest list getting out of control, you can always choose a reception site with limited capacity as an excuse to keep the numbers down.

If one set of parents is truly upset that they cannot invite as many friends and family members as they would like, why not suggest that they host a separate party, at a later date, to which they can invite whomever they want? It doesn't need to be fancy or formal, just an occasion to invite their friends to meet and celebrate with you. Sometimes this solution works best when couples' families live on opposite sides of the country.

One important decision that you will need to make is whether to invite young children. There is no right or wrong decision when it comes to children at a wedding; it is simply a matter of preference. Many couples find ways to make compromises for their guests with young children, such as hiring babysitters to stay with the children during the ceremony. When you and your partner think about the style and approach you want to take in planning your wedding, consider how kid-friendly you want your wedding to be.

One more bit of advice: As you gather names and addresses for your guest list, enter them in a database in your computer. That way, you will have a list of all the people important to you, your partner, and your respective families. It can be exciting to merge the names and information of the people you love most in the world with the people your partner feels closest to. You can use that list to keep in touch with everyone if you send out annual Rosh Hashanah cards or announcements or invitations to future *simchas* (joyful occasions). Also, you can easily use the database to print out labels for your wedding gift thank you notes.

Green Jewish Weddings

Over the last thirty or so years, a growing number of Jews have turned to texts within our tradition for wisdom about contemporary ecological crises. Within Jewish texts, there are many teachings about the relationships between human beings and the natural world, from the first chapter of the Torah (Bereshit) in which human beings are created from the earth and are given responsibility to care for it to the rabbinic injunction *ba'al taschit*—do not destroy needlessly.

From these texts has emerged a movement of passionate Jewish environmentalists, who are committed to creating a healthier Jewish world and healthier planet. Religious leader Rabbi Arthur Waskow, the Founder of the Shalom Center and author of *Torah of the Earth: Exploring 4,000 Years of Ecology in Jewish Thought* (Jewish Lights), describes this movement as the "insights of a spiritually-rooted caring for the endangered web of life on this planet, leading to a conscious eco-Judaism."

If you find yourself connecting to the Jewish environmental movement, there are many ways to bring your consciousness to your special day and make your Jewish wedding into a *green* wedding. Here are some ideas:

> *Your chuppah:* As a symbol of the home you and your partner are creating, your *chuppah* is a wonderful place to go green. Select a 100 percent organic cotton or linen fabric as a base. If you want to add color, choose vegetable dyes. You can also decorate around your *chuppah* with local potted plants and flowers that can go into a garden after your nuptials.

> *Your clothing:* Just as with choosing fabric for your *chuppah*, you can also be eco-conscious in the clothing that you choose. Organic cotton and linen can make incredible dresses and suits. Hemp silk is another sustainable fabric that makes gorgeous clothes. Ask a local dressmaker if they can get organ-

ic fabric or order some online. (Also, look in the appendix for a list of places to order ready made eco-gowns). Another very fun way to go is to "recycle" vintage wedding clothes. Poke around in vintage shops for dresses and suits that appeal to your sense of style. You can also find "recycled" gowns on eBay!

Your food choices: The food you serve at your wedding is a wonderful place to show your eco-Jewish values. Eco-*kashrut* is part of the Jewish ecological movement and interprets the laws of *kashrut* in a way that focuses on contemporary sustainability, animal rights and both personal and global health. For a full explanation of eco-*kashrut*, see p. 180 in Wedding Delicacies and check out a sample Jewish vegan menu on page 184.

Your flowers: Many couples are making their weddings greener by how they make choices around flowers and other greens. Buying locally grown means reducing carbon emissions from flowers that are flown in from around the world. Using as many potted plants vs. cut flowers for centerpieces and decorations means that they will find a home in someone's garden. Small potted plants make wonderful take-home favors.

Your invites: Using recycled paper is the choice for many couples who want to bring an eco-consciousness to their wedding invitations. You can also check out tree free paper, made from materials like hemp and bamboo, that can be specially ordered. Some couples are also avoiding paper altogether and designing and sending electronic invitations.

Your location: As you plan the "where" of your wedding, you have another opportunity to think green. If you're wedding at the synagogue and choose to have your reception in the social hall there, you'll be cutting down on the carbon emissions that would have been emitted with guests driving to get to another location. You could also have your ceremony and reception at a place that supports the green economy, like a local organic farm, a green hotel, a nonprofit space or at an outdoor setting that will fill your whole wedding with a natural sensibility. As long as you've got a *chuppah* there, you can create a Jewish space anywhere.

chapter two

Hear Ye, Hear Ye

Setting the Stage with Unique Invitations

When many couples begin planning the Jewish aspects of their wedding, their thoughts turn to the ceremony or the ritual objects essential to a Jewish wedding, such as the *chuppah* or the *ketubah*. But there are many ways for couples to express their connections to Judaism even before the wedding arrives. Creating a distinctive wedding allows you to explore your Jewishness in an important and meaningful way and to transmit your *kavannah* to your wedding guests.

Your wedding invitation should reflect your original vision of your *simcha* and the *kavannah* that you are bringing to your wedding. Ideally, the colors, symbols, design, and language that you choose for your invitation will exude the thoughtfulness and care that you are bringing to the process of designing your wedding.

Fashioning your wedding invitation can be one of the most fun and creative tasks of your wedding planning. Your unique invitation sets the stage for your wedding, letting your guests know what kind of wedding you are planning—formal or casual, intimate or with a certain theme. The details that make up your invitation—the color and style of lettering, the wording, the paper, and any visual symbols or literary quotations—offer a wealth of opportunities to express yourselves as a couple, both Jewishly and creatively, and to express what you hope your wedding will be.

So *nu*—what is Jewish in all the decision making that goes into your invitation design? Well, plenty. From the design and quotations to the phrasing of the language, your invitation can anchor you and your guests in Jewish tradition. It is up to you how much of that tradition you choose to include.

Envisioning Your Invitation

Before you start planning the details of your invitation, such as its style and wording, take some time to clear your mind and see what "invitation visions" come to you. Sit down; take out your wedding journal. Put on some soft music, if you like. One of you can read the following visualization out loud, then you can both take some time to write a response.

The mail arrives. You pick it up and sort through the usual junk, bills, catalogs. At the bottom of the pile, a special envelope catches your eye. Pick it up, hold it in your hands. Look closely at the envelope. What color do you see? Look at the stamp, at the way it's addressed. Open the envelope and take out your ideal wedding invitation. Hold it in your hands. What images grace the invitation? Is there a certain design, symbol, or other visual nuance that catches your eye? How does the use of color enhance the feeling of the text? What does the wording of the text express about the event? What feelings surface as you read through it? When you have had a good look, imagine that you are putting the invitation back in its envelope. You are free to open the envelope and take out the invitation for another look whenever you need inspiration. As you open your eyes, record all that you saw and felt.

When you finish journaling your visualization, compare notes. You may have had very different visions. That's okay. Now you can begin discussing your ideas and incorporating parts of both your imaginings into an invitation design. If nothing specific came to you, don't worry about it. This chapter will guide you through different options and choices relating to your invitation.

English and Hebrew?

In most traditionally observant communities in the United States and Canada, Jewish wedding invitations are printed in both Hebrew and English. Many non-Orthodox couples are also taking on this custom as a way of expressing their Jewish identity. You and your partner definitely want to discuss whether this option makes sense for you. On the one hand, if very few of your guests read Hebrew, it may seem like a superfluous addition. On the other hand, even if people can't understand what it says, the very presence of Hebrew makes a powerful statement. Throughout Jewish history, Hebrew has been cherished as a sacred, even mystical, language; today, it is both a classical tongue and a living, breathing form of communication.

The Hebrew/English decision doesn't need to be an all-or-nothing proposition: There are places in which the "two civilizations" can intermingle fluidly. You can easily insert Hebrew phrases within English text. For example, your names could appear in English, followed by or beside your Hebrew names. Your wedding date could be written in both English and Hebrew. This addition introduces Jewish time and language, while acknowledging the reality that your guests primarily speak English. Many couples report that their non-Jewish friends were especially interested in the Hebrew that appeared on their invitations and were curious about its significance.

Contemporary invitations can be simple and tailored or as ornate as you prefer. Designed by Jonathan Kremer, this one is mostly in English with just a few uses of Hebrew text.

Working with Hebrew Text

If you want to include Hebrew on your invitations—either in a side-by-side panel with the English text or integrated into it—there are lots of easy ways to do so. First, if you're planning to purchase rather than make your invitations, you can find a stationery company that prints in Hebrew. If you live in a major metropolitan area, browse around and ask at stationery/party stores. If you live in a smaller community with fewer resources, have no fear: Shopping on the Internet puts these resources at your fingertips. Check out the resource section in Appendix I for a list of online invitation companies that print Hebrew text.

Another option is to find a calligrapher experienced in writing Hebrew who can create an original invitation for you in the form of camera-ready art. Once you have the artwork, an invitation company can print from it as a model, or you can reproduce it yourself. Many *ketubah* artists (listed in Appendix I) also design custom invitations.

If you are concerned about saving money but want original, handwritten lettering, you might look for a talented art student who would welcome the opportunity to create your invitation without charging you a fortune. Put up a flyer in local art schools/studios advertising for someone experienced in calligraphy, preferably in both English and Hebrew, and see who responds. Finding a talented student is a win-win situation: You save some money and get a great invitation design, while the student gains experience, a sample for a portfolio, and some remuneration.

With the amazing selection of fonts and the high quality of today's laser printers, lots of couples choose to create their wedding invitation on a computer. If you want to add Hebrew wording in the Hebrew alphabet (as opposed to transliterated Hebrew), no problem: You can use a Hebrew word processor such as Davka (available at www.davka.com) that will allow you to type in Hebrew. If you aren't interested in purchasing a Hebrew word processing program, you might see whether your rabbi or a Jewish friend has one on her computer and will allow you to use it.

If you're not an experienced Hebrew speaker or reader, be sure to show your text to someone who is and who has an excellent eye for proofreading. Even if you think you remember how to spell your Hebrew names correctly, it is always a good idea just to make sure that you've got it right.

Options for Wording Your Invitations

Wedding invitations are a modern innovation, so there is no Jewish law or tradition that governs the phrasing of your invitation. You should include the basics:

> *Who:* The names of the couple (as decided) and, traditionally, the names of both sets of parents. Jewish tradition looks at a marriage as a joining of two families, as well as two people,

so the groom's and the bride's parents' names usually appear on wedding invitations. When there has been a divorce, death, or separation in the family, wording options can be tailored to address the specific situation (see "Family Dynamics" later in this chapter for examples).

What: Let your guests know whether they are being invited to any events taking place before the ceremony, such as a *tisch* or *ketubah* signing. (See chapter 5 for explanations of pre-wedding festivities.)

Where: Your wedding invitation should make clear whether the ceremony and reception will be held at the same place or at two different locations. Directions to all wedding-related events should be included with the invitation.

When: You'll need to let guests know how early to arrive before the ceremony if festivities are planned beforehand.

Why: That's the part of the invitation that draws on your creative side and will allow you to share your wedding *kavannah* with your guests. You can choose a Jewish quote and/or a visual symbol for your invitation that speaks to the "why" of the moment.

You have a lot of freedom in how you choose to integrate this information into a text. Your wording can incorporate the landscape, geography, or theme of your wedding. It can also emphasize or include references to ground it in Jewish time. For example:

On the tenth day of Nissan,
Corresponding to the seventeenth day of June,
Alexandra Rochelle Goldman,
Elianna Bat Shmuel V'Golda,
and Michael David Cohen,

Micha'el David Ben Simcha Yosef V'Rivka Haya,

invite you, along with their families,

to rejoice as they celebrate their love

under the chuppah

in the meadow, beside Lake Wappanatuck,

one of the first places they ever went camping together.

2 p.m. at Wappanatuck State Park (directions enclosed).

A picnic lunch will follow.

Many couples like to use the wording on their invitations to specify why they decided to get married. For example:

Joshua Michael Zimmerman

and Kevin Fink

are honoring their longtime devotion to

and deep love for each other

in a commitment ceremony

on Saturday evening, November 10th,

At 7:30 p.m.

Please join with us

to bless and witness our union.

At Temple Ohev Tzedek,

550 Fairview Parkway, Springfield, Massachusetts.

Dinner and dancing immediately to follow.

As you choose your wording, consider the degree of formality you wish to express. You have the option to do away with the third-person voice if you choose. For example:

We hope you'll come dance with us

at our wedding

'til the cows come home!

Please join us, Jennifer and Matt,

along with our folks, Rachel and Jay

and Paula and Lou,

for a celebration of love, life, and the pursuit of marital bliss!

Sunday, October 1/10 Cheshvan

at the Sunnyside Inne in Waynesboro

Kabbalat Panim (Welcoming the Bride) and Groom's Tisch

begin at Noon.

When parents are paying for a wedding, it is customary to phrase the wording so that they are clearly the hosts (see "Family Dynamics" later in this chapter). Write a draft of what you would like your invitation to say and run it by the family. You can still be informal and original in your wording, while acknowledging the parents as hosts:

Won't you come light the last Hanukkah candle with us

as our beloved children

Jessica Lynn Marx

Yoelet Leah Bat Shifra V' David Ya'akov

and Ethan David Weiner

Eitan Ben Yoni V'Rut

stand together under the chuppah.

On 2 Tevet / 27 December,

the last night of Hanukkah.

Steve and Sallie Marx   Joseph and Bev Weiner

A wedding invitation can read as poetically, dramatically, or simply as you choose. Create clear, concise wording that captures your feelings and intentions.

A Note on Hebrew Names

What's in a name? We use our secular names in a variety of utilitarian and personal functions—on our bank accounts and credit cards, shortened into nicknames, as the signature in our e-mails. For an American Jew, a Hebrew name generally serves a different function: It is a name you may forget in day-to-day life, but it was chosen to link your life to a loved one's memory or to acknowledge your Jewish heritage. It is the name that's used on sacred occasions, such as when you are called up to read from the Torah or when you are standing under the *chuppah* on your wedding day.

However, if you were never given a Hebrew name, you're not alone. Parents who aren't particularly observant or Jewishly connected when children are born may not have considered the significance of giving them a Hebrew name. If you find yourself in that situation, not to worry: Consider choosing your own Hebrew name. First, talk with your parents (or other older relatives if your parents aren't living). Are you named after someone special? Do they know that person's Hebrew name? If you weren't named for someone in particular, you may want to choose a name that carries special meaning for you. Choosing a Hebrew name is not something that should be done quickly or lightly. If you have a rabbi with whom you are close, make an appointment to talk with him about some name possibilities. Take some time and look at a book of Hebrew names. You might want to pick a name that corresponds to your English name or begins with the same sound. Because a Hebrew name is your name for sacred as opposed to utilitarian matters, you may want to take some time to meditate about your name. Read through the choices of names. Biblical names embody beautiful imagery and poetry; contemporary Hebrew names often refer to elements in nature, such as *Gal* (wave) or *Elanna* (tree).

When you choose a rabbi to officiate at your wedding, let her know that you were not given a Hebrew name at birth but would like to take one on. She can help you create a simple ritual to "cement" your name. Choosing a Hebrew name, reminding yourself of what your Hebrew name is, using your Hebrew name on your invitation beside your English one, and joining your Hebrew names together in your wedding ceremony can evoke powerful feelings, linking you to tradition. Do not feel bad if you do not have or do not know your name: Your upcoming wedding is an opportunity to reconnect and expand your connections to being Jewish.

Creative Options for Designing Your Invitation

Text, images, or both can be used to make invitations that let your guests know something about you and your partner, and about the ceremony you're creating. Choosing the words and designs is an exciting early step in the wedding-planning process, and can be a fun activity for a couple to work on together.

A Jewish Literary Journey

Many couples incorporate a literary quotation in their invitation design to capture the essence of their love. There are a whole host of Jewish literary sources that can be used to find a meaningful excerpt or quotation. If you have an interest in poetry and literature, searching for the right quotation can take you on a wonderful journey through works of Jewish literature both familiar and new. If you have a background in sacred and secular Jewish literature, you may already have some ideas about where to begin. If you are less familiar with the Hebrew Bible as literature or cannot name a contemporary Jewish poet, this foray into religious works may open up a new way for you to connect to Jewish culture. Keep in mind that as you search for a quotation, you may also find passages that you could include later on as readings in your wedding ceremony. There are lots of places to find beautiful Jewish poetry, and the following guide will hopefully make your search a bit simpler.

Also designed by Jonathan Kremer, this invitation shows how effective using a Jewish quotation can be.

The Hebrew Bible

You may not associate the Torah with love and romance, but don't reject it without checking it out first. *Shir HaShirim*, the Song of Songs, is probably the most frequently used source of love poetry in the Hebrew Bible. Many couples use the quotation *"Ani l'dodi V'dodi li"* ("I am my beloved's and my beloved is mine") on their invitations. Within the Song of Songs, though, are many other stanzas filled with sensual, passionate imagery. For example, "As a lily among thorns, so is my beloved among the daughters. As an apple-tree among trees of wood, so is my beloved among the sons" (Song of Songs 2:2). What makes it even easier to find a beautiful quote from *Shir HaShirim* is that several contemporary poets have created their own compelling translations of the text. Ariel and Chana Bloch's *The Song of Songs* and Marcia Falk's *Song of Songs: A New Translation* are two of the sources that you'll want to check out. Browse through a synagogue library, Jewish bookstore, or the Internet to find copies of both texts.

"You have put a joy in my heart greater than all the world's riches." Pretty good love poetry, yes? If you are still skeptical about the Bible as a source of lovely poetry, you should know that this quote comes from the Book of Psalms (Psalm 4:1). Although the Psalms are sacred literature that express love for and connection to God—along with the human emotions of anger, grief, and joy—there is nothing wrong with applying a quotation from Psalms to your personal relationship. There are some translations of Psalms that are especially poetic, including Stephen Mitchell's *A Book of Psalms: Selected and Adapted from the Hebrew* and David Rosenberg's *Blues of the Sky: Interpreted from the Original Hebrew Book of Psalms*. The Book of Psalms contains a wealth of quotations that could beautifully capture the essence of your love. Another favorite of mine is, "In the rightness of the world, I behold your face as I wake and your image sustains me" (Psalm 17:15).

Some same-sex couples (and heterosexual couples as well) like to use quotations from stories in the Bible that capture the essence of relationship and devotion between partners of the same gender. Faced with a tradition that has silenced and oppressed same-sex love relationships, gays and lesbians have searched the tradition for models that they can use to celebrate their unions. Two examples that are frequently used are the stories of Naomi and Ruth (found in the Book of Ruth) and David and Jonathan (found in the Book of Samuel).

Although Ruth and Naomi were not lesbian lovers, and though Jonathan and David's profound and abiding love for each other is not universally interpreted as homosexual in nature, these examples offer a point of connection for many same-sex couples. One popular expression of love is Ruth's famous exclamation of dedication to Naomi, "Wherever you go, I shall go. Your people are my people, Your God is my God" (Ruth 1:16–17).

Ladino poetry

Did you know that there exists another uniquely Jewish language besides Hebrew and Yiddish? The Jews of Sepharad—originally from Spain and Portugal—created a language called Ladino, which mixes Spanish and Hebrew (sometimes called Judeo-Spanish). There are many beautiful love poems written in Ladino. Check out *A Treasury of Jewish Love: Poems, Quotations & Proverbs in Yiddish, Hebrew, Ladino and English* for a variety of Ladino love poems. If your family or your partner's family has some Sephardic roots, including Ladino poetry, music, and customs in your wedding is a great way to honor that part of your heritage (more information on Sephardic wedding customs can be found in chapter 5).

Yiddish poetry

Although the Yiddish language is usually associated with comedy, serious Yiddish writers explored every literary style, including poetry. Particularly in the nineteenth and twentieth centuries, there was a great Yiddish literary blossoming in Eastern Europe, which included both male and female writers. Their works can be found in the above-mentioned anthology as well as in the *Penguin Book of Modern Yiddish Literature*. If you have Yiddish-speaking relatives, it might be very touching for them to see a quotation from a Yiddish writer as an expression of your love. For more information on Yiddish poetry, contact the Yiddish Book Center at www.yiddishbookcenter.org.

Contemporary Jewish poetry

From the last century through today we have seen a resurgence of poets whose identity as Jews naturally and organically flows into their work. Some of these poets, such as Marge Piercy, write intentionally for Jewish sacred moments, from interpretations of daily prayers to poems to mark life-cycle events. Her book *The Art of Blessing the Day* compiles her Jewish-themed poems, including an entire section of poems about marriage. Poet Merle Feld, whose spiritual autobiography and poetry is contained in *A Spiritual Life,* also incorporates a Jewish background and sensibility into her work. And well-known Jewish poet Adrienne Rich is also a great source of contemporary love poetry (particularly from a lesbian perspective).

Using Israeli poetry is another wonderful way to make a Jewish literary connection. Perhaps no Israeli poet is better known and loved than the late Yehuda Amichai, whose poems were said to be carried by soldiers in the fields of battle. Amichai's love poetry is sensual and highly imagistic. Amichai wrote many books of poems; for beginning reading, you might want to start with *Selected Poems of Yehuda Amichai.*

Other sources

There are many living, breathing Jewish poets whose work might speak to you. A great way to find them is by checking out back issues of *The Jewish Women's Literary Annual* (available at www.ncjwny.org), *Bridges* journal (www.bridgesjournal.org), and a great website called www.ritualwell.org, which provides a range of poetry and other readings to be used for ritual moments.

Creating a Design

A literary quotation is one way to capture the essence of your relationship, and a visual symbol can do the same thing. Your invitation may include a visual image in myriad ways: It may open or unfold to showcase the image; the image may appear as a border around your text; it may even grace the outside of your envelope. You may choose a meaningful design for your invitation that you want to carry through your wedding by including it on your wedding programs, *ketubah*, and thank you notes. The use of color and visual symbols adds value and richness that can speak to people in a different way than words can. Jewish ritual art employs certain visual symbols over and over again. Pomegranates are symbols of fertility and abundance, for example. You do not have to be an artist to plan your design or come up with colors and graphic styles that appeal to you and can

CARRA AND SCOTT

Invitations like this one created by Susan Leviton can have both pretty designs and meaningful quotations.

help you express your wedding *kavannah*. The choice is ultimately about your personal aesthetic. As you think through your design, consider the following range of options.

A *visual symbol*

You might want to choose a visual symbol to adorn the front of your invitation or to be woven in or around the text. My husband and I asked our calligrapher to draw a lotus flower above our text. The lotus is a powerful Buddhist symbol that represents the nature of cause and effect. The lotus flower both seeds and blossoms at the same time. It needs a muddy swamp to root in so it can rise to the surface as a beautiful flower. The lotus is an incredibly inspiring symbol to both of us, and this symbolic reference is also one way that we honored Fred's Buddhist path in our Jewish wedding. You might want to include visuals that suggest Jewish meaning—from an illustration of a *chuppah* to a sketch of the fields of Jerusalem. Take a look at Jewish art books, such as *Jewish Art* by Grace Cohen Grossman, to get some ideas.

This design was used on the invitation by Jonathan Kremer and incorporated into other wedding-related materials.

Color

The use of color in your invitation can be as bold or as subtle as you want. Your text can be printed in a color that will appear as a recurring theme in your wedding décor. You can choose paper in a wild shade, such as magenta or tangerine, even though those aren't traditional wedding colors. Take a look at a color palette and talk through with your partner which colors most appeal to you and what nuances each suggests. If your wedding is being held on or around a specific Jewish holiday, color can be a great way of making a connection: silver lettering for a Rosh Hodesh wedding, shimmering paper in gold or yellow to symbolize the Hanukkah lights.

Paper

There are many wonderful paper styles and textures available today. Before you make a decision about what kind of paper you'd like, take some time to

Simple Steps for Making Paper

Materials

- Paper scraps of your choice: computer paper (unprinted), newspaper (if you want a grayish-colored paper), old cards (for heavier paper), tissue paper (for finer paper), napkins, or construction paper

- Blender/food processor (for making paper pulp)

- Flowers, leaves, and branches for interesting color and texture

- Window screening (large enough to lay your paper on)

- Wood frame (an old picture frame can be used)

- Staples or tacks (for tacking screen on frame)

- Plastic basin/tub (large enough to totally immerse the frame)

- Stirring spoon

- Measuring spoons

- Liquid starch

- White felt or flannel fabric (at least 8 x 11 inches, or larger than the size paper you plan to make), in as many sheets of paper you plan to make, plus one

- Sponge

- 2 cookie sheets

- Sieve

browse through a stationery store or look at craft stores online (see resources in Appendix I). If you are really brave—and have some time on your hands and someone who can help you—you could even consider making your own paper. Although it takes some practice to get really comfortable with the technique, making paper can be a thoroughly satisfying craft project. You get to play with texture and color, adding different amount of flowers, leaves, or other natural objects to create the kind of paper that you want. If you are planning to use roses to adorn your *chuppah*, you might want to include rose petals in your paper. (See "Simple Steps for Making Paper" sidebar on this page.)

Making paper is also a great way to recycle old paper (one of the needed ingredients). If you want to honor the Jewish value of *bal taschit* (not wasting) in your wedding, creating your own paper for your invitations is a great place to start. You can let guests know that your invitations were made out of recycled paper and that you did the recycling!

Papermaking may be a more realistic project for someone having a wedding on the smaller side, with fifty or fewer guests. If you want to try making your own paper but have more than fifty invitations to create, I suggest asking a friend or two to help out. You could also throw a party with a papermaking theme and get a bunch of folks to help you.

Connection to Ketubah

You may not have given any thought yet to what kind of design you want for your *ketubah*, but thinking through a graphic for your invitation might inspire some ideas. Marsha and Dave Kleiner, for instance, came up with a very original idea that both graced their invitations and became the design for their *ketubah*. They asked a close artist friend to sketch the outdoor grove where their wedding would be taking place. On the invitation, the drawing gave their guests a sense of the place they would be coming to for the wedding, and on their *ketubah* the drawing reminds them of their special day.

How Other Couples Personalized Their Invitations

When Felicia Herman and David Ben Ur were planning their wedding, they wanted to go with a simple, elegant garden theme that incorporated their love of flowers and gardening. To set the stage, Felicia began by making her own invitations. "A creative friend of mine showed me a lot of different options, different sizes of paper, envelopes, colors, orientation of the print, and so on," she recalls. "That helped me to get out of the white card stock, 5 x 7 standard thing."

To create an original botanical design, Felicia took flowers, branches, and leaves from her garden and flattened them. She then used a roller to cover them with black ink and pressed the ink side onto white paper to make an imprint of the design. Next she scanned the design into the computer and printed it out on sage-colored paper. The text of the invitation, also created on the computer, was printed on parchment-style paper. "I think the total time I spent on it was a day and a half, from beginning to end," Felicia says. "But this is the kind of project that, now that I have a child, I can't imagine having the time to do!"

Kevin Haworth and Danielle LeShaw also wanted to break away from the white, standard-issue invitation. They first thought about finding a sacred Jewish quotation that could appear on their invitation, which would let their guests know about their intentions for their marriage, their connection to Jewish tradition, and their love for each other. After much study, the couple chose, "Blessed is the Generous One, God of our ancestors, who sent you this very day to meet me" (I Samuel 85:32). They asked an artistic friend to incorporate the quotation, written in Hebrew and English, in an arbor surrounding their wedding invitation text.

Kevin and Danielle decided to play with the form of their invitation. Danielle had read a blurb in the Style section of the *New York Times* about invitations for a high-end gala that were sent in pretty little boxes containing chocolates. She thought that some kind of interesting container, rather than a traditional envelope, might be a fun way to go for their wedding invitations. They mailed their vellum invitations in sturdy, cylindrical containers that Danielle found at an art-supply store. "We put little jelly beans inside for sweetness," she recalls. "That was like a little preview of the custom of throwing candy at the bride and groom during the *aufruf*, which is also for sweetness." Kevin and Danielle put labels on

Instructions

1. Select the pieces of paper to be recycled. Mix different types to create your own unique color and texture of paper.
2. Rip the paper into small bits and put into the blender (about half full). Fill the blender with warm water. Run the blender slowly at first, then increase the speed until the pulp looks smooth and well blended (30–40 seconds). Make at least three blenders full of pulp. Make sure that no flakes of paper remain. If you are adding flowers or leaves, put them into the blender now and run it slowly until they are mixed into the pulp.
3. The next step is to make a mold. The mold is made simply by stretching fiberglass screening (plain old door and window screening) over a wooden frame and stapling it. It should be as tight as possible.
4. Fill the basin about halfway with water. Add three blender loads of pulp (the more pulp you add, the thicker the finished paper will be). Stir the mixture with a spoon.
5. Stir two teaspoons of liquid starch into the pulp.
6. Place the mold into the pulp and then level it out while it is submerged. Gently wiggle it side to side until the pulp on top of the screen looks even.
7. Slowly lift the mold up until it is above the level of the water. Wait until most of the water

has drained from the new paper sheet. If the paper is very thick, remove some pulp from the tub. If it is too thin, add more pulp and stir the mixture again.

8. When the mold stops dripping, gently place one edge on the side of a fabric square (such as a felt or flannel square). Gently ease the mold down flat, with the paper directly on the fabric. Use a sponge to press out as much water as possible. Wring the excess water from the sponge back into the large plastic tub.

9. Now comes the tricky part. Hold the fabric square flat and slowly lift the edge of the mold. The wet sheet of paper should remain on the fabric. If it sticks to the mold, you may have pulled too fast or not pressed out enough water. It takes a little practice. You can gently press out any bubbles and loose edges at this point.

10. Repeat the steps above for each sheet of paper, and stack the fabric squares with the sheets on a cookie sheet. Save one fabric square to place on the top of the stack to cover the last piece of paper. Use another cookie sheet to press the remaining water out of the stack. (Do this outside or in the bathtub, as it can make a mess.) Run the excess water through a sieve before pouring it into your sink so that it won't clog your drain.

11. After you press the stack, gently separate the sheets.

the cylinders and took them to the post office to mail. Their guests responded warmly to these unique invitations.

Family Dynamics and Your Wedding Invitation

A seemingly simple task such as writing your invitations can become explosive when you consider the complexity of today's families. Approaching the issue with sensitivity can help you in the long run.

Traditionally, if a bride's parents were paying for a wedding, the invitation would come from them. Today, there are no hard and fast rules about who pays for a wedding. If you're in a situation in which the groom's parents are better able to foot the bill, they may want their names to appear in the host position. Talk through the best way to honor everyone: Perhaps the names of the parents could appear side by side. Another option might be the following:

Mr. and Mrs. Eric Goldstein

along with Mr. and Mrs. David Wachs

Invite you . . .

Jewish values teach us that *lo leviyesh*—not embarrassing another person—is a critical injunction. Although times have changed, there is often still an expectation that a bride's parents will foot the wedding bill, so if financial circumstances make it impossible for them to do so, they may be feeling both ashamed and uncomfortable. Considerate wording can ease everyone's minds.

Another complex situation occurs when parents on either or both sides are divorced and/or remarried. Some parents may be contributing as hosts, while others are not. In this case, you and your partner might need to be creative in the wording. You could be general, and just say "together with our families," or you could include all the names. For example:

Milt and Suzanne Siegel

and Jason and Elyse Wexler

Invite you to rejoice at the wedding of their daughter

Elizabeth Nicole

To

Jonathan Michael Mayer,

Son of

Alice Cohen

And David and Jessica Mayer

The exercise of figuring out the best wording for your particular families can help prepare you for the coming dynamics that occur when you bring all sides together. You will need to find a way to acknowledge and honor your families. Because many couples are marrying later in life and hosting their own weddings, they may feel silly mentioning parents at all. One way to honor parents while still making it clear that you are the hosts is to list both parents in the way that was traditionally reserved for the groom's parents:

Rachel Lee Adler

Daughter of Stephen Adler and Marci Smith

and

Benjamin Cohen-Lekowski

Son of Jack Cohen and Jane Cohen-Lekowski

invite you to join us

at the simcha of our wedding!

Many people who are remarrying, especially those with growing or grown children, like to list their children's names on the invitations. This gesture shows that the marrying of the two individuals will create ties among all their children. Seeing their name in print on the invitation can really help children gain a sense

They can be dried by hanging on a clothesline or laying them out flat on sheets of newspaper. When they have dried (it may take anywhere from a few hours to a whole day, depending on how thick your paper is and how humid a day it is), peel them off the fabric and voilà! You have paper! Don't be discouraged if your paper didn't come out exactly as you would have liked. Papermaking is not an exact science; it requires experimentation and practice.

Don't Forget the Thank you Notes!

While you are designing, making, or ordering your invitations, you might want to do the same for your thank you cards. You can use the same quotation, design, or symbol for your thank you cards, or create something in a similar vein but with a little twist. For example, if your invitations feature an illustration of assorted pomegranates, your thank you card might feature a close-up of one pomegranate.

You may want to go with thank you postcards, which will save you money on postage and also honor the Jewish value of *bal taschit*, since you're not wasting envelopes. You can print up a sample postcard and take it to a copy shop to be reproduced.

Have your thank you notes on hand so that you can write them as gifts come in, before, during, and after the wedding. In this day of digital communication, people really savor a handwritten message, and writing thank you notes is one occasion when you can offer this kind touch. It does take time and some couples prefer to divide up the pile, while others each write a line or two on each note. You don't have to write a long note to make it a meaningful one. If you can add a personal detail for each gift—either about how much you love the gift or about the gift of that person's presence at your wedding—it will be greatly appreciated.

of ownership and involvement in what may feel like an otherwise anxiety-provoking event. For example:

Dear friends and family,
We, along with our beloved children,
invite you to join us
to celebrate the simcha of our wedding!
Festivities will take place on the 15th day of Kislev,
the 8th day of December,
at Temple Brit Shalom,
Annapolis, Maryland.
Chuppah will begin at Noon.
Helen Jane Sussman
and her children, Mark, David and Lisa,
and
Dr. Leo Rothman
and his children, Michael and Sara

In cases when a parent has died, the bride or groom may still find it important to list that parent's name on the invitation, as a way of honoring her memory and feeling connected to her presence during such an important time in life. One way to make clear that a person is deceased is to add the abbreviation *z"l*, after the name. *Z"l* stands for *zichrono livracha*, meaning "of blessed memory."

Today's families may look more complicated than those in generations past, but a wedding, handled with sensitivity, tact, and patience, can be an opportunity for healing and rejoicing. Most important, you and your partner should talk openly and honestly about issues that surface concerning family dynamics, and you may wish to talk with your rabbi as well.

chapter three

Let's Make a Deal
Crafting Your *Ketubah*

One of the most essential objects in a contemporary Jewish wedding ceremony is the *ketubah*, the Jewish marriage contract. The government sanctions marriages by issuing marriage licenses; Jewish law has historically used the *ketubah* in much the same way.

In addition to serving a legal purpose, *ketubot* (pl.) have long been an expression of Jewish creativity, with artists employing the value of *hiddur mitzvah* to make the *ketubah* a document of incredible beauty. Today, with the exception of the Orthodox community, original *ketubot* are being created for both same-sex and heterosexual couples. Couples can create art for their *ketubah* that is expressive of their relationship, as well as adapt the traditional *ketubah* text to better reflect the nature of their commitments to each other.

For many couples, creating an original *ketubah* is one of the most rich and profound processes associated with planning their wedding. Because there are many serious decisions neccessary to create the best *ketubah* for you, I recommend that couples allow plenty of time—optimally at least six months before the wedding—to think seriously about all the issues surrounding their *ketubah*. This chapter contains many suggestions for ways in which you and your partner might choose the right kind of *ketubah* text and art for you.

Ketubah literally means "writing" or "written" and came to refer to the written marriage contract that is signed and read as part of the Jewish wedding.

Scholars are not exactly sure when *ketubot* first surfaced, but they do know that the standard text of an Orthodox *ketubah* was composed around 200 B.C.E. It was—and is—written in Aramaic, the secular language for the Jewish community at that time.

In 200 B.C.E., when Middle Eastern cultures were clearly patriarchal in nature, the language and concept inherent in a *ketubah* was certainly innovative. Throughout Jewish history, when a woman got married, the *ketubah* became her property and she held on to it dearly, as it served to protect her financially in case of divorce or death. It is essentially the first prenuptial agreement in history. The *ketubah* was also created to protect the bride's ongoing rights in the marriage: It declares the wife's rights to food, clothing, and even sex throughout the course of the marriage.

Although the language of the original *ketubah* may not always speak to the issues of today's couples, it was a great step forward at the time toward acknowledging women as human beings with real physical and financial needs. For that giant step forward we can feel very proud of our Jewish heritage.

What many couples choose to add to the rather matter-of-fact original text is an expression of spiritual and emotional needs—not just for the bride, but for both partners. Just ahead, I will share many of the innovative kinds of texts that couples are using in contemporary *ketubot*. A *ketubah* today can honor the legacy of our past while adding new components to ground it as a sacred, living document for our present times.

The Complexity of the *Ketubah's* Legacy

Although the *ketubah* was an innovation when it first appeared, many modern couples cannot condone using the standard text of a traditional *ketubah*. Even though it speaks to the bride's rights, the text considers the bride herself as property. Traditional language states that a groom "acquires" a bride. In the narrative of the *ketubah*, it is the groom who is speaking, while the bride merely consents. The text also assumes the virginity of the bride (while saying nothing about the state of the groom's virginity).

Again, it is helpful to consider the times in which the document was written and to step back and realize the extent to which women's equality has evolved (in most cultures). While many couples want to carry on the tradition of a Jewish legal document affirming their marriage, they will not use one that represents the patriarchal thinking of the past. For a long time, Reform rabbis did away with the concept of a *ketubah* altogether and are only now reclaiming the tradition with creative innovation.

In her groundbreaking book *Engendering Judaism*, scholar and critic Rachel Adler suggests that the notion of "acquiring" and the language of the *ketubah* be done away with altogether. As an alternative, Adler has created the concept of *brit ahuvim*, a covenant of love, that couples make to each other to sign on the occasion of their wedding. Adler composed a new text using sources from Jewish texts, along with contemporary writing, that speaks to a bride and groom or to same-sex couples making a covenant to each other. Her *brit ahuvim* describes the spiritual, emotional, physical, and financial commitments that a couple pledge to one another. (Sample text appears later in this chapter.)

Adler's innovation is one way to work with the complex history of a tradition that is evolving to reflect the changes in women's status in most Jewish communities. There are other ways to approach this issue as well; for example, some couples choose to include the standard Aramaic text as a way of honoring tradition, while adding their own personal vows and commitments in English. Other couples look for a prewritten *ketubah* that uses some of the original language and updates other parts of it.

By presenting the range of alternatives and innovations in contemporary *ketubot*, I am not suggesting that couples who choose to use a traditional *ketubah* are wrong in any way. For many couples, using a traditional *ketubah* gives them a sense of connection to their ancestors, who used the very same document in their wedding ceremony, and to a sense of *klal Yisrael*—the Jewish community all over the world.

Perhaps no other time in Jewish history has seen such a diversity in terms of styles of worship and observance as ours, and the wide range of *ketubot* being created today attest to that. Deciding what kind of *ketubah* is right for you depends on your personal philosophy. Whether you consider yourself feminist or not, whether you are gay or straight, even whether you want God language in your text or not, you can find or create a *ketubah* to meet your needs.

Types of Texts

Because of the variety of *ketubah* texts available, I have provided an outline and examples of some of the different types. If you choose to write part or all of your own text, you might use elements of any or all of the following options.

Please note: Your *ketubah* is one element of your wedding that you should be sure to discuss with the rabbi who is marrying you well in advance of the ceremony. Some rabbis have very strong feelings about using a halachically suitable *ketubah*, the kind that follows traditional Jewish law. Other rabbis may feel very strongly that a *ketubah* be egalitarian—written in modern Hebrew and English and expressing the sentiments of the couple. Make sure you have an idea about the kind of *ketubah* text that you prefer when you first choose an officiant.

Orthodox

It is important for all couples to know that in the Orthodox world, only the traditional, Orthodox *ketubah* is recognized as valid. By Orthodox *ketubah*, I mean the version of the text (sample on the next page) that has been the same word-for-word text for approximately the past two thousand years. If you are Orthodox, that is obviously a very important fact for you to know.

What does this mean for couples who are not Orthodox? It means that at some point in your life, an Orthodox rabbi could question your *ketubah*. It also means that if one member of the couple comes from a family that includes Orthodox relatives and wants them to give their approval to the marriage, they might feel strongly that an Orthodox *ketubah* be signed and read as part of the wedding ceremony.

Unfortunately, misunderstanding and miscommunication abound among the various Jewish movements today. Orthodox Jews live by a certain set of laws that make up their world of values, beliefs, and behaviors. Liberal (non-Orthodox) Jews see those sets of laws as being important guides, but they are willing to see Judaism as an evolving culture, with some laws needing to be changed under certain circumstances.

Most non-Orthodox couples do not feel the need to use an Orthodox *ketubah*, while some couples prefer it because of its very link to tradition. Another option, if you and/or your rabbi feels that it is important to have an Orthodox *ketubah*, is to use one and also to create your own, contemporary *ketubah*. If you make that choice, you can add additional text in the second document that expresses your spiritual and emotional commitments to each other. Both documents can be signed and incorporated into the wedding ceremony.

A translation of a standard Orthodox *ketubah* reads:

On the _____ day of the week, the _____ day of the month _____ in the year five thousand seven hundred and _____ since the creation of the world according to the reckoning which we are accustomed to using here in the city of _____ in _____. That _____ son of _____ of the family _____ said to this maiden _____ daughter of _____ of the family _____ "Be my wife according to the laws of Moses and Israel, and I will cherish you in accordance with the custom of Jewish husbands, who cherish, honor, support, and maintain their wives faithfully. And I here present you with the marriage gift of virgins, two hundred silver *zuzim*, which belongs to you, according to the law of Moses and Israel; and I will also give you your food, clothing, and neccessities, and live with you as husband and wife according to the universal custom." And _____ , this maiden, consented and became his wife. The trousseau that she brought to him from her father's house in silver, gold and valuables, clothing, furniture, and bedclothes, all this _____ , the bridegroom, accepted in the sum of one hundred silver pieces, making in all two hundred silver pieces. And thus said _____ , the bridegroom, "The responsibility of this contract, of this trousseau, and of this additional sum, I take upon myself and my heirs after me, so that they shall be paid from the best part of my property and possessions that I have beneath the whole heaven, that which I now possess or may hereafter acquire. All my property, real and personal, even the shirt from my back, shall be mortgaged to secure the payment of this marriage contract, of the trousseau, and of the addition made to it, during my lifetime and after my death, from the present day and forever." _____ , the bridegroom, has taken upon himself the responsibility of this marriage contract, of the trousseau, and the addition made to it, according to the restrictive usages of all marriage contracts and the additions to them made for the daughters of Israel, according to the institutions of our sages of blessed memory. It is not to be regarded as an indecisive contractual obligation or as a mere formula of a document. We have followed the legal formula of a document. We have followed the legal formality of symbolic delivery between _____, son of _____, and _____, daughter of _____, this maiden, and we have used a garment legally fit for the purpose, to strengthen all that is stated above,

AND EVERYTHING IS VALID AND CONFIRMED.

Attested to _____

          Witness

Attested to _____

          Witness

Note: A traditional Orthodox *ketubah* is signed by two male Jewishly observant witnesses. A non-Orthodox *ketubah* does not have any special constraints regarding the number of witnesses who must sign it; it might be signed by two male and two female witnesses, or any number of witnesses that the couple chooses. In some communities, the bride and groom also sign their own *ketubah,* as does the rabbi officiating at the wedding. (For more about the place of *ketubah* signing in the wedding ceremony, see chapter 5.)

Conservative

Often referred to as the "Lieberman" *ketubah* after the scholar who modified it, this *ketubah* is identical to the Orthodox version, except that it includes a special provision at the end of the document stating that the groom promises to give the bride a divorce should she ask for one. Within the Orthodox world, there is a tragic situation that occurs when a man won't give his wife a divorce—the woman becomes what is called an *agunah* (a chained wife) and is not legally able to marry again. This Conservative modification was put forth by Professor Saul Lieberman of the Jewish Theological Seminary in 1953; his concern, at that point, was that a *ketubah* should be a viable legal document in American as well as Jewish courts. Supported by the Rabbinical Assembly (the professional association for Conservative rabbis), a *ketubah* with the Lieberman clause is generally the preferred document among Conservative rabbis today. This does not mean that if you are planning to be married by a Conservative rabbi you shouldn't discuss the idea of adding any creative interpretation to your *ketubah*. Many Conservative rabbis encourage couples to write a statement about love and respect in English that can follow the traditional Aramaic text. The Lieberman clause reads:

> _____, the groom, and _____, the bride, further agreed that should either contemplate dissolution of the marriage, or following the dissolution of their marriage in the civil courts, each may summon the other to the Bet Din of the Rabbinical Assembly and the Jewish Theological Seminary, or its representative, and that each will abide by its instructions so that throughout life each will be able to live according to the laws of the Torah.

Reform/Reconstructionist/Egalitarian

Within the Reform and Reconstructionist movements, there are a number of popular ways to work creatively with *ketubah* text. Some couples choose to write original text in English that may also be translated into modern Hebrew. The texts usually speak to the couples' spiritual and emotional commitments, but may include physical and financial obligations as well.

One approach that blends tradition with modernity is to keep the literary style of the *ketubah* text traditional in its tone, while personal/spiritual vows are inserted in appropriate places to make the content of the document contemporary in feeling.

Within this version of an updated *ketubah*, language may also be used to reflect egalitarian ideals: Instead of speaking of the groom promising to pay the marriage gift, for example, both the bride and groom can be mentioned as paying the gift.

When my husband, Fred, and I were working with Rabbi Shai Gluskin in preparation for our marriage, Shai shared with us the *ketubah* that he and his wife, Sarah Braun, created for their wedding. Shai spoke about wanting to feel connected to the creative literary style of our ancestors—he appreciated the way the *ketubah* reads like a story. By preserving the intent of the original language, but by updating its content to reflect their values and ideals, Shai and Sarah struck a balance between tradition and innovation. Fred and I used this model to create our *ketubah*, which reads:

On the third day of Tammuz in the year 5761 since the creation of the world as we reckon time here in Altoona, Pennsylvania, in the valley of the Upper Appalachia mountains, in the United States of America

The bride, Gabrielle Suzanne, daughter of Lynn and Stephen, said to the groom Fred, son of Gladys and Joe, *"Harai ata mekudash li, k'dat Miriam, Moshe, v'Yisrael."*

The groom, Frederic Abraham, son of Gladys and Joe, said to the bride Gabrielle, daughter of Stephen and Lynn, *"Harai at mekudeshet li, k'dat Moshe, Miriam, v'Yisrael."*

The bride, groom, the parents of the bride and groom, and their families and friends contributed to the establishment of the couple's household. They brought "silver, gold, valuables, and household furnishings.

She also said, "I take it upon myself to provide for your needs, physical, emotional, and spiritual, to the best of my abilities.

"I take it upon myself to bring a sense of humor and playfulness, a willingness to communicate, and a promise to always listen to your feelings, to our marriage.

"I will support you when you're sick or tired. I will strive to create nutritious meals to nurture our bodies and souls, and I will do my fair share of housework.

He also said, "I take it upon myself to provide for your needs, physical, emotional, and spiritual, to the best of my abilities.

"I take it upon myself to hold life in the highest regard. With the deepest appreciation for the fortune that life has to offer, I will continually strive to make the love I have for you manifest in our daily life. I will value our time together and strive to bring quality, respect, encouragement, dedication, and compassion to our relationship in all its forms.

"I will strive to take account of my actions so that I can always grow and develop to be the best possible partner.

"I will love and respect you, our pets, our future children (God willing), and our collective families and communities. I will strive to live a life of balance and simplicity and so bring joy and happiness to our home."

"I take it upon myself to consider the legacy of our ancestors and anticipate the future of our descendants, seven generations into the future, when acting for myself and for our family."

The bride and groom said to each other, "We promise to strive for honesty with each other, to respect the ways we are different from each other, and to comfort and challenge each other through life's joys and sorrows.
"We also sanctify our lives through the appreciation of each other's faith, the support of each other's spiritual practice, and in our joint belief in repairing the world through the reformation and revolution of our lives. We rejoice in our love and are thankful for all the events and blessings that lead us to each other."

The groom, Frederic Abraham, and the bride, Gabrielle Suzanne, accept upon themselves the responsibility for the ketubah. Everything is valid and established.

If you compare this text with the Orthodox version, you can see where the language is the same and where it differs. It was important to us, for example, to honor the role of women in Jewish tradition, so we added Miriam to Moses and Israel (which we also did when reciting the *"harai at"* statement during the exchange of wedding rings part of our ceremony). We chose to have our *ketubah* text written in traditional Aramaic where the language is the same as in a traditional *ketubah*, but we added a modern Hebrew translation for the original parts that we wrote. An Israeli friend was able to translate our English into poetic, natural-sounding Hebrew. Our *ketubah* is written in calligraphy in both that Aramaic/Hebrew combination and in English.

Gender Neutral

Gender-neutral texts, written without masculine or feminine pronouns, are a successful way for same-sex partners to create *ketubah* texts without needing to specify gender or use the terms "bride and groom." Gender-neutral texts generally refer to the partners in the first person, rather than in the third person, as the traditional texts do. One example of such a *ketubah* was written by calligrapher Betsy Platkin Teutsch. It reads:

> With hearts full of joy, we stand together under the *huppah*, linking past to future uniting our lives. In exchanging these rings, we consecrate ourselves to one another, entering into a sacred covenant of love, trust and commitment. We promise to cherish, honor and support each other, striving ever to be loving, patient, and loyal partners. Respecting our differences and sharing our strengths, may we together meet life's challenges. Nurtured by our union, may our souls blossom, our talents flower and our dreams bear fruit.
>
> As a Jewish family, we will weave a tapestry of celebration, sanctifying the cycles of our years and the seasons of our lives. May the Holy One protect and guide us on our life's journey, blessing our hearts with happiness and wisdom and our home with openness, friendship, abundance and peace. And may we always share these blessings with our family and community, the Jewish people, and all who dwell on earth.
>
> And duly witnessed, all is established and confirmed.

Humanistic

Humanistic Judaism embraces a human-centered philosophy that combines the celebration of Jewish culture and identity with an adherence to humanistic values and ideas, focusing on the way humans treat one another as opposed to the relationship between human beings and God. The Association of Humanistic Rabbis has created a modern *ketubah* that emphasizes a couple's pledge of love and support to each other and to the Jewish community but does not contain any mention of God. It reads:

On the _____ day of the month of _____, in the year _____ of the Jewish calendar, corresponding to the _____ day of the month of _____, in the year _____ of the secular calendar as recorded in _____, _____, _____ and _____ entered into this Covenant of marriage.

We hereby pledge to trust, respect and support each other throughout our married life together. We shall always endeavour to be open and honest, understanding and accepting, loving and forgiving, and loyal to one another.

We hereby promise to work together to build a harmonious relationship of equality. We shall respect each other's uniqueness and help one another to grow to our fullest potential. We will comfort and support each other through life's sorrows and joys.

Together, we shall create a home filled with learning, laughter and compassion, a home wherein we will honour each other's cherished family traditions and values. Let us join hands to help build a world filled with peace and love.

_____

Witness

_____

Witness

_____

Rabbi/Officiating Clergy

Interfaith

A Good Company's interfaith *ketubah* design

A *ketubah* written for a Jew and a non-Jew is not considered legally valid in the Orthodox and Conservative world. Some Reform, Reconstructionist, and Jewish Renewal rabbis, however, do encourage interfaith couples to create a document in the style of a *ketubah* to express the couple's commitment to each other. A very popular interfaith *ketubah*, produced by a firm called A Good Company, seeks to integrate the background of both members of the interfaith couple. It reads:

> From every human being there rises a light that reaches straight to heaven. And when two souls that are destined to be together find each other, their streams of light flow together and a single, brighter light goes forth from their united being. —Baal Shem Tov

> This certificate celebrates before God and all those present that on the _____ day of the week, the _____ day of _____ in the year _____ corresponding to _____ at _____, the holy covenant of marriage was entered into between the Groom, _____, and the Bride, _____. We pledge to each other to be loving friends and partners in marriage, to talk and listen, to trust and appreciate one another, to respect and cherish each other's uniqueness, and to support, comfort and strengthen each other through life's sorrows and joys. We further promise to share hopes, thoughts, and dreams as we build our life together. May we grow our lives ever intertwined, our love bringing us closer. We shall endeavor to establish a home that is compassionate to all, wherein the flow of the seasons and the passages of life, as witnessed by our mutual traditions, are revered and honored. May our home be forever filled with peace, happiness, and love.

Public/Private *Ketubah* or *Tennaim*

Rabbi Arthur Ocean Waskow and spiritual leader Phyllis Ocean Berman have created another interesting model of a contemporary egalitarian *ketubah*—one that is actually two *ketubot*, a public and a private version. The private version, which the couple may want to share only with each other, and perhaps with a few very close friends, involves making certain personal commitments to each other. Then they may create a second, less personal *ketubah*, which can be read in public during the wedding ceremony.

The intent of writing the private *ketubah* is for the couple to really think about and write out their pledges to each other and to have them witnessed and honored in a sacred, albeit private, ritual as part of their wedding ceremony. Berman and Waskow suggest that items to consider writing about in a private *ketubah* include sex, money, geography, work, children, previous families, spiritual life, Jewish life, society, politics, *tikkun olam* (literally "repairing the world" or social action), change of names, and also provisions for rethinking and making changes to these commitments by mutual consent further down the road. In its concept, the private *ketubah* takes on more of the weight of the traditional *ketubah*, in that it concerns very pragmatic realities that will directly affect the couple's lives. The public *ketubah* might use language that speaks in more general, rather than specific, terms.

If the idea of drafting two documents appeals to you, you may want to write your more personal commitments in another related document called the *tennaim* (literally "conditions"). Jewish marriage tradition offers another opportunity for writing up some personal hopes and promises to each other in the *tennaim* text. In many Jewish communities of days gone by, the *tennaim* were pledges, written into a legally binding document, specifying such information as the agreed-upon date of the wedding and what would happen if one partner backed out. The *tennaim* were generally drafted at the time of engagement, and in many Eastern European countries it was customary for the mothers of the intended bride and groom to break a plate after the *tennaim* were signed, which was said to symbolize the irreparable conditions of the deal.

Today, some couples write out contemporary-style *tennaim* and share them at an engagement party. You and your partner might want to draft *tennaim* shortly after your engagement, as a way of addressing the various issues that you need to work through and the commitments you are willing to make to each other about your marriage plans. You can use the topics that Waskow and Berman suggest and write your own promises and conditions. Again, the document could be completely personal, between only the two of you, or you could share it with a few close friends or relatives.

Brit Ahuvim

As mentioned earlier, Rachel Adler's concept of *brit ahuvim* replaces the traditional *ketubah* with a document that expresses a couple's commitment to each other and to the Jewish people. This is for couples who reject the ideas put forth in the traditional *ketubah* and feel strongly that, rather than making modifications in the traditional text, a new text should be written altogether. Adler's innovative document may be the right choice. It is also a good (and popular) choice for same-sex couples. Her suggested *brit ahuvim* text reads:

On _____ (day of week), the _____ day of _____ (month), 57 _____ according to Jewish reckoning (_____ [month]_____ [day,] _____ [year], according to secular reckoning), in the city of _____ (state or region), _____ (country), _____ , (Hebrew name) daughter/son of _____ and _____, whose surname is _____ , and _____ , (Hebrew name) daughter/son of _____ and _____, whose surname is _____ , confirm in the presence of witnesses a lovers' covenant between them and declare a partnership to establish a household among the People of Israel.

The agreement into which_____ and _____ are entering is a holy covenant like the ancient covenants of our people, made in faithfulness and peace to stand forever. It is a covenant of protection and hope like the covenant God swore to Noah and his descendants, saying, "When the bow is in the clouds, I will see it and remember the everlasting covenant between God and all living creatures, all flesh that is on earth. That," God said to Noah, "shall be the sign of the covenant that I have established between me and all flesh" (Gen. 9:16–17).

It is a covenant of distinction, like the covenant God made with Israel, saying, "You shall be My people, and I shall be your God" (Jer. 30:22).

It is a covenant of devotion, joining hearts like the covenant David and Jonathan made, as it is said, "And Jonathan's soul was bound up with the soul of David. Jonathan made a covenant with David because he loved him as himself" (1 Sam. 18:1–3).

It is a covenant of mutual lovingkindness like the wedding covenant between God and Zion, as it is said, "I will espouse you forever. I will espouse you with righteousness and justice and lovingkindness and compassion. I will espouse you in faithfulness and you shall know God" (Hosea 2:21–22).

The following are the provisions of the lovers' covenant into which _____ (Hebrew name), daughter/son of _____ and _____ , and _____ (Hebrew name), daughter/son of _____ and _____ , now enter:

1. _____ and _____ declare that they have chosen each other as companions, as our rabbis teach: Get yourself a companion. This teaches that a person should get a companion to eat with, to drink with, to study Bible with, to study Mishnah with, to sleep with, to confide all one's secrets, secrets of Torah and secrets of worldly things. —Avot D'Rabbi Natan 8

2. _____ and _____ declare that they are setting themselves apart for each other and will take no other lover.

3. _____ and _____ hereby assume all the rights and obligations that apply to family members: to attend, care, and provide for one another [and for any children with which they may be blessed] [and for _____ _____ child/children of _____]

4. _____ and _____ commit themselves to a life of kindness and righteousness as a Jewish family and to work together toward the communal task of mending the world.

5. _____ and _____ pledge that one will help the other at the time of dying, by carrying out the last rational requests of the dying partner, protecting him/her from indignity or abandonment and by tender, faithful presence with the beloved until the end, fulfilling what has been written: "Set me as a seal upon your arm, for love is stronger than death" (Song of Songs 8:6).

To this covenant we affix our signatures.

The partners:

_____

_____

Witnessed this day the _____ day of Parashat _____ (Hebrew date).

The witnesses:

_____

_____

Should You Write Your Own *Ketubah*?

Deciding, as a couple, which kind of *ketubah* text is right for you may seem daunting and a bit overwhelming. The good news is that if you start thinking about it early on, you will have the opportunity to create a document that holds real spiritual significance—not only for use in your wedding but also as part of your home—to reflect on throughout your life.

Making the *Ketubah* Text Your Own

If you do not want to write an original text, do not feel pressured to do so. There are many egalitarian *ketubot* out there with great variations in language. Search for texts that speak to you by looking at *ketubot* online (resources are listed in Appendix I) or at your local Judaica store.

If you write an original *ketubah* in English, discuss with each other the decision to translate the text into modern Hebrew as well. In some cases, your rabbi might offer to help you with the translation. But don't assume that the rabbi will do so: Some rabbis' skills in modern Hebrew (which is different from prayer book and biblical Hebrew) may not be up to the task. Other rabbis might consider the translation an extra job above and beyond performing the wedding and may charge extra for it.

Again, always discuss your ideas about your *ketubah* text with your rabbi in advance so that you are all on the same page. She can talk with you about options that have worked well for other couples that she has married.

You will also want to start thinking about how the art and text of your *ketubah* dovetail, a topic addressed in the next section of this chapter.

If you are reading this book and are inspired by the variety of *ketubot* available today, but are already married, don't despair. Many couples are creating anniversary *ketubot* as a special way to mark their commitment and covenant to each other over the years.

The Art of the *Ketubah*

Although the text of the *ketubah* clearly originated as a legal document, the art that came to ornament the text served a different function: to make the *ketubah* an object of beauty. For centuries, in all the countries where Jewish communities flourished, decorating *ketubot* became a distinctive art form. It is as if there were an unspoken acknowledgment that, above and beyond the legal need for the document, there was a deeper need for aesthetic beauty to mark the momentous occasion of bride and groom joining together. The ornate art of the *ketubah* softens the legality of the text it adorns.

The art of the *ketubah* exemplifies *hiddur mitzvah*—making a *mitzvah* more holy by beautifying it. Because there were no laws to govern the creative expression of decorating a *ketubah*, the art itself could thrive without limitations. Looking at *ketubot* from various countries and periods is truly inspiring: The art ranges from illuminated manuscripts to elaborate paper-cut designs, from folk art with native designs and symbols to illustrations of Jerusalem and other holy sites.

The art of beautifying a *ketubah* continues to thrive today. In Jewish communities all over the world, serious artists are creating a wide range of designs, using mediums from watercolor to paper-cutting. In this chapter, you will learn about some of the magnificent, contemporary artists who specialize in illustrating *ketubot*. I will also present various options and ideas to help you create a unique *ketubah* design on your own.

Envisioning Your *Ketubah*

Although the decisions about choosing the most appropriate kind of *ketubah* text may feel particularly cerebral, they are balanced by the right-brain task of selecting visual imagery to adorn the text. Again, no matter what your Jewish affiliation—from Orthodox to liberal—your options for *ketubah* design are limitless. Selecting the style, color, and imagery for the design allows you to focus on the kind of art that speaks to you.

For many couples, a *ketubah* is the first work of art they are buying together. Where do you begin? What if your aesthetic senses diverge? How will you find the artist to carry out your vision? What if you have a deep desire to illustrate your *ketubah* on your own?

It may take some time to find the right *ketubah* design for you. Again, I recommend beginning this project with a visualization exercise. For this exercise, sit back and relax. Take turns, with one partner slowly reading the following questions to the other partner. Then switch roles. When both partners have had a chance to "vision," talk about your responses.

Who are your favorite artists? Do you have a favorite painting? What is it in the painting, or in the artist's work, that resonates for you?

Are there colors that are particularly meaningful to you or that you really love? Bold colors, soft colors?

Are you drawn to older styles of art? Modern art? Impressionism? Abstract expressionism?

What are your favorite flowers, animals, and trees?

Are there any symbols that have personal meaning for you? What are they and what do they represent?

As you listen to each other's responses, don't worry if your tastes don't seem to mesh; there are ways to integrate different stylistic preferences into amazing works of art. Hopefully, this visualization helped make you more aware of each other's tastes. Now comes the really fun part. The following assignments can help you gain a better sense of each other's aesthetic preferences and crystallize your ideas about the ideal *ketubah*.

Go to an art museum or gallery together. It doesn't matter whether you are a frequent museum-goer or you can't remember the last time you've been to an exhibit. This time, as you walk through the museum or gallery together, stop and talk about the colors and styles that really speak to you. Jot down the names of any artists whose work you admire.

See whether your local library or bookstore carries books that feature examples of *ketubot* throughout history, such as *Ketubah: The Art of the Jewish Marriage Contract* by Shalom Sabar or *Treasures of Jewish Art* by Grace Cohen Grossman. Look through the books together and note the kinds of *ketubot* that strike you as beautiful or moving.

If you live in an area that has Judaica stores or synagogue gift shops, stop by and browse through the variety of lithograph *ketubot* that they carry. Or you can look online at such sites as www.artketubah.com and www.ketubahtree.com (more websites are listed in Appendix I). Talk about which artists/designs you prefer.

As you explore together, you'll learn more about each other's aesthetic styles. Focus on your similarities; for example, you may both love a certain color palette, even if one of you likes modern art and the other prefers more traditional styles. Look for the ways that your styles and tastes overlap. As you browse together, listen to what kind of art your partner is passionate about. You may find yourself understanding and appreciating that style in a new way. By spending time looking at art together, you will be more likely to find common ground.

The more you browse and think about the kind of art that speaks to you, the closer you come to choosing the *ketubah* that will truly grace your home. The right *ketubah* is both an aesthetic and a literary work of art, carrying the legacy of our ancestors while shining as a work of originality and innovation, fresh in its spirit and beauty.

Choosing Visual Symbols

Whether you are planning to create your own art for your *ketubah* or commission an original work from an artist, you'll want to consider the kind of visual symbols and design that will adorn your text. A wonderful resource to help you start thinking about visual symbols is Ellen Frankel and Betsy Platkin Teutsch's *The Encyclopedia of Jewish Symbols,* which collects and explains the meaning of all symbols in Jewish religious, literary, and folk tradition. This book can be an invaluable resource for couples who are seeking the right symbol(s) to illustrate their *ketubah* (or incorporate into their invitation or *chuppah* design). The book includes every Jewish symbol imaginable, but you might want to focus on a few symbols that would be meaningful for you.

Religious Resonances

> *Torah Portion:* Find out what the Torah *parashah* (portion) and Haftarah portion will be the week of your wedding. Often there can be symbolic meaning in the text that you can incorporate into the *ketubah* to ground it in Jewish time. For example, if the *parashah* is Noach, you might want to incorporate the symbol of the rainbow.

> *Names:* Consider the symbolism of the couple's Hebrew names, which can contain wonderful imagery.

Family Origin: There are certain Jewish symbols that were important to Eastern European Jews, others that were important to Middle Eastern Jews, and others that resonate with Jews of Sephardic heritage. Look for a symbol that might have specific meaning for your family of origin.

Themes from Nature

Location: Incorporate symbols connected to where and when the wedding will take place. Use state flowers, birds, and local trees and vegetation. Such symbols have historical precedence: Many *ketubot* from years ago featured local birds and flowers as a way of displaying the couple's regional roots.

Seasonality: Feature the flora and fauna that will be in bloom at the time of the wedding. For example, a May wedding on the East Coast might take place when lilacs are in bloom. The smell of lilac each year can conjure up memories of your wedding day.

Phase of the Moon: Because Judaism follows a lunar calendar, you could illustrate the phase of the moon that will occur when the wedding takes place.

Artist Anna Fine Foer uses another kind of visual symbolism in the *ketubot* that she creates. Her specialty is creating what she refers to as "biographical landscapes," which are collage maps highlighting the most significant places in each of your lives and showcasing the places that brought you together. Some couples even commission map collages that hearken back to their ancestors—the Pale of Settlement, for example. You might consider creating an original *ketubah* with a personal map of your lives—the places you went to camp and to college, where you met your partner, where you hope to live someday, and so on.

This Jonathan Kremer *ketubah* captures the image of Jerusalem, a popular design for *ketubot* through the ages.

Creative Options for Making Your *Ketubah*

Commissioning a *ketubah* from an artist or purchasing a lithograph are two ways to go when it comes to selecting your *ketubah*. But these are not the only ways to create a really meaningful work of art. Even if you don't consider yourself to be an artist, making your own *ketubah* can fill you with a sense of ongoing connection to the text. The following suggestions are some of the creative ways you can participate in making your *ketubah*.

Calligraphy

Do you enjoy playing around with fancy pens? Have people commented on your nice penmanship? If so, you might consider doing your own calligraphy for your *ketubah*. Many people who have never done calligraphy before embrace this as a way of making their *ketubah* more meaningful and contributing to something that will last beyond the wedding day—something that will be a permanent fixture in their home. If learning to do calligraphy interests but also overwhelms you, here are a few tips to help you decide whether doing your *ketubah* calligraphy is right for you:

- Play around early. Months before your wedding, buy some calligraphy pens and an introductory book, such as *Learn Calligraphy* by Margaret Shepherd. See how you feel as you experiment with the pens and browse through Shepherd's book; if it's a fun and enjoyable experience, keep going.

- If you find you enjoy working from the book, sign up for an introductory calligraphy class at a local JCC or art studio. You might also look for a calligrapher in your area who would be willing to give you a few private lessons.

- If you're feeling confident about trying out your new calligraphy skills for your *ketubah*, go for it! Just make sure you begin drafting the actual *ketubah* text in plenty of time (a good three months before your wedding). You may be surprised by how much time it takes to write a few lines.

Betsy Platkin Teutsch at work on one of her original *ketubot*.

- "Give yourself an out," suggests professional calligrapher and *ketubah* artist Betsy Platkin Teutsch. Teutsch has seen brides scrambling to finish the calligraphy on their *ketubot* the night before their weddings. "Not a fun way to spend that night! You should line up someone who could help you out, just in case it takes much longer than you initially thought and you get stuck," she recommends.

- Accept that the calligraphy may not be perfect. It will certainly be beautiful, but don't expect your work to look like that of a professional artist who has been doing calligraphy for years. Be proud of the work you do, and don't beat yourself up if you have made a little mistake here or there; most likely, you'll be the only one to notice it.

- *The First Jewish Catalog*, which was first published in 1973 and soon became a revolutionary how-to manual for a generation of Jews interested in a hands-on approach to Jewish living, includes a fantastic guide for beginner calligraphers interested in the art of Hebrew letter-making. Thirty years later, it is still a marvelous resource for anyone doing Hebrew calligraphy.

When Geoff Sternlieb and his wife Shoshanah Feher Sternlieb were planning their wedding, Geoff remembered how much he enjoyed doing calligraphy seventeen years earlier at a Jewish summer camp. Geoff decided he wanted to try his hand at drafting their *ketubah* text, so he took a handful of private lessons from a professional calligrapher and was on his way. "I can't remember exactly how long it took me to write our *ketubah*," he says, "but I would allow at least sixty hours for learning, practicing, and writing." If you invest in a few pens or lessons and then decide it's too much pressure to do your calligraphy, no harm done. Just make sure you have a back-up plan in mind so that you're not scrambling to find a calligrapher at the last minute.

The Frame's the Thing

Don't forget to think about the frame that will surround your *ketubah*. There are so many creative options for framing today. If you enjoy wood restoration, you could prowl through antique shops or flea markets for a unique frame that might need a little tender loving care. The frame could be sanded and painted to complement the color and/or design of the text.

When my husband Fred and I were considering our *ketubah* design, we fell in love with a folk art company called Stix that makes everything from furniture to chess sets. We were browsing in a shop that carried their work when Fred pointed out that the size of their mirror frames was roughly the size we imagined our *ketubah* would be. We decided that the art of our *ketubah* would be the Stix frame itself, rather than a design adorning the text. Stix allows its customers to select the words, graphics, and colors that appear on their work. We chose themes for our frame that complemented our *ketubah* text. Our frame reads: "The Secret to Life Is to Enjoy the Passing of Time," followed by a list of ways that we celebrate and live our life.

One couple I know bought a shadow-box frame at an art shop; this contains little boxes to hold small objects. Their *ketubah* text stands in the middle of the frame, surrounded by personal objects that have great meaning to them, including a perfume bottle from the bride's great-great-grandmother and stamps from Argentina, where the groom comes from.

If choosing a special frame interests you as a way to adorn your *ketubah*, start out by looking everywhere—from galleries to garage sales—to find a unique frame that speaks to you.

An original frame made especially by or for the couple can complement any *ketubah*.

Collaborative Art

It may take guts to choose this next option, but remember that great art often involves risks! If you and your partner would like others to contribute to your *ketubah* design, you might invite some friends over for an illustrating party.

A Group Effort

- Decide ahead of time how big your *ketubah* text will be.

- Purchase a frame with a large area of matting that can surround the text. The art your friends create will go on the matting part of the frame.

- Assemble a range of writing implements—calligraphy pens, fancy markers, and the like—in the colors that you prefer.

- Give your friends some basic instructions. Let them know that whatever they create is great (that's the only attitude to have if you are considering this option). For example, do you want their art to be a collage of all their different designs? Or should they work together on a common theme?

- You should probably go out of the room while they are working so that their creation will be a surprise—unless you can hang out in a relaxed, no-pressure kind of way.

This kind of design works best if a tapestry effect appeals to you and you are not expecting a professional outcome. It doesn't hurt, either, if you have a few artsy friends who will take the lead and have fun with this idea!

Another way to involve a group in your *ketubah* design is even more spontaneous. Instead of hosting a party in advance, you could invite all the guests at your wedding to sign and/or illustrate the mat. The art that adorns your *ketubah* will be the names, drawings, and even messages of the people who were present to witness and participate in your wedding day.

Original *Ketubot* Created by Other Couples

The originality that goes into creating a *ketubah* today is truly breathtaking. Many of the couples I interviewed while researching this book showed remarkable creative energy in planning their *ketubah*—from learning to do their own calligraphy to researching the perfect symbols that artistically represented their interests. The following two couples' creative *ketubah* journeys deserve special mention.

The art that Hilarie and Brian Pozesky chose for their *ketubah* holds special meaning for the couple. Hilarie and Brian come from different religious backgrounds—Hilarie was raised Catholic, although she had left the church ten years before she met Brian, who is Jewish. As they got to know each other more deeply and fell in love, Hilarie also became very interested in Judaism, and after Brian proposed to her, she decided to convert. The piece of art that inspired their *ketubah* was originally a gift that Brian gave Hilarie for Christmas the first year they were dating.

"The painting now hangs in our living room," Hilarie says. "When we met, I was celebrating Christmas, so Brian bought me this painting as a gift." As Hilarie describes the painting, it is clear that she and Brian have thought deeply about its significance. "It's an abstract piece of work that shows two figures who are almost touching. There arms are raised above their heads as if in joy," she explains. "But there is a black line that seems to separate the two. To us, it's been a symbol of the challenge of relationships. Sharing a life together and yet being two whole, independent people. I think that the tendency is for that line to get blurred or for the line to be too harsh. You have to walk that line carefully in order for a relationship to really work."

As they were originally planning their wedding, neither Hilarie nor Brian had thought much about what kind of *ketubah* they wanted; choosing one was just one more thing to check off on their wedding "to do" list. But when Brian's stepmother told the couple that she would like to give them a custom-made *ketubah* as a Hanukkah gift, they had to give the decision more thought. "I hadn't really thought of doing something custom. To be honest, it seemed a bit extravagant," Hilarie recalls. However, when Brian's stepmother sent them to the artist Nishima's website and they saw that she had created *ketubot* based on pieces of art that were important to couples, they thought

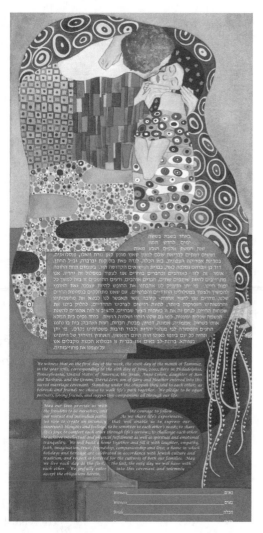

One option for choosing art for your *ketubah* is to think about your favorite artist. This *ketubah* designed by Nishima captures Klimt's famous painting, *The Kiss*.

of their painting. It seemed perfect to take the symbols from a painting that was so meaningful to them and incorporate those symbols into their *ketubah*.

Brian and Hilarie really liked and clicked with Nishima after talking to her. She was flexible, and her utmost concern was making a beautiful *ketubah* that said something about them as a unique couple. Brian and Hilarie gave Nishima an egalitarian text that their rabbi recommended to them, which she integrated into her art. In addition to the symbols from their favorite painting, Nishima also added the images of Hilarie's family's barn that still stands in rural western Illinois (she comes from a long line of farmers who settled there in the 1830s) and Brian's synagogue, where he celebrated his bar mitzvah and where his parents were married as well. To Hilarie and Brian, these touches make the *ketubah* feel as if it represents a continuum encompassing their individual pasts, their present life together, and their future as a married couple.

"There was nothing like the feeling that we both had as we opened our *ketubah*. It was more beautiful and special than we imagined it would be," Hilarie says. Evolving from simply an item "to do" into a work of art just for them, the *ketubah* enriched their wedding and now graces their home.

As noted, the Pozesky's custom-made *ketubah* was a gift to the couple. If you really want a custom-made *ketubah* but are concerned about the cost to commission one from an artist, you might think about asking for a *ketubah* as a gift. Certain friends or relatives may want to give you a really special gift but aren't sure what to purchase. You might voice your desire for an original *ketubah* and see what happens. It could be a great group gift, with a number of friends contributing to the cost of its creation.

Kevin Haworth and Danielle LeShaw took an interesting route in creating their *ketubah*. They considered using Adler's *brit ahuvim* as well as writing their own original text, but instead decided to create a *ketubah* that uses Jewish texts to support their commitments to each other. Both Kevin, a freelance writer and editor, and Danielle, then a rabbinical student and now a rabbi, are steeped in Jewish texts, so their decision to study and select Jewish texts seemed natural to them. "I wanted the words of our *ketubah* to be timeless," Kevin explains. "If we wrote 'I promise to,' those promises might change at one point or another in our lives. But the words of the texts that we chose can be reinterpreted time and again, and looked at with fresh eyes each time you read them." Danielle also appreciated the fact that Jewish texts lent a feeling of authenticity to their innovation. "Since we were doing something really new," she says, "I wanted it to be anchored in Jewish tradition."

The time they spent choosing the right texts for their *ketubah* became some of the best time they spent together during their engagement. They both feel that setting aside time in their busy lives to study sacred texts together—to discuss their meaning and how they applied to their relationship—was one of the holiest aspects of planning their wedding.

The couple eventually chose nine quotations and wrote an introduction to each quote, outlining the pledge to each other that the quote represented. Their *ketubah* text reads:

> At Sabbath's wane, the 19th day of the month of Av, corresponding to the 19th day of the month of August, in the city of Philadelphia, Pennsylvania, Danielle, daughter of Paula and Jeff, and Kevin, son of Eileen, Barry and Andy, confirm in the presence of witnesses a lovers' covenant and declare a partnership to establish a household among the people of Israel.
>
> It is a covenant of companionship:
> "Acquire for yourself a friend. How so? This teaches that one should find a friend to eat with, to drink with, to study with, to sleep with, and to reveal all one's secrets to—holy secrets and mundane secrets alike." —Avot D'Rabbi Natan 8
>
> It is a covenant of love and devotion:
> "And Jonathan's soul was bound up with the soul of David. Jonathan made a covenant with David because he loved him as himself." —1 Samuel 18:1–3
>
> It is a covenant of comfort:
> "My heart is a place for you, as you are mine." —Morning Blessings
>
> It is a covenant of holiness:
> "These are the things which have no prescribed measure: the corner of the field, the offering of first fruits, the journey, acts of loving-kindness, and the study of Torah." —Mishnah Peah 1:1

Shopping for a Lithograph

Many couples prefer to look online or at local Judaica shops for a *ketubah* lithograph that they love. If this sounds like the best route for you, here are a few pointers to keep in mind as you browse:

- *Size and space for witnesses:* You will have at least two witnesses sign your *ketubah*, but you may choose more. Questions to consider: Has the artist left space for more than two witnesses to sign? Is the space for signatures big enough for everyone to write their Hebrew names with ease? Is there a place to add additional names without interfering with the design?

- *Hebrew language:* You may need a rabbi or someone else who reads Hebrew fluently to help you here. Is the Hebrew language poetic and accurate? Is it grammatically correct?

- *Both the text and art that you want:* Suppose you find a lithograph design you love, but do not want the text that accompanies it. Can you order the same art with different text? Contact the artist to find out; she may have versions available with language that you prefer.

It is a covenant of protection:
"Reveal yourself . . . spread over me your canopy of peace." —Yedid Nefesh

It is a covenant of community:
"Be seated, be seated exalted guests, holy guests, guests of faithfulness, be seated in the shade of the Holy One." —Ushpizin

It is a covenant of growth and support:
"Stand by the roads and consider, inquire about ancient paths: which way is good? Travel it and find rest for your soul." —Jeremiah 6:16

It is a covenant of abundance:
"May it be your will that our merits increase as the seeds of a pomegranate." —Rosh Hashanah Blessing

It is a covenant of gratitude:
"Blessed is the Generous One, God of our ancestors, who sent you this very day to me." —1 Samuel 25:32

And everything is valid and confirmed.

To complement their carefully selected words, Kevin and Danielle turned to Kevin's friend, artist Michael Lewy. Michael is Jewish, but he had never done any kind of sacred or ritual art before, and his art doesn't express any particular Jewish themes. "We loved Michael's artwork," Kevin says. "We trusted him as an artist and as a friend, and we liked that he is a Jewish artist, even if his art isn't specifically 'Jewish.'"

Lewy uses recycled objects in his art and chose an old piece of wood as the surface on which to paint Kevin and Danielle's *ketubah*. He asked them their favorite colors, interests, and likes from their childhoods and integrated all these elements into his design. The only constraint he had was to leave space for the text, which would be attached to the wood and put under a glass frame once it was signed.

"The art was a total surprise to us on our wedding and we absolutely loved it," Kevin recalls. "The art and the text were connected in that the text of a *ketubah* has been around forever and we found a new way to use it. The wood Michael used was probably around forever too, and he found a new way to use it."

Danielle and Kevin love this original work of literary and visual art that so well expresses their commitments to each other and their connection to both Jewish tradition and Jewish innovation. Their decision to use a "non-*ketubah*" artist presents one more choice to consider: You may have a close friend or relative who is an artist and would also be excited to take on this new kind of project. Although not every artist would embrace a new creative project in the way that Michael did, it doesn't hurt to ask! Many professional *ketubah* artists (including Nishima) got their start when a friend asked them to make a *ketubah*. Just clearly explain to your friend in advance your ideas and expectations. Creating a *ketubah* is a major investment of

Another of Nishima's creations, this joyous *ketubah* celebrates the union of two women, here portrayed wearing *kippot* and sharing *kiddush* wine.

creative time and energy—you should certainly offer to pay your friend for their time. Your friend may decide that she or he would rather give you the *ketubah* as a wedding gift than accept payment. That is up to them. But it is only fair to offer to pay for a friend's art, as you would when you commission a work of art from someone you don't know personally. And remember: An artistic friend may not necessarily be comfortable with or experienced in doing calligraphy. You may want to have your friend create the art and hire a professional calligrapher to do the text.

Family Dynamics and Your *Ketubah*

The nature of family relationships is relevant to all aspects of your wedding. In creating original *ketubah* text, it is the nature of the new family you are forming with your partner—or, if either of you are remarrying, your evolving family—that needs consideration.

Divorce

There is one important decision regarding your *ketubah* text that I have not mentioned so far. If you are not planning to use an Orthodox *ketubah* or one that includes the Lieberman clause, you and your partner should discuss whether you want to include any mention of divorce in your *ketubah* text. On one hand, you may feel that when drafting a text about your love and commitments to each other any mention of divorce may weaken the intent of your pledges. On the other hand, one of the historical strengths of the *ketubah* is the way that it honestly acknowledges that not all marriages work out as the couple would hope, and that it protects both parties in the event that the marriage dissolves. If you do include a line about divorce, it can be brief and to the point, such as, "The bride and groom agree that in case, God forbid, of divorce, common assets would be divided so that neither party would bear undue hardship."

Even talking about this issue may feel uncomfortable to you, which is natural. No one entering a marriage wants to think about this outcome. You might bring it up in a meeting with your rabbi—ask her whether she prefers that couples write in or use a text that mentions provisions should a divorce occur. Talk to a few close friends and find out how they addressed this issue in their *ketubot*. Ultimately, it will be your decision as to whether your *ketubah* deals with the divorce issue.

Marrying Later in Life

When people choose to marry at midlife or later, their lives often involve different configurations than the lives of people in their twenties or early thirties. A marriage between people in their twenties or thirties is about building a life together—dreaming about their goals and visions and making choices about children, career, and whatever else the couple hopes for in their life together. The *ketubah* text that such a couple drafts will reflect those hopes; it will be full of their dreams and yearnings.

People who meet at midlife or later and choose to marry also have hopes and dreams for their relationship, but they bring with them a different kind of life experience. They may have children already grown or growing, issues concerning their aging parents, and very concrete thoughts about financial demands related to college tuition and retirement. When couples at this life stage choose to marry, it is always recommended that they spend some serious time figuring out how they are going to balance their own life responsibilities while creating a new partnership and home.

If you and your partner are at this life stage, writing an original *ketubah* text gives you an opportunity to look at some very real issues and figure out how you hope to work with them. Drafting them on paper and having them signed by witnesses and read aloud in your ceremony honors your commitments in a sacred manner. Your *ketubah* text will be full of hopes and promises, enriched by the wisdom of your life experience. Hearing people at midlife making serious commitments to learn from their experiences and do all they can to build a new life with their partner can be a profound moment in a wedding ceremony.

Couples with children from a previous marriage might think about the idea of drafting an original "family *ketubah*" that outlines the promises and commitments that blended parents and children make to one another. The family *ketubah* could be read aloud during the wedding ceremony, along with the couple's *ketubah*, or it could be a personal document to be displayed in the home.

A Remedy for Fighting

After getting married, many couples keep their *ketubah* displayed in a place in their home where they can see it often. Some couples like to keep it in their bedroom, while others prefer to showcase it in a more public place where guests will see it. Either way, it's important not only to look at the art but also to read the text every once in a while, to reconnect to those promises that you made.

"Our rabbi suggested that we read our *ketubah* together, out loud, as part of making up from a fight," says Emily Goldstein, who has been married to her husband Steve for eight years. "We actually don't fight that often, but we have had some really harsh fights from time to time. I remember once when we really couldn't see eye to eye, and Steve remembered the rabbi's instructions. We were both really pissed when we started reading it, but we were crying and holding each other as we got through it. It sounds so corny, but it really worked . . . what we were fighting about was stupid ego stuff, and reading our *ketubah* just helped us step back and get some perspective."

Other couples read their *ketubah* out loud together as part of their annual anniversary celebration. For couples who have children, it's also wonderful to share your *ketubah* with them and talk about the promises and commitments that you made to each other when you got married, as well as the promises and commitments that you have to them as parents. Your *ketubah* reflects your covenantal relationship, one in which both partners have entered the marriage with commitments to uphold.

chapter four

Chuppah Hooplah

Creative Possibilities for Your Wedding Canopy

The Origin and Purpose of a *Chuppah*

Aside from breaking a glass, the one association that most people have with Jewish weddings is where they take place: under a special canopy—the *chuppah*. As long as you wed under a *chuppah*, your wedding can take place anywhere you like—at a synagogue, a park, the beach, or any other favorite place. During the Middle Ages, Jewish weddings took place in the street or in the marketplace, and the *chuppah* set apart private space from the hustle and bustle for the bride and groom. As you and your partner consider various options for your wedding location, you can feel confident that as long as you have a *chuppah*, you can mark off sacred space wherever you prefer.

The *chuppah* is one of the most ancient parts of a contemporary Jewish wedding. Originally, in ancient Israel, after the betrothal period, the bride was taken to the groom's tent—or *chuppah*—where the wedding was consummated. Throughout Jewish history, the *chuppah* has been most commonly interpreted as a symbol of our matriarch and patriarch, Sarah and Abraham. It is said that Sarah and Abraham's tent was open on all sides to let guests know that they were always welcome to come in. Because both Sarah and Abraham were thought of as having special relationships with God, their tents marked sacred space where God's presence could be felt upon entering. So, too, in contemporary weddings, the *chuppah* serves to create a sacred space, both open and private. It is open for all the bride and groom's friends and relatives who are present to witness their covenant to each other. At the same time it is private, creating a feeling of warmth and intimacy that surrounds the special couple.

Jewish tradition tells us that prayers of the bride and groom uttered under the *chuppah* have a special gateway directly to God. However one may imagine the Divine, many brides and grooms report that once they step under the *chuppah*, they feel as if they have entered an "altered" space, a space in which all the stress and craziness of wedding planning and drama magically melt away, and all that is left is the love that brought them to that moment.

You, too, can create a wedding canopy that circumscribes a sacred space, allowing the Divine Presence to bless your union. Your *chuppah* can speak to your unique spiritual vision as a couple, and it can help invoke a loving, beautiful presence to surround you at your wedding ceremony.

For many couples—past and present—finding a *chuppah* was another chore on the wedding checklist, something provided by the synagogue or rented from a florist. There's nothing wrong with that, but if you are looking for meaningful ways to express yourselves creatively at your wedding, the act of creating an original *chuppah* is a wonderful way to do so. And not only will the beauty of your *chuppah* be there for you on your wedding day, but it might also become a lovely wallhanging in your first home or even a new family heirloom to be shared with your siblings, future children, cousins, or others dear to you on their wedding day.

Creating an original *chuppah* can be a fun project: There are absolutely no limits in terms of creative design and vision, as long as the canopy hangs above the bride and groom and is carried on four poles. You and your partner may want to design a *chuppah* together or come up with some general ideas relating to colors, fabrics, and design, and then turn over the project of making the *chuppah* to a friend or relative who would love to assemble it. There is no rush to decide now: First, take some time for the following two-part visualization exercise.

Envisioning Your *Chuppah*, Part One

The key to creating a distinctive wedding canopy is figuring out what you want your *chuppah* to look and feel like. One way to approach this is to consider the metaphor of the *chuppah* as a symbol of the bride and groom coming together to make a new home. Imagine your wedding as a new beginning, a fresh start of two individuals creating one home out of combined interests, values, hopes, and ideals. Your *chuppah* can be a visual, tactile celebration of this union—a symbolic tapestry of who you are and what you dream of becoming. Your *chuppah* can be a work of art, representing a theme that reflects your marriage and the home you are building together.

Take a few quiet moments together. Sit down, breathe deeply, and let yourself forget about whatever cares or concerns are on your mind. Just focus on your breath. When you feel ready, one of you can read the following questions out loud. If you are the listener, you may want to record your partner's responses in your wedding journal.

> In your ideal home, shared with your partner, what do you see when you wake up in the morning?

> Describe a typical gathering of guests in your home. What type of food is everyone eating? What kind of music echoes through the house? What are people talking about?

> What colors and textures characterize your home's décor? Would a stranger describe it as cozy, elegant, minimalist, eclectic? What are the most distinctive elements (design or otherwise) in your home?

When you are ready, switch roles and allow the other partner to spend time answering the questions. Afterward, you can share your responses together. Note both the similarities and the differences. Acknowledge ways that your styles and visions match, and where they might grow together to forge a symbiotic blend.

What does all of this imagining have to do with making a *chuppah*? You may discover a certain color theme that says "home" to you, a color scheme that you can carry through the design. Identifying your taste as cozy or elegant may help you pick out the best style for your *chuppah*. Most important, don't rush into any quick decisions. Talk, sketch, and take some time to allow your *chuppah* dreams to bubble to the surface.

Thinking of home is only one way to begin envisioning your ideal *chuppah*. You might instead focus your visualizations on the ways each of you connects with God, and then design your *chuppah* as a way to express that. You might see it as a canopy that carries your values and expresses your dreams. You might imagine it as a tapestry that represents your immediate and extended families and your ancestors reaching back in time.

Of course, whatever *chuppah* you end up creating, remember that its symbolism also reminds us that it is a temporary structure; it is really love and spirit, rather than material items or structure, that make a home.

Envisioning Your *Chuppah*, Part Two

Hopefully, the exercise above helped you to start imagining some ideas for your *chuppah* design. The next exercise will help you visualize more specifically being under the *chuppah* at the moment of your wedding. (Note: You may want to do the two exercises a day or even a week apart to allow ideas and images to surface.) When you're ready, take out your journals again, relax, get quiet, put on some music, maybe pour a glass of wine—whatever will allow you to dream some more. You can take turns reading the questions out loud.

> When you look up at your *chuppah*, what do you see? Which colors, textures, images, and words come to mind?

> Imagine being a guest at your wedding. You look at the bride and groom together under the *chuppah*. What do you see? What do you feel?

You are standing under the *chuppah* on your wedding day. As you turn to your right and to your left, who do you see standing there with you?

Allowing yourself to visualize from both your own perspective and that of a guest can help you plan the ideal design. Should your *chuppah* be surrounded by flowers or plants? Should it be very open, with few people surrounding it, so more people can see in? How close will your *chuppah* be to your guests? How large of a space will it occupy?

There is no right way to create a *chuppah*, just as there is no right way to create a wedding. Again, depending on your personal style and comfort level, you may hand over some of your initial ideas and let a friend create a *chuppah* for you. Or you may work together as a couple to make this dream tangible.

Creative Options for *Chuppah* Styles

The possibilities for *chuppah* design are as far-ranging as your imagination, but here are a few tried and true methods that you can use, adapt, and experiment with.

Embroidery: a classic, elegant look. Choose words to be embroidered that have meaning for you as a couple. You could embroider the quote you selected for your invitation, a selection from Psalms or Song of Songs, or other poetry/music that you cherish. Embroidery looks most beautiful on flaps that hang down on all four sides so that your guests can read your words. A floral design incorporating your wedding colors is also lovely. You could combine embroidery with another art form, such as fabric

A commissioned family heirloom *chuppah,* created by fabric artist Elsa Wachs, features antique fabrics donated by the Braman family.

painting, on the underside of the *chuppah* that the bride and groom see.

Fabric Paint: Do either of you love to paint or is there someone close to you who does? One of the most beautiful, original *chuppot* that I've seen was painted for my friend Sheila's wedding by her friend Jill. Jill used the wedding colors—shades of lavender and rose—and painted a floral explosion of freesias on the underside of the canopy. The flowers matched the actual flowers that were surrounding the *chuppah,* and the blending of the symbolic and real flowers created a magnificent effect, giving those of us standing under the *chuppah* a sense of how the Garden of Eden might have looked and smelled. The *chuppah* is now a prized piece of art in Sheila and Michael's home.

Flowers: Standing poles adorned with beautiful flowers can create a stunning *chuppah* effect. Even if you don't have a fortune to spend on flowers, consider simple ways to create a natural, floral design. For example, one couple I know was moving to a house that had a magnificent grape arbor. For their autumn wedding, they cut vines loaded with purple grapes from the grape arbor and wrapped them around the *chuppah* poles using craft wire. At the base of each pole was a beautiful pot of purplish chrysanthemums. The actual fabric of their *chuppah* was simple white cotton, and they had stenciled with fabric markers a *kiddush* cup with their names and wedding date on the underside.

Based on which season and location your wedding will take place in, you can be as simple or as lavish as you like in choosing a floral design. With a little craft wire and imagination, you don't have to spend a fortune at the floral shop.

Collage: This type of *chuppah* involves friends, family, and anyone else you want to help create your design. It is the perfect project if you want to bring your loved ones into the wedding-designing process and you're not afraid to relinquish some control. You don't know what kind of designs you'll get back! For me, that element of surprise was all part of the fun, and our collage *chuppah* turned out to be more beautiful than I could have imagined. A step-by-step plan for creating a collage-style *chuppah* is featured in the "How-to" section beginning on page 104.

Quilting: This is similar in process to the collage *chuppah*, except that evenly cut squares in a quilt style are sewn together in a neat pattern. If you or someone you know is a quilter, you can make your *chuppah* into an actual quilt and use it later on your bed. Another quilting option is to skip the collaborative part and work from one pattern, perhaps with a Jewish symbol or design. Again, if you are considering this option, leave plenty of time for the creation process! Many couples have chosen to include squares that represent someone they love who has passed away. It is a great honor to ask a friend or loved one to design a square in someone's memory, and this can add great meaning to your *chuppah*.

Stenciling: Stenciling is another wonderful way to create a great visual design without having to study at a fine arts academy. Be forewarned, though, that if you have never tried your hand at stenciling, it is more exacting than it may first appear. If you are not familiar with stenciling, you can walk into any crafts store and go to the stencil aisle. There you will find a great variety of plastic stencils, with myriad designs to choose from. You simply lay a stencil down on fabric and paint or color the spaces that are cut out of the plastic.

Good stenciling requires a steady hand and an eye for detail. If you think you might like to stencil a design onto fabric for your *chuppah*, you'll find a huge variety of designs—

particularly floral and heart themes—that could beautifully grace your *chuppah*. Be sure to practice stenciling on paper until you have a feel for it before you go ahead and do your actual *chuppah*. Hebrew letter stencils are available through Judaica shops and Hebrew education catalogs; you might want to stencil a Hebrew quote or your Hebrew names onto your *chuppah*.

Lace and Heirloom Fabrics: A *chuppah* made from beautiful lace conjures up an antique feeling. You can either shop around at fabric stores for the kind of lace you want or try for a more authentic look. I have a friend who spends hours searching out beautiful old lace tablecloths at thrift stores. By sifting through piles of junk, she finds some amazing treasures.

You may have an easier way of tracking down heirloom lace right in your own family. If you are blessed to have grandmothers, aunts, or other older relatives still alive, ask them whether they have any old tablecloths or other pieces of antique fabric tucked away that they might be honored to contribute as part of your *chuppah*. Professional *chuppah* artist Elsa Wachs, for example, asks couples who commission *chuppot* to bring her any meaningful fabric they can find. The fabrics might include handkerchiefs, neckties, or even antique wedding gowns worn by grandmothers or other relatives.

If one partner is not Jewish or comes from a non-Jewish family, using special fabric from that side of the family for the *chuppah* is a wonderful way to make that family feel involved and included in the wedding and more connected to the experience of the ceremony.

Inspired by Nature: If you are getting married outdoors, you might want to create a *chuppah* that will blend in with the natural setting around you. For her northern California wedding, for example, Lisa Schwartz wanted to create a *chuppah* that would match the outdoor surroundings, so she chose simple bamboo poles with a white organza canopy. Because they were getting married in the afternoon, Lisa wanted to use only light fabric that would pick up the sun during that time of day. Consider the season, time of day, and location where your wedding will take place, and think about what kind of fabric and poles would best complement the beauty of your natural setting.

Picture Stories: Using quilting, appliqué, or simple fabric paints, you can create a picture on your *chuppah* that symbolizes your relationship. Think about the symbols covered in the last chapter; you might choose seasonal flowers or an image from the *parashah* that will be read on your wedding week. You and your partner may want to choose the same symbols that adorn your invitation and/or your *ketubah*.

Professional *chuppah* designers Margery and Eli Langner made their very first *chuppah* for their own wedding. "We used a round, 6-by-6 foot fabric, with a collage of symbols in vibrant colors—blues, reds, purples," Margery explains. "In the center there is a moon for Eli and a lotus for me. The earth's arms are opening to embrace our union. There are two flames, joining together to make one larger flame, representing the Baal Shem Tov's quote that when two souls join together, their individual flames make one larger flame. Those flames are surrounded and protected by thirty-two smaller flames, because in Hebrew, the number thirty-two spells *lev*, 'heart.' To us, the symbols represent our love and passion."

Tie-dye can create a fantastic blend of color for your *chuppah*. Practice makes perfect—work on some old T-shirts before you try it on your *chuppah* fabric.

Tie-dye: Tie-dye is not just for hippies anymore! You can create wonderful, colorful designs by simply tie-dying cotton fabric. Choose dye colors that will complement your flowers. By using rubber bands, you can create simple designs, including hearts and Jewish stars. Tie-dyeing is a fairly inexpensive process, so you can buy the dyes you need and practice your technique on some old T-shirts until you get the hang of it. See the "How-to" section on page 104 for step-by-step instructions on creating your own tie-dye *chuppah*.

Tallitot: A *tallit* is the traditional Jewish prayer shawl worn for morning prayers. Traditionally, brides would present their new husbands with a special wedding gift of a new *tallit*, which might also be used as the wedding canopy. Today in many liberal circles, both men and women wear *tallitot* for morning worship. *Tallitot* come in a vast array of colors, styles, and intricate designs. If you and your fiancée are people who cherish wearing a *tallit* (or are thinking about starting to do so), you may want to buy each other a *tallit* as a way to update this tradition. The two of them can be simply pinned together to make a lovely canopy. Alternatively, many professional *chuppah* artists create *chuppot* that can then be divided into two *tallitot* afterward. If you are feeling ambitious, you can even make your own *tallitot*. Most Judaica shops carry the *tzitzit* (fringes) needed to make a *tallit*. You can even order a basic "make your own *tallit*" kit, featuring fabric, *tzitzit*, and instructions, through www.judaicartkits.com.

Don't Forget the Poles

While perusing the above design ideas, one thought may have been gnawing at you: How do we actually attach the *chuppah* to four poles? Fortunately, connecting the fabric to the poles is easier than you'd think.

Some people like to find their own poles—by taking wood branches from trees that are being trimmed, for example, or by going on a hike and finding four sturdy branches of the right height. In years gone by, it was traditional for a cedar tree to be planted at a Jewish boy's birth and a cypress tree to be planted for a girl. When children reached marrying age, branches from their trees were cut and used for *chuppah* poles. If you have such a significant tree in your life, you may want to cut branches from it in this tradition.

However, you can also easily buy wooden curtain rods and paint them any color you like. Or use plain old PVC pipes, available at your local hardware store. Just make sure that your poles are long enough: at least 6-feet-5 inches (depending on your and your spouse's height). It is no fun for anyone if the *chuppah* keeps landing on your head!

You can dress up your poles by covering them with fabric, painting them in colors to match your canopy and/or flowers, or using craft wire to attach real or silk flowers up the length of the pole. You might want to experiment with different options and see what looks most complementary with your canopy. If your poles are made of nice wood, don't be afraid to let them stand alone. Especially if your canopy is very elaborate, overly decorated poles can detract from the effect.

One very simple, effective way to attach the poles to the fabric is to cut four small holes in the corners of the *chuppah*, about 2 inches from the actual corner. Reinforce the material around the holes with extra stitches. Attach eyelets to the *chuppah* poles (which need to be flat on the top and bottom). Take pretty-colored yet sturdy ribbon and thread it through the holes in the eyelets, then through the holes in the *chuppah*. Tie the ribbon.

Some couples prefer using four vertical poles with connected horizontal crossbars to hang their canopy fabric over. To make this kind of structure, simply put a bolt with a wing nut through one crossbar and the corner pole, and then put another bolt with a wing nut through the second crossbar and the same corner pole. Repeat until all the corner poles are connected to the crossbars. You can sew small ribbons to the front and back edges of your canopy, spreading across the length of the crossbars. When you lay the *chuppah* across the top of the poles, you can tie the ribbons to the front and back crossbars so that the fabric lies nicely on top.

If your *chuppah* is going to be held exclusively by four people, you don't need to worry about what the legs of the poles will go in. However, if you want your *chuppah* to be self-supporting, the poles must be placed in something nice

A close-up view of the *chuppah* pole that Elsa Wachs created for the Braman family *chuppah*.

How to Create a Collage-Style Quilt

Buy a very large piece of pretty fabric (cotton, muslin, or even silk) to serve as the base. How big? This depends on how many folks will be standing under it. Start with a 6-by-8 foot piece, and by eyeballing it, approximate whether you will need more or less fabric. Make sure that the fabric takes a needle easily, especially if you're hand-sewing.

Buy another piece of fabric the same size in a neutral color (white or beige). Cut it into whatever shapes you like—hearts, ovals, squares, and so on.

Send the pieces to people you love with a short explanation of your project (see sample letter on the next page). They can beautify their fabric piece any way they like: with fabric paints or markers, embroidery, stencils, collages, or any other means of decoration. They may also want to attach small three-dimensional objects, such as a treasured piece of jewelry or a souvenir from a family trip, to their fabric piece. Ask them to leave space (at least a ½-inch) around the edges for hemming. Make sure it is absolutely clear in your letter what the deadline is for sending their decorated fabric piece back. You may want to include a stamped, self-addressed envelope for easy return.

When you get the pieces back, arrange them on the larger fabric

and sturdy. One option is to place the poles into ceramic pots filled with heavy dirt. Another option is to attach the bottom of your poles to sturdy PVC pipes that can fit into patio umbrella stands, which can also be decorated with pretty fabric or flowers.

Practical Considerations

Creativity is important, but when it comes to wedding planning, organization is critical. Taking on too many tasks without proper organization can make wedding planning a stressful rather than joyous process. There are many practical considerations that go into creating a *chuppah*. After reading through the following section, you will be able to talk honestly with each other about whether this is a project that you want to undertake. You may find that you both prefer to rent, borrow, or commission someone else to make a *chuppah* for you.

Time

Depending on which method of *chuppah* making you choose, you need to set aside an appropriate amount of time. If you are going to choose a collage or quilt style of *chuppah*, which involves asking friends and family to design elements of it, you want to allow at least a three-month turnaround time from when you ask them to contribute a fabric square to when someone actually starts assembling the squares. I know one couple who did not leave quite enough time for family to do their part (and who also tolerated extreme lateness) and so consequently had someone sewing together their *chuppah* the night before the wedding! Professional *chuppah* artists generally prefer meeting with couples at least six months before their wedding to talk about design and then go to work creating the *chuppah*. By giving yourself six months to work on this kind of project, you can do it at a relaxed pace and avoid last-minute scrambling.

Sharing the Work

One option for creating your own *chuppah* without putting yourself under unneeded stress is to find a friend or relative who would delight in helping with this important project. Once you figure out the design/style you want, you could ask the person to do the actual work of creating the *chuppah*. This is a great honor, especially for a friend with an artistic flair. Again, depending on which kind of *chuppah* design you prefer, you may want to choose someone who loves (and has experience in) sewing, embroidery, or another fabric art. Make sure that you give this special person plenty of advance notice so that she doesn't feel rushed or pressured. Being a considerate bride or groom will yield a much happier wedding all around!

Size

You need to figure out ahead of time how many people are going to be standing under the *chuppah* with you so that you can create a canopy of appropriate size. Some couples choose to have their parents standing with them under the *chuppah* (a traditional practice), while others want to stand under the *chuppah* with only the wedding officiant and maybe one attendant each for the bride and groom. People can always surround the *chuppah*, standing just outside it. But if you plan now, you will be able to fit everyone you want to have right there under the *chuppah* with you.

Freestanding or Requiring Holders

The honor of holding the *chuppah* poles during the ceremony is another important factor for partners to discuss. Depending on the style of *chuppah* you choose, it could be walked in as part of the wedding processional, or it may need to be set up in advance with poles that stand independently (or you could do a combination of both). For example, a *chuppah* designed with elaborate floral décor will most likely need to be set up hours before the ceremony. Even if you choose such an option, you may still select four people to walk in with you and stand

any way you like. Play around and see what arrangement looks best. You may want to cut and add additional fabric shapes, ribbon, bells—anything you like!

Hem both the big and smaller pieces as needed. Attach smaller pieces to the big pieces with fabric glue or stitches (or both).

Sample Letter to Family and Friends

Dear _____:

As you know, our wedding day is fast approaching! We have deeply appreciated all the love and support we've received from friends and family as we plan for our special day.

We have a very sacred project, involving all of you, that will make our wedding all the more meaningful. In this package is a square [or heart or oval] of white muslin; that square is for you to decorate and design, and it will become part of our chuppah. *For us, the* chuppah *symbolizes our intentions to start a new home and life together. By having our families and friends design patches of our* chuppah, *we are affirming that although our wedding ceremony sanctifies our relationship as a couple, we could not really create a home together without the love and support of our friends and extended families.*

Your chuppah *square does not need to be fancy—we're looking for your original contribution, not perfection. You can decorate your square with a design, a symbol, a motif, a picture, a poem, or anything that reflects your wishes for us. You can use fabric paints or markers, do embroidery, sew sequins—whatever you like. You are truly honoring us through this collaborative creation.*

Our dear friend Sallie Cohen has graciously offered to assemble the chuppah. *Please return your square to her no later than MARCH 15th. Her address is listed below.*

Please contact us with any questions or concerns. Thanks again!
Love,
The Happy Couple

How to Create a Tie-Dye *Chuppah*

Before you begin: If you have never experimented with tie-dyeing before, use the following directions to play around on some old T-shirts so that you are comfortable with the technique before actually trying it out on your *chuppah.*

Materials:

- Large square of cotton, linen, silk, rayon, or hemp (avoid 100 percent polyester at all costs) at least 6-by-4 feet.
- Sodium carbonate (soda ash)
- Rubber bands
- Plastic soda bottles or squeeze bottles
- Dye in colors of your choices (check out companies such as Rit, Dharma, and Prochem; see Appendix I).

"holding" the poles and so surround you with their loving presence. My husband and I wanted to give this honor to four of the most important people in the world to us. Each of us chose one of our very best friends, and together we chose the couple who introduced us and who are like family to us. It was so wonderful to have those four friends holding our *chuppah* poles and feeling their support and smiles throughout our ceremony.

Regulations at Your Wedding Site

When thinking through the kind of *chuppah* you want, it is critical to find out when you will be able to set up your *chuppah*. Every site's rules will vary, depending on the schedule of parties and functions. If you are designing something in your mind that will take many hours to assemble, but in reality you will have only two hours on the morning of your wedding to do the assembling, you're setting yourself up for a whole lot of stress. Get the details on how much time you have to set things up, and use this information to think in realistic terms.

Setting It Up and Taking It Down

The last thing that a bride or groom wants to be doing just before or after the wedding is worrying about the logistics of transporting, assembling, and taking down the *chuppah*. Make sure that you ask a friend or family member, way in advance of the wedding, to take on this important job for you. Ideally, this person should be someone with prior *chuppah*-setting-up experience or someone who is just a handy person you trust completely. Let this person know where you want your *chuppah* to go once it has been taken down. Some couples like to pin up or hang their canopy on an easel during their reception for all their guests to see. Another option is to pin it to the wall behind the bride and groom's seats at the reception.

Commissioning a Professional *Chuppah*

If you have your heart set on standing under an original *chuppah* but you don't have the time, the energy, or a friend who can help you create it, another option is to hire a professional Judaica artist to take on the job. Today, more and more artists are expressing themselves through amazing works of Judaica that bring new meaning to the traditional notion of *hiddur mitzvah;* that is, by beautifying a commandment, it extends the commandment. Among these Judaica artists is a subset of professionals who specialize in creating original *chuppot.*

Using a professional is obviously more expensive than creating a *chuppah* on your own. But remember, a *chuppah* is something that you can keep as a family heirloom long after the wedding day is over. Many of the couples who work with professional artists are given their original *chuppah* as a wedding present from one or both sets of parents. If you are interested in this option, see the artists listed in Appendix I.

Chuppot Created by Other Couples

When Joellyn and Ron Zollman were planning their wedding, they had the challenge of making both their families—who live on opposite coasts—feel involved and included. The wedding was held in Joellyn's hometown of Altoona, Pennsylvania, while Ron's family was based in Los Angeles. But for their *chuppah,* both mothers—one in Pennsylvania and one in California—worked on their own, simultaneously embroidering pieces of matching fabric. Their embroidery included text from the *Sheva Brachot* (Seven Blessings) part of the Jewish wedding ceremony, "Voices of Joy and of Gladness, of the Bride and the Bridegroom," along with the names of the couple and their wedding date. When everyone came together for the wedding weekend, the two moms pieced together the fabric and hung the tapestry on four poles. Their individual long-distance efforts came together to make a gorgeous *chuppah.*

When Carra and Scott Minkoff were planning their wedding, they envisioned their *chuppah* as one day serving as a canopy for their bed. Carra asked her future mother-in-law to look for lace tablecloths that would create a light, airy feeling. Carra and Scott wanted four friends to hold the *chuppah* and walk it into the ceremony as part of the processional, but knowing that it would be a long ceremony, they wanted the poles to be self-supporting so that their friends wouldn't have to be supporting the poles on their own. Mrs. Minkoff bought four

- Newspapers
- Rubber gloves
- Plastic gloves

Note: It is best to tie-dye outdoors to avoid any spilling/splashing mess. If you are tie-dyeing indoors, be sure to put newspapers down under your work area.

Instructions

1. Before you start the actual dyeing, take some time to think about what kind of design you prefer. By tying rubber bands around your fabric you can create a variety of effects, from spirals to sunbursts to stripes and more. Check out ww.ritdye.com for specific instructions for each kind of tie-dye.
2. Wash and dry your fabric.
3. Just before dyeing, pre-soak the fabric for fifteen minutes to an hour in a solution of 1 cup of sodium carbonate per gallon of water. Use the kind that is sold for swimming pools. The brand known as "pH Up" is excellent.
4. Tie your rubber bands around the fabric according to the desired effect that you want to achieve.
5. In a plastic soda or squeeze bottle, dissolve 4 teaspoons of dye into 1 cup of water. If you are dyeing a large amount of the fabric in one color, double or triple the above proportions as needed.
6. Lay the fabric nearly flat on newspaper, or pleated loosely,

and drip the dye from the bottle directly onto the fabric. Be sure to wear gloves! The sodium carbonate is slightly caustic and must be washed or at least wiped off your skin immediately after contact.

7. Repeat steps 5 and 6 with each color.

8. The fabric needs to stay damp for at least two and up to twenty-four hours. You can wrap the fabric in a plastic bag to ensure dampness.

9. When your fabric has dried, you can wash it in cold water on the gentle cycle. Silk must be dry cleaned only.

10. To complete your *chuppah*, see instructions on page 102 for attaching it to poles. You might want to use ribbons matching the colors in your tie-dye to attach it to the poles and/or paint a design on top of the tie-dye with fabric paints to add a more textured look. Consider tie-dyeing *kippot* to match your *chuppah*.

simple patio-umbrella stands and used the bases of them as the places where the *chuppah* poles (light but sturdy PVC pipes, covered in white fabric) would be inserted. She covered the umbrella stands with pretty white material that was aesthetically pleasing, while allowing them to serve their primary purpose of containing the poles. Their *chuppah*, in the end, captured the antique, canopy feeling that the couple had envisioned.

Several couples I spoke with are creating "family *chuppot*" in which original canopies are being shared by extended families. When one sibling gets married, his name and wedding date are embroidered onto the *chuppah*; when the next sibling marries, her name and date are added, and so on. The *chuppot* are sometimes also used for other family milestones, such as baby namings. Some families create their *chuppot* with fabric panels that can be rearranged for each new occasion. By creating the fabric as panels, it can be taken apart and rearranged for each sibling or relative, making the design connected to the family but unique for each particular couple.

Family Dynamics and Your *Chuppah*

As mentioned previously, creating an original *chuppah* can be a wonderful way to involve both families in a truly meaningful project. Whether you choose to do a collage-style *chuppah* that draws on the talents of lots of friends and family members, or an embroidery project created by someone from each family, you are setting the stage to make both families feel valued and welcomed as part of your wedding planning. If you and/or your partner are not close to your family of origin, calling on your extended community of friends can serve the same purpose.

If you have children from a previous marriage, invite them to create part of your *chuppah* as a way of making them feel that their contributions—to your wedding and your new life as a blended family—matter. You might have them individually design fabric squares, for example. Then bring the children together to talk about how best to lay out the squares. Listen to everyone's opinion and let yourself be guided by their suggestions.

If you and your family are considering creating an heirloom *chuppah* to be shared among your siblings, try to be sensitive to your partner's family in the process. Be sure to include both sides of the family in the design process. When the mother of a groom came to *chuppah* artists Margery and Eli Langner and wanted them to create something special because the bride's family was giving an original *chuppah* to the couple as a gift, Margery suggested that they create a matching piece of fabric art to serve as the tablecloth for the small table holding the wine and glasses that would stand under the *chuppah*. This innovation helped the groom's family feel included and it created even more beauty for the couple as they stood under their *chuppah*. There is always a creative way to make both sides of the family feel part of the wedding, as long as you approach your wedding designing with sensitivity, an open mind, and good communication skills. (But keep in mind that, even with the best intentions, it is completely normal to have a few meltdowns along the way.)

This embroidered *chuppah* was created by two mothers—one in Pennsylvania and one in California—and then sewn together a few days before the wedding.

You or your partner may have experienced a recent loss, or you may be feeling with special poignancy the loss of someone such as a cherished grandparent who died some time ago. Consider honoring that person's memory in your *chuppah* design. Use a tablecloth that your grandmother made for the *chuppah* base; attach your grandfather's *tzitzit* to the *chuppah's* ends; or adorn your poles with scarves or handkerchiefs that belonged to someone you are missing at this milestone moment. These are just a few ways to bring the presence of that special person to your wedding through your *chuppah* design.

As you plan your *chuppah*, another issue to consider is who will stand under the canopy with you. It used to be customary for both the bride's and the groom's parents to stand with them under the *chuppah* during the ceremony. Your own parents may have had their parents under the *chuppah* with them, and may therefore assume that they will do the same with you. Talk about this ahead of time with your partner and with both sets of parents to avoid any hard feelings.

Some couples who have divorced parents find it easier not to invite parents to stand under the *chuppah*. If two ex-spouses are on bad terms and haven't seen each other for years, their son or daughter might prefer not to bring that baggage under the *chuppah*. Each couple needs to look at their family dynamics and determine what makes the most sense for their situation. If you have four (or more) parents who will stand proudly with you under the *chuppah*, it is a most powerful feeling and a real gift to share that intimate space and time together. But if you prefer your *chuppah* space to be held by just you, the couple, and your rabbi, that is a fine choice, too. Arrange the chairs surrounding your *chuppah* so that parents and other relatives can be as close as possible and can experience the beauty of the ceremony from their seats.

Your children from a previous marriage will also feel honored and involved in your wedding by standing right there under the *chuppah* with you and your new partner. If they are old enough and capable of holding the *chuppah* poles, that is a wonderful role for them to take on as well. Remember, the honor of holding a *chuppah* pole is reserved for people closest to you, so decide together who will serve in those important roles.

In the end, whatever *chuppah* you choose should have one overriding goal: to create a sacred space surrounding you during your wedding ceremony.

chapter five

The Truth about the Aufruf . . .
and Other Jewish Pre-Wedding Rituals

One thing that I really enjoyed about my own wedding experience was that there were lots of celebratory events that took place prior to the wedding day. Excitement was building toward the wedding, and these lovely celebrations gave me a chance to be with people who all wished us well. It is challenging to have meaningful interactions with so many people you love from all facets of your life when they are gathered together for the one brief afternoon or evening of your wedding. During pre-wedding festivities, you can actually talk to and connect with people. Jewish tradition understands this phenomenon and offers many opportunities to celebrate and renew ties—opportunities for both spiritual reflection and social engagement with the people you love—before your wedding day. You and your partner can thoughtfully choose the pre-wedding rituals that will infuse your entire wedding experience with the most meaning.

Traditionally, the engagement of a Jewish couple was celebrated with a party. These parties were often an opportunity for the families to meet for the first time and get to know each other. Years ago, this was also the setting where *tennaim* (marriage conditions) were signed to commit both families to the wedding date and other provisions for the upcoming marriage.

Today, engagement parties still allow both families to meet each other, if they haven't done so before. Even if both sets of parents have met, it's nice for siblings and other extended relatives to meet and mingle so they are all acquainted with one another before the wedding. Engagement parties often take place way in advance of the wedding—especially when couples plan a long engagement period so they can each finish school, establish a career, and so on. If the couple's families live in different parts of the country, it is sometimes easiest for everyone if two engagement parties are held. That way, if people are unable to travel a long distance for both an engagement party and a wedding, both sides of the family still get to celebrate with the bride and groom.

When the time finally comes for the wedding festivities, the celebration may start off with any or all of the following customs and rituals.

Henna Party

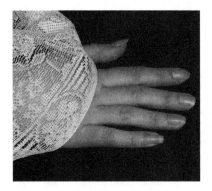

Using lace is one way to create a fancy henna design.

Whereas going to the *mikvah* is a serious ritual designed for spiritual purity (read more about it later in this chapter), this pre-wedding custom—the henna party—is more about fun and celebration. When many people in the West think about Jewish customs and traditions, most often we focus on elements passed down from Ashkenazi Jews, our ancestors from Central and Eastern Europe. But Jewish civilization also comprises a rich heritage from Sephardic and Mizrachi Jews—our co-religionists whose roots go back to Spain, Portugal, North Africa, and the Middle East. One especially enjoyable pre-wedding custom that comes from our Sephardic and Mizrachi sisters is the henna party. Henna is a red dye made from vegetables that women in the Middle East have been using for thousands of years, both as a hair dye and as a way to create beautiful, nonpermanent decorative motifs on their skin. It is customary for Middle Eastern and North African brides—Jewish, Muslim, and Christian alike—to be showered with a henna party a few days before the wedding ceremony.

The traditional henna party was hosted by the mother and mother-in-law, and all the bride's women friends and relatives were invited. The women would create elaborate designs with henna on the bride's hands and feet to make her more beautiful for her wedding. The designs would often be very ornate, using fancy lace as a pattern to lay the henna over. Because henna takes some time to dry (twenty-four hours to completely set), the bride just had to sit still and rest for a while. The other women would feed her all sorts of delicacies—nuts, olives, honey, pastries—and bless her with good wishes for her marriage.

If you live in a major metropolitan area, you can probably locate a professional henna artist who could come to your henna party. If you would like to include a henna party as part of your pre-wedding rituals but don't live in an area where henna artists are available, you can still buy some henna at a health-food or beauty-supply store and ask a handy friend to try giving you a design. If you're worried about how the design might come out, you could schedule your party a week or so before the wedding, so the henna can wash off before the big day arrives. In Sephardic/Mizrachi communities, the groom was also celebrated by his father, his father-in-law, and his male relatives and friends with a festive party, minus the henna.

Immersing in the *Mikvah*

The *mikvah* (Hebrew for "gathering of water") is the ritual bath that a traditional Jewish bride immerses in before her wedding day as a way of acknowledging her change in status from a single to a married woman. In Jewish tradition, one of the main functions of immersion in the *mikvah* is to purify a woman after her menstrual cycle. Although this tradition offers a complex challenge for many contemporary women who do not view their menstrual cycle as dirty or something from which they need to purify themselves, the ritual of immersing in a *mikvah* still has strong spiritual resonance for many women. Some of them have taken on the tradition of going to the *mikvah* either before their wedding or as a regular ritual, dunking in the bath to wash off stress and negative energy. Many women embrace the *mikvah* as a "woman's space," separate from daily responsibilities, a special place to reconnect with the Divine Presence.

One bride that I spoke with, Jill Levy, found the experience of going to the *mikvah* the night before her wedding to be one of the most spiritually powerful experiences of her life. "My mother-in-law told me about a new *mikvah* that had been built at her temple (where we were getting married), so I thought I'd try it," Jill recalls. "The changing room for the *mikvah* was quite posh and as I undressed

Everything You Need to Throw a Fantastic Henna Shower

If you are the mother, sister, or best friend of a bride and want to lavish her with a most festive shower, consider throwing a henna party. Here's what you need:

Tasty finger foods: Start with traditional Sephardic fare, including almonds, olives, pistachio nuts, and feta cheese. Add plenty of sweet baked goods, such as baklava, to complement the salty treats. Be sure to include any of the bride's favorite nuts or candy.

Sephardic music: Set the party tone with some contemporary Sephardic-influenced Israeli pop music, such as that of crooner Yehoram Gaon. Be sure to assign someone as the DJ and make sure you mix in any of the bride's other favorite tunes, especially sappy love songs (in whatever genre she prefers).

Gorgeous lace: On your shower invitations, ask each guest to bring a small piece of lace. You will use that lace to cover the bride's hands and feet and create a henna design.

Lots of pillows: Place big, comfy pillows, preferably in bright colors, all over your floor so everyone can sit on the ground. Make sure the bride is comfortable and encourage her to sit back and relax: She will be waited on.

Henna: Check out your local health-food store or order online. For best results, practice on another guinea pig before you adorn the bride!

Blessings: In addition to bringing the lace, ask your guests to bring some kind of blessing (in writing) to share with the bride. It might be a special song, a poem, or an original blessing. After each guest offers her blessing to the bride, you can put the written copies into a special scrapbook so she can remember the day.

Plenty of wine: What's a Jewish party without some good red wine? You might also try some specialty Sephardic liquors, such as etrog liquor, which can be imported from Israel. See kosher wine listings in Appendix I.

Mix it all together and you have a fun-filled henna shower! Make sure that the bride reclines and is waited on, no matter how much she protests. This is her time to bask in the celebration of her happy event.

I felt like I was at a day spa or a fancy hotel. When I went into the clean, blue *mikvah* and immersed, I felt really free. My time in the *mikvah* was quiet and peaceful. I said the traditional *bracha* (blessing) and made an internal *kavannah* (intention) for each dunking about what I was thankful for in getting married to my amazing husband and for my family, who had all supported me so much in planning the wedding. I also said the *Shehecheyanu* (the blessing to celebrate new and special occasions). I stayed in the changing room by myself for a little while and suddenly I started to cry. It was a mixture of sadness and happiness, just taking the time out to realize that I was about to start a new part of my life, and how excited and thankful I was."

For many brides today, going to the *mikvah* on the night before their wedding (or a few nights before) can be a great opportunity to connect with a mother or a special friend in an intimate way, apart from the wedding anxiety. "Going to the *mikvah* for the first time, the night before my wedding, was a real cleansing for me," says Carra Minkoff. "It was just my Mom and me, late at night. From that moment on, I put all the planning and details aside and just let myself focus on being present for the wedding. It was so special that Mom and I had that time to connect."

Some women like to invite a group of friends and relatives and make a party/shower of the experience of going to the *mikvah*. In some Sephardic traditions, sisters and friends would give the bride special perfumes and soaps when she went to the *mikvah*, and the women would all sit around and sing and laugh together as they walked the bride back home from the ritual bath. Going to the *mikvah* can be a fun experience for brides who crave a social experience with their gal pals just before their wedding. Of course, you can create your *mikvah* moment anywhere you'd like on the spectrum from private and introspective to public and social; it doesn't need to be an either/or choice.

Your town may or may not have a *mikvah*, depending on the size of the Jewish community there. Years ago, only Orthodox communities had public *mikvahs*, but today many communities have Conservative or Reform-affiliated *mikvahs*. These ritual baths are often used for people going through conversion to Judaism, but they can be used for pre-wedding rituals as well. Be sure to call the *mikvah* ahead of time to ask about availability and any associated fees.

According to Jewish law, a *mikvah* does not need to be indoors; it just needs to contain a flowing source of water. This means that any flowing water source— a river, a lake, the ocean—could become your *mikvah*. You may not want to go completely nude if you're in a public place, but some clever brides have been known to go out fairly deep in the ocean, drop their bathing suit, and dunk three times, as the ritual prescribes, totally in the buff, then pull their suit back on and swim gracefully to shore, their fellow beachgoers completely oblivious to the powerful ritual that just took place in their midst.

The *mikvah* is not a ritual for women only. It is customary that Jewish men go to the *mikvah* to immerse for purposes of spiritual purity as well. Grooms may want to set aside time, shortly before the wedding or on the morning of their wedding day, to engage in this tradition. Make it a reflective time, when you are able to let go of the worries and constraints that have been on your mind. The act of dunking in the water can be a way of letting go of your identity as a single man and embracing your new status as part of a committed covenant. If you are an outdoorsy kind of guy, you might want to go on a hike with a best friend and find a natural source of running water for your *mikvah*. Whether you choose an indoor or an outdoor *mikvah*, allow some time for prayer, meditation, and reflection before and after the experience.

Many people compose new poems and prayers to accompany their pre-wedding dunking; you can find an assortment of these at www.ritualwell.org. Both men and women can take the opportunity of going to the *mikvah* to write an original prayer or poem. Your prayer does not need to be in formal or fancy language.

Questions to Inspire an Original Prayer

What do you remember most about the special moments you've shared with your partner? Where were they? What details can you recall in terms of colors, scents, and textures during those special moments?

What do you feel most thankful for at this moment in your life?

What are you most excited about as you enter this new phase of your life?

Do you have any emotional baggage or fears that you are carrying with you that you want to release before your wedding?

If you could say anything at all to God at this moment, what would it be?

You can shape your responses into a poem or prayer to read at the *mikvah* or you can simply use the traditional blessing when you immerse. The traditional blessing recited when dunking in the *mikvah* is:

בָּרוּךְ אַתָּה יְיָ

אֱלֹהֵינוּ מֶלֶךְ הָעוֹלָם,

אֲשֶׁר קִדְּשָׁנוּ בְּמִצְוֹתָיו וְצִוָּנוּ עַל הַטְּבִילָה.

Baruch atah Adonai,
Elohaynu melech haOlam,
asher kidshanu b'mitzvotav v'tzivanu al haTevilah.

Blessed are you, Adonai our God,
Sovereign of the Universe,
who made us holy with *mitzvot*
and commanded us concerning immersion.

Envisioning Your *Mikvah*

Whether or not you are interested in actually going to a *mikvah*, the following visualization exercise can help you let go of some of the worries that you may be carrying with you before your wedding. You can take some time to do this exercise as a way to prepare for your visit to the *mikvah*, or you can simply use it for its own sake. Find a quiet place to sit and relax. Breathe deeply. Ask your partner to read the following scenario. There is no need to take notes; just allow yourself to go on a journey.

Sit back, close your eyes. Let your muscles relax, your breathing slow down. Imagine yourself walking along the beach. The sun is vibrant in the sky, the sand is warm between your toes. The wind is calm, gently brushing your face. As you walk along the beach, you look out to the sea stretching before you. You notice how incredibly blue and sparkling the water is. You have never seen such clear blue water before. The sun is making your whole body feel warm and relaxed. You walk to the water's edge and let the water run over your toes. The water feels so good, so warm, bathing and caressing you. You walk deeper into the water so that it covers your feet, ankles, shins, knees. You look up at the sun—it seems to radiate its warm light right into your heart, filling your whole body with light. You walk deeper into the water; it comes up to your waist, your chest, then your shoulders. It is a warm bath of a water. You feel incredibly safe and calm. When you are ready, you dunk your whole body into the water, and you float beneath the surface. The water holds you and caresses you. You emerge back to the air feeling lighter, as if any worries or concerns have floated free from your body. You dunk again, feeling safe and nurtured once more. You rise peacefully to the surface and look at the blue water around you. Before you dunk again, you decide to say a prayer. It may be a prayer of thanks, a prayer asking for help, or a prayer appreciating the beauty of the world that surrounds you. It is your prayer. When you are ready, dunk again and release it. When you feel it is time, you can walk out of the water, letting your body dry in the sun's warmth. Take some time basking in the sun. Know that this warm, nurturing water is there for you to dunk in, any time that you desire. When you are ready, gently open your eyes and return to the room.

Aufruf—The Pre-Wedding Aliyah

This ritual is probably the best known and most commonly practiced pre-wedding ritual among American Jews today. In traditional Jewish communities, a groom is called to the Torah to receive an *aliyah* on the Shabbat immediately prior to his wedding. Yiddish for "calling up," the *aufruf* (pronounced "oof-roof") celebrated in non-Orthodox communities today includes both the groom and the bride going up for an *aliyah*, which generally means that they receive the honor of chanting the blessing before and after the Torah reading. After doing so, the rabbi usually offers them a special blessing for their marriage, and then the real fun takes place: The congregation showers them with candy. This custom is always a big hit with the under-five set, who scurry around the *bimah* collecting as much candy as possible. (Word to the wise: Look out for any nephews in the ten-to-twelve age range, who often get a kick out of pelting and whipping the candy as hard as possible. I have never heard, thank goodness, about a bride who received a hard-candy black eye the day before her wedding, but I certainly think a little defensive ducking couldn't hurt! Make sure you take a defensive strategy and buy only soft, individually wrapped candies.)

If you and your partner are comfortable doing more, the honor of being called up for an *aliyah* can be extended into other honors as well. Some couples like to read from the Torah and/or give a *d'var* Torah (a commentary about the Torah portion that is being read) at their *aufruf*. An *aufruf* can also be a time to honor other relatives who may want to participate in the worship service. Offer them the opportunity to say some words of Torah or one of the blessings. Talk with your rabbi ahead of time about all the possibilities. Just remember: You don't want to take on anything that would cause you extra stress just before your wedding.

One especially nice thing about inviting your wedding guests to your *aufruf* is that it gives non-Jewish guests an opportunity to experience a Jewish ritual before the wedding. Although many of your non-Jewish guests may have attended other Jewish weddings, there will probably be some for whom your wedding is their first experience of Jewish worship. Going to your *aufruf* gives them the chance to hear Hebrew, hold a Jewish prayer book, and take in the surroundings of a Jewish sanctuary. Just having that small bit of exposure beforehand may make your wedding ceremony an even richer experience for them.

Creating a Wedding *Shabbaton*

Rather than just inviting guests to an *aufruf,* some couples like to use the opportunity for Shabbat worship and celebration to hold a sort of wedding *Shabbaton.* That is, they invite guests to participate in a series of events that might include a Friday night Shabbat dinner and/or *oneg* (reception), a Saturday morning *aufruf* followed by a *kiddush* luncheon, and perhaps a *havdalah* ceremony Saturday night, marking the close of Shabbat. A *Shabbaton* can be a wonderful way of extending your wedding celebration so that you get a chance to interact with as many loved ones and friends as possible.

Rabbi Arthur Ocean Waskow and Phyllis Ocean Berman have officiated together at many weddings over the years and have found that couples who make their wedding into a *Shabbaton* have very special experiences. "It really takes the pressure off the bride and groom on the wedding day," Berman says, "if they have had the chance to be with their guests during the weekend. This way, people really get to know each other and circles of friends and families start to mix. By the wedding day, everyone is feeling the buildup for the big celebration."

Such a series of events takes planning and coordinating on your end. Considering the following:

> Can we schedule all the events in close proximity so that guests are able to get from one to the other with ease? Will friends who are religiously observant be able to walk easily from hotel to synagogue?

> Are there friends or relatives who can host, set up, and coordinate the *oneg,* luncheon, or *havdalah*?

> How many guests should we realistically expect at the *Shabbaton*?

> How much will it cost to host these events? Will we, the couple, pay for these events, or will we ask parents/family to help defray the cost?

> Does our schedule build in any downtime for our guests? How programmed do we want the weekend to be?

Of course, you don't need to make your wedding weekend into an all-or-nothing proposition. You might host a Friday night *oneg* and have an *aufruf* on Saturday morning, but leave the rest of Saturday totally open for people to do sightseeing, hang out together informally, or just relax.

Another way to create a relaxed *Shabbaton* is to hold your wedding at a retreat center, where everything will take place on the premises. Everyone sleeps and eats at the center, Shabbat services are held on site, and folks have the opportunity to take walks, swim, shoot hoops, or take part in whatever leisure activities the center offers. You may be surprised by how economical this alternative can be: Oftentimes, retreat centers have no programming scheduled during their off seasons and will give you a great deal. Many non-Jewish retreat centers are able to bring in kosher food, if you like, and make accommodations for Jewish weddings.

Separation/Fasting

Traditionally, bride and groom would not see each other at all during the week before the wedding in order to enhance the joy of their wedding through their separation. This custom makes a lot of sense, considering the many emotions that arise during that week; the last thing either partner needs is to pick up on the other person's stress (it is challenging enough to deal with your own stress). But you will probably be dealing with some last-minute details that will require your mutual cooperation, and you may also want to take part in some of the celebrations together. Today's couples come up with a variety of ways to build in some separation before the wedding. If you are living together already, for example, it may be that one of you sleeps over with a friend the week before the wedding, so that you only see each other during the day. Or you do things together up until the *aufruf*, then say good-bye to each other until the wedding. Talk to each other ahead of time about what possibilities for separation make the most sense for you. While separating from each other may pose some logistical challenges, something magical happens when you finally come together again after a separation and first see each other dressed and ready for your wedding.

It is also traditional for brides and grooms to fast, starting at sundown the night before their wedding. Just as with fasting on Yom Kippur, this custom serves as a way to purify oneself before marriage, so that bride and groom can stand under the *chuppah* in a pure state. Fasting helps set apart your wedding day from any other day in your life: The seriousness of the ritual focuses your intention on the sacredness of the commitment you are about to make.

Many couples today do indeed fast before their wedding, while others choose to modify this ritual. You know yourself best: If you think that not eating at all might cause you to pass out under the *chuppah*, for example, then you should probably avoid fasting. Another alternative is to eat some light crackers and water, rather than eating a heavy meal, just to tide you over. Consult with your rabbi about choosing this ritual.

Whether you choose to fast or not, a Jewish wedding is still a sort of personal Yom Kippur for the bride and groom. That doesn't mean that it's a somber day, but rather a time for personal prayer and reflection. You may consciously want to block out some time, even if it's only fifteen or twenty minutes, when you can sit alone and meditate or simply reflect about your life and the gratitude you are feeling. The High Holy Days are also a time when Jews actively participate in *teshuvah* (literally "returning") work. *Teshuvah* is about examining our actions and taking responsibility so that we can grow and change. *Teshuvah* may mean apologizing to someone we have hurt, either intentionally or not. This is a wonderful practice to bring into your wedding. Even with the best intentions, we sometimes hurt someone we love dearly during the time we are planning our wedding. Take some time before your wedding—it doesn't need to be on your wedding day—to take anyone aside to whom you want to say "I'm sorry." Just clearing the air that way will not only benefit the other person but will also allow you to enter your wedding with a lighter spirit. The loving support around you will be even stronger when you approach your *chuppah*. You and your partner may have had a million stupid fights during the course of your wedding planning. Take time, before you separate, to let each other know how much you love and appreciate each other and to ask forgiveness for hurting each other during this emotionally stressful time.

With careful planning, the week before your wedding can be a time to reflect personally, to connect with family and friends, to create meaningful rituals and celebrations, and to ground yourself and your guests in Jewish time. Whatever celebrations you plan, however, make sure you build in some downtime for yourself to rest and relax. The best advice anyone gave me was to schedule a massage for the day before my wedding. That half-hour helped me be present for my ceremony the next day more than anything else!

Family Dynamics During the Pre-Wedding Stage

If you and your partner both come from Jewish families who are active members of a synagogue, you may want to schedule two *aufrufs* to honor both your families. If your wedding is being held in the hometown of one partner, the other family may be feeling slightly left out, and holding an *aufruf* at their synagogue sometime before the wedding can help make them feel more included. If families live far away from each other, this idea probably won't be possible. But if it's a matter of a few hours' drive, talk to both sets of parents and ask them whether holding an *aufruf* at their congregation is important to them. Especially if you still have ties to a rabbi there or to many of the congregants, you'll be doing a *mitzvah* by inviting the congregation you grew up with to celebrate this milestone in your life. Talk with the rabbi (or ask one of your parents to) and see whether you can schedule the *aufruf* as close to the wedding as possible—maybe a couple of weeks in advance. Then on the actual Shabbat before your wedding, you can do *aufruf* number 2. What's there to lose? I say more candy and happiness for everyone!

chapter six

Reckon You'll Bedecken?
A Creative Look at the Jewish Wedding Ceremony

When I first envisioned writing a creative Jewish wedding book, I thought about all the tangible ritual objects connected to the wedding—from the *ketubah* to the *kiddush* cup, from the invitations to the *chuppah*. I considered all the ways that people could express their personal style in creating those physical objects that can last a lifetime and be passed down to future generations.

But as I began to do research for the book, and reflect more deeply on my own wedding experience, I realized that the most significant area to bring your creative energy to bear is in the planning of your wedding ceremony. The ceremony is a ritual—a living enactment of your covenant, spoken in front of and witnessed by your collective community of family and friends. It is not something that you will be able to hold years after, not something you can show to your grandchildren in years to come. Yes, photographs and certainly video can capture the memories of your ceremony, but even as close as it comes, watching it on tape is not like being there, experiencing the magic in present time. Your ceremony will happen in its moment and be gone, yet its impact may change you forever.

A ritual such as a wedding ceremony calls our deepest selves to come forward and rise above our earthly problems and egotistical concerns. A wedding ceremony joins us together—two beloveds making a commitment and covenant to each other—on a spiritual level, a place inside us where we may not often travel and may not have traveled together before. The feelings of love and awe, of memories and connections to the past, present, and future that arise under the *chuppah* are powerful stuff, not to be taken lightly.

You have the opportunity in creating your ceremony to work with and honor Jewish tradition and its powerful rituals, while adding or incorporating new elements into the ceremony that will help reach the deepest place in your soul. Whether you are a traditionally observant or a completely secular person, you can use the ideas, encounters, and experiences in this chapter to think through your ceremony in a way that will make it the most meaningful experience possible.

For some couples, the ceremony is nothing more than some words that have to be uttered to satisfy parents before moving on to the party. If you are feeling cynical or alienated by the idea of the wedding ceremony, know that you're not alone in that attitude. We have few opportunities in contemporary society to experience transformative rituals, so it is not at all surprising that when many of us come to major ritual moments, we freak out a bit and want to move through them as quickly and painlessly as possible. On top of that, for people alienated by religion, the idea of taking part in a religious ceremony is annoying at best and deeply troubling at worst.

Again, let me remind you that Judaism, in the words of the late Rabbi Mordechai Kaplan, has always been an evolving civilization, learning and shifting and innovating through time. When the Jews were exiled from Israel and moved away from the holy Temple, the center of religious life, the Rabbis of the Diaspora had to create new ways of practicing Judaism, based on the synagogue as a place of community and learning and the home as the center of ritual life. From that point on, each generation of Jews has contributed to Judaism's innovation and growth, leading us to present times and the current wealth and diversity of Jewish thought and practices. Whatever your belief system or form of religious expression, there is a place for you in the world of contemporary Judaism. Whether you are bringing egalitarian ideals to the ceremony, a consciousness for the rights of gays and lesbians, or a skepticism about religion in general, there is a way for you to create a meaningful Jewish wedding ceremony. The Humanistic Judaism movement even makes room for Jews who openly state that they don't believe in God, but who do believe in the Jewish religion's embrace of humanistic values. Your Jewish wedding ceremony should be a creative expression of who you are. Unless you take ownership of the ceremony and make it personally meaningful, the most creative *chuppah* or the most beautiful *ketubah* won't mean a thing.

You may have a very clear sense already of where you fit in to the spectrum of Jewish belief and observance. Or you may be approaching your wedding with a sense of doubt, curiosity, or even confusion. As individuals and as a couple, planning your ceremony will help you clarify your beliefs and the way you are most comfortable expressing your Jewish identity. What you experience during your wedding ceremony may have a profound effect on the way you view religion in your life from that point forward, as well as on your relationship with your partner.

As you begin to think about the rituals associated with your ceremony, it is natural for differences to arise between you and your partner. Whenever possible, you should start from common ground, from a place that both of you can agree on. If you each imagine God in a different way, for example, talk to your officiant about finding God language within Jewish tradition that makes sense for both of you.

Before the Ceremony

The Jewish wedding begins before the actual moment when the partners stand together under the *chuppah*. Many different rituals occur prior to the ceremony.

Kabbalat Panim

In Jewish tradition, the bride and groom are treated as king and queen for the day, and this begins with guests going to separate rooms to pay their respects to the "royal couple" as part of what's called *kabbalat panim* (literally "receiving of the faces").

For the groom, this meeting takes the form of a *tisch*. The *tisch* (table) is a gathering of men who basically joke and roast the poor groom, who is supposed to offer some words of Torah to the group but who keeps getting interrupted with

Reckon You'll Bedecken? A Creative Look at the Jewish Wedding Ceremony

125

songs and jokes. The purpose of the *tisch* is for the men to celebrate with their friend and take his mind off what is about to come. If the groom is supposed to be treated like a king, his friends take on the role of the court jesters. In traditional communities, while the groom is at his *tisch*, the bride is dressed and sits in another room, on a fancy chair, to receive her guests who come to offer her good wishes for her marriage (and, of course, compliment her on how beautiful she looks).

The essence of these traditions is that both bride and groom are separated from each other and are surrounded by friends. This is a concept that can be modified to meet the needs of you and your community. If you aren't skilled in words of Torah, for example, don't worry about it: Your *tisch* could be more about hanging out with the guys, while they tell embarrassing stories from your high school days. Some women like to hold a *tisch*, too, rather than a traditional *kabbalat panim*, if they prefer the energy of laughter and joking. You can ask one of your most outgoing, lively friends to lead the *tisch* and keep the stories, jokes, and songs moving along. Often couples do not break down their *tisches* across gender lines but will invite all their guests to move back and forth between separate rooms. If you would like to schedule a *tisch* before the wedding, make sure that your ceremony site has rooms where it can take place. Also, be sure to let guests know what time to arrive for this pre-wedding event.

If you think you would prefer a more quiet introduction to your wedding, you could use the tradition of *kabbalat panim* as a way to schedule some private time before the wedding to exchange words with the people who are closest to you. You might ask a few friends, your parents, your siblings, or other cherished relatives to stop by and quietly chat with you for a few moments before the ceremony begins.

Some couples, either right after a *tisch* or instead of it, take some quiet time just before their ceremony to sit and meditate. They might sit with their rabbi, who can be a calming presence at a time when emotions tend to run high. They might choose to sit with their partner or to have each partner take time with the rabbi alone. Even sitting quietly for ten minutes can have a calming effect on wedding day nerves and one's ability to be really present for the ceremony. Some couples like to say a few words, spontaneously from their heart, to each other before they rejoin their guests for the rest of the pre-ceremony rituals.

Ketubah Signing

In traditional circles, the signing of the *ketubah* marks the official beginning of the wedding ceremony. It is read aloud and signed by two male witnesses, and the groom takes hold of some ritual object, usually a handkerchief, to acknowledge that he accepts the obligations laid out in the document.

In many contemporary non-Orthodox communities, the *ketubah* signing involves both bride and groom, along with their witnesses. The *ketubah* signing may be the first moment that day that bride and groom lay eyes on each other. They may invite all of their guests to witness the signing, or just invite a small group of family and friends to participate. Again, in non-Orthodox communities, both men and women can serve as witnesses, and the *ketubah* might also be signed by the bride and groom. Make sure that

The groom, in a homemade Grateful Dead *kippah*, signs his *ketubah*.

you and/or your witnesses know how to sign your Hebrew names (in Hebrew letters) in advance of the moment; you can also carry a "cheat sheet" to take the pressure off.

Also, you will want to designate someone to carry the *ketubah* from the signing to its place under the *chuppah* if it is going to be displayed and read as part of the ceremony (this person can also pick it up after the ceremony and take it to the reception to be displayed there). The *ketubah* signing can be a real celebratory moment, enhanced by a song or two. If you are planning to include a lot of readings or songs in your ceremony and are worried about how long it will run, you might want to read the *ketubah* at this point rather than during the ceremony. Some couples also skip reading the *ketubah* altogether, but include a copy of its text in their wedding program for guests to read.

Bedecken

This couple used the *bedecken*—veiling—as a time to look deeply into each other's eyes.

Bedecken (or "veiling the bride") comes next. Traditionally, the groom would place the veil over his bride's face. This custom arose in a reference to two biblical stories: (1) Rebekah veiled herself as a sign of modesty when she met Isaac, her intended, and (2) Jacob was tricked by his father-in-law Laban, who hid his daughter Leah under a veil when he had promised Jacob his daughter Rachel. The veil symbolizes modesty, and the *bedecken* ritual ensures the groom that he is going to marry the right woman. Usually, men would dance the groom to his bride, who was sitting on a thronelike chair; he would then lower the veil over her face, and then the men would dance him off to his place under the *chuppah*. Many traditional communities follow this ritual more or less as described.

But many couples concerned with egalitarianism take issue with the traditional *bedecken*. Many women—and men—have viewed the veil as a symbol of a woman's being silenced in marriage. It seems unfair, too, that the groom has a way to check out that his bride is the authentic one, while the bride is given no such ritual. So over the past thirty years or so, many non-Orthodox couples have looked for ways to infuse the *bedecken* ritual with contemporary meaning.

Our rabbi, Shai Gluskin, for example, created a lovely ritual in which he asked us to take a moment "to really see one another." Rabbi Shai's ritual gave us an opportunity to look into each other's eyes and confirm that we were, in fact, seeing one another as the people that we are. It worked well for us, especially because I chose not to wear a traditional veil.

Rabbi Marcia Prager, a rabbi and teacher in the Jewish Renewal movement, structures the pre-ceremony rituals so that they move from a large group to a more intimate one. They begin with a large circle of family and friends gathered together for the *ketubah* signing. Then the rabbi asks just the parents of the couple (and/or the children of a previously married couple) to stay for a moment of *kabbalat panim*, when she offers the parents a blessing, as a way of acknowledging that the wedding of their children is also a major milestone in their lives and filled with emotion. Following that ritual, she asks that only the couple stay with her for the *bedecken,* so that the ritual may be as intimate as possible. She asks the couple to look into each other's eyes and see each other as they were at age thirteen, twenty, and so on, and also to envision each other at age sixty, eighty, and onward. She asks them to see each other for all they have been and all that they will become. Her *bedecken* ritual allows the couple to really take a moment before going to the *chuppah* to connect to each other and to the love that brought them to this moment.

Rabbi Zalman Schachter-Shalomi offers another approach to the *bedecken.* He asks couples to imagine that the veil represents everything that keeps them separate from each other, and also separated from God. As the groom lifts the veil to see the bride's face, he asks the couple to imagine that all the things that keep them separated from each other are being lifted away.

There are many women who love wearing a veil and have interpreted it not as a symbol of silence but as a way to recognize God's presence surrounding them on their wedding day. Danielle LeShaw remembers that she initially had doubts about wearing her mother's bridal veil, but then "was so happy to be under it, in a place of holiness and privacy during such a public moment." For brides who choose to wear a veil, the *bedecken* can still become a very egalitarian ritual: When the groom places a veil on the bride, she can place a *kippah* (skullcap) on his head. Some couples like not to use a veil at all, but prefer that both partners wear *kippot.* Lesbian couples can both choose to wear a veil or other head coverings, and many gay men have created *bedecken* ceremonies in which they crown each other with a *kippah.*

The Ceremony

The Jewish wedding ceremony is more than an exchange of vows and rings. It is made up of a number of rituals, beginning with the processional and culminating in the breaking of the glass.

Processional

The Jewish wedding processional leaves a lot of room for creativity and fun. According to tradition, the pageantry of the processional is meant to evoke the ancient practice of treating the bride and groom like royalty.

There are no hard and fast rules governing the order of the processional. Very often, the best man and/or groomsmen walk out first, leading grandparents to their seats. After the best man, the groom and his parents usually come next; they may walk with him to stand under the *chuppah*, or kiss him at the *chuppah* and take their seats. (It is a lovely moment to watch parents embrace and kiss a grown son. Although it is a very public experience, many grooms have commented to me about what a moment of intimacy it is.)

Next in the processional come any bridesmaids, followed by the maid/matron of honor and then, finally, the bride and her parents. Some couples prefer having all the attendants walk in first, followed by the groom and his parents, and then the bride and her parents. Even among couples concerned with creating an egalitarian ritual, the custom of leaving the bride's entrance as the most dramatic, most highly anticipated moment endures and is still held as sacred. There is something simply magical about the bride's entrance. Some couples like to connect their eyes as the bride walks in, so that as she walks to the groom, they are holding each other's gaze. There is some confusion as to whether or not the guests should stand for the bride's entrance at a Jewish wedding. Your officiant can let the guests know just before the processional if you would like them to stand.

Depending on family circumstances for both bride and groom, there are many alternatives to walking down the aisle besides doing so with one or both parents. None of these configurations is set in stone and can be easily adapted in the cases of couples who have complex parental configurations or are dealing with the loss of a parent (see "When a Parent Has Died," at the end of this chapter). Many couples who marry in middle age have grown (or growing) children, and it is most meaningful for them to be walked down the aisle by their children.

Many gay and lesbian couples choose to create a processional in which both partners enter the room simultaneously from different entry points. Both partners then walk to the *chuppah*, escorted by parents or other significant people in their lives. It creates a beautiful, dramatic moment to watch as the partners come together to meet each other under the *chuppah*.

Some couples today are even including their canine friends in their processionals. I have some friends who would never have walked down the aisle without their puppies, dressed up and ready to join them. If you want to consider this option, just make sure that you have someone who will walk out with the pets after they come in. Much as you may love your pet, you can't predict how quiet he or she will be during the ceremony.

Your processional should set the stage for your unique ceremony—from the music you choose for your entrance to the number of attendants you choose to walk to the *chuppah*. Robin and Max Minkoff chose to have what they referred to as "the world's largest wedding party." They chose a collection of thirty-six friends and family members, whom they referred to as their "ambassadors of joy." The wedding party walked down the aisle in pairs and during the ceremony surrounded the couple (in a circle of chairs, not under the *chuppah*). The Minkoffs chose thirty-six attendants because of "double *chai*," the Hebrew word for "life," whose numerical equivalent is eighteen. Max and Robin appreciated the positive energy generated by their special wedding party of thirty-six during their ceremony.

You also need to think about how you will end up standing once you reach the *chuppah*. It was originally a Catholic tradition to have bride and groom face the priest, with their backs toward the congregation. In Jewish tradition, weddings were held outdoors, in the street, with bride and groom facing the community. It is very powerful to have the couple standing so that everyone can see the expressions on their faces and see the details of the rituals, such as sipping from a *kiddush* cup.

Rituals During the Ceremony

The traditional Jewish wedding ceremony is actually composed of two separate and distinct parts. The first part of the ceremony is generally known as *erusin* (betrothal) or *kiddushin* (holiness) and this ceremony calls on the groom to recite a certain formula and then give his bride something of value (the ring); through this process, she would then be "acquired" by him as his wife. The ancient motive behind this legal initiative was to set a woman apart exclusively for one man for the purpose of procreation. The betrothal ceremony often took place as much as one year before the second part of the wedding ceremony; it was more of what we would think of today as an engagement.

The second part of the marriage ceremony, known as *nesuin* (Hebrew for "marriage," from the verb "to carry"), contrasts greatly from the legal nature of *erusin*. This is where love, spirituality, and connection to God enter the picture; its main component—the chanting of the *Sheva Brachot* (Seven Blessings)—is a liturgical celebration of the joining of bride and groom. By the eleventh century the two ceremonies were united into one, which is still the standard ceremony used by Orthodox Jews today. Over time, in some Jewish communities, the legalities comprising the *erusin* section—the betrothal blessings and the giving of a wedding ring—grew to be interpreted symbolically, rather than literally.

Yet with the rise of scholarship and practical leadership among Jewish feminists—both male and female—in the past thirty years, serious attention has been paid to the nature of the *erusin* ceremony. Making changes to a ritual that has come down to us as the traditional Jewish wedding ceremony is complicated. On one hand, those of us concerned with equality in marriage want to create a ceremony that is full of integrity and honesty and that treats women as more than property. On the other hand, we recognize the immense archetypal power inherent in traditions and rituals that have been used for countless generations. In seeking answers to questions raised about the role of women in the Jewish wedding ceremony, those who have most successfully created new rituals and new adaptions of prayers and blessings have done so by balancing the demands of tradition and innovation.

Hakafot (Circling)

Traditionally, the wedding ceremony begins with the bride circling the groom seven times. Throughout history, circling has been used by many cultures to set aside a sacred space and to ward off evil spirits. This is a powerful, ancient gesture.

In Jewish tradition, the number seven holds great mystical power. It took seven days for God to create the world (six days of creating plus one day of rest). Kabbalists—scholars who have studied and created a mystical understanding of

Jewish tradition—attach many meanings to the number seven. The custom of the bride circling her groom in the Jewish wedding ceremony is said to stem from a line of text in the Book of Jeremiah that states, "A woman encompasses her man" (Jeremiah 31:22). In many communities, the bride's mother and/or her mother-in-law-to-be would escort her as she circled the groom.

Some feminists have interpreted this circling as sexist, a sign that the groom is checking out the property he is about to purchase before agreeing to do so. Many people find it problematic that the bride would do the circling for all to see, while the groom just stood and watched.

Fortunately, there are many ways to reclaim the custom of circling to make it a powerful and egalitarian ritual for everyone. First of all, many couples are just fine with the bride circling the groom, and they accept it as a beautiful woman's ritual, for which there is no male counterpart. Other couples choose to join hands and walk seven circles together, either in a side-by-side manner or with both partners extending arms and leaning back. Another popular option is for one partner to do three circles, the other to do three, and then to join hands together for the seventh circle.

As a *kavannah*—intention behind the ritual—many couples imagine that with each circle they are creating a stronger "force field" of love that will surround them during their ceremony and in their new life together as committed partners. Other couples try to look deeper into each other's eyes with every circle. A circle represents completeness, and making a circle around each other starts off your wedding ceremony with a feeling of wholeness and connection.

Some couples add a modern twist to a traditional ritual: *hakafot*, or circling, is no longer done only by brides.

When Rabbi Marcia Prager talks to couples she is marrying about the *hakafot* (circling), she offers the kabbalistic image of the Divine masculine energy and the Divine feminine energy circling to meet each other. "This takes the idea from just walking around each other in a circle and allows the bride and groom to imagine themselves carrying Divine energy," Reb Marcia says.

If you are not entirely comfortable with movement, take a few moments some time before the ceremony just to practice your circling with your partner.

Take it lightly and have fun. It doesn't need to be a performance or even look a certain way. In one wedding, the bride and groom held hands and sort of skipped around together seven times. Don't worry if you stumble a bit or feel goofy. When the time comes, just keep breathing and enjoy the circles. If a bride is going to be wearing a long train, be sure to ask an attendant to hold it during the circling or to at least straighten it once the circling is done.

Note: Some couples prefer that their rabbi say a few opening remarks before they do the circling. The rabbi may ask everyone present to focus their love and blessings on the couple as they circle. This request can ground everyone in the present moment and connect the guests to the couple's ritual.

Welcome

After the circling, the rabbi usually greets the bride and groom, along with the guests, with a few traditional recitations. The rabbi and/or cantor may elect to sing the words of welcome. They are:

בָּרוּךְ הַבָּא (בְּרוּכִים הַבָּאִים) בְּשֵׁם יְיָ.

Baruch haBa b'Shem Adonai.

Welcome in the name of Adonai.

בֵּרַכְנוּכֶם מִבֵּית יְיָ.

Bayrachnuchem miBayt Adonai.

We welcome you from God's house.

מִי אַדִּיר עַל הַכֹּל,
מִי בָּרוּךְ עַל הַכֹּל,
מִי גָּדוֹל עַל הַכֹּל,
הוּא יְבָרֵךְ הֶחָתָן וְהַכַּלָּה.

Mi adir al haKol,
mi baruch al haKol,
mi gadol al haKol,
hu y'varech heChatan v'haKallah.

May the One who is more adored than all,
May the One who is more blessed than all,
May the One who is greater than all
bless this groom and bride.

After the welcoming blessing, some couples like to insert the *Shehecheyanu*—
the blessing that Jews recite for a special or momentous occasion:

בָּרוּךְ אַתָּה יְיָ

אֱלֹהֵינוּ מֶלֶךְ הָעוֹלָם,

שֶׁהֶחֱיָנוּ וְקִיְּמָנוּ וְהִגִּיעָנוּ לַזְּמַן הַזֶּה.

Baruch atah Adonai,
Elohaynu melech haOlam, shehecheyanu,
v'kiyimanu, v'higianu, lazman hazeh.

Blessed are You, Adonai our God,
Sovereign of the Universe, who gives us life,
sustains us, and enables us to reach this moment.

As you plan your ceremony with your rabbi, you may elect to change some
of the God language to reflect images of God that work for you. *Adonai* (Lord) is
a traditional way of referring to God, but many names for God appear in the
Hebrew Bible and are now used as part of Jewish liturgy. Some common alternatives rooted in Jewish tradition include *Makor Chayyim* (Source of Life) or *Chai
HaOlamiem* (Life of the World). Simply voicing conscious choices in the way you
refer to God can make the liturgy feel more poetic and precise.

Kiddush and *Birkat Erusin*
(Blessing over the Wine and Betrothal Blessing)

It is no surprise that blessing a cup of wine comes toward the beginning of the Jewish wedding ceremony; wine is our people's symbol for joy and celebration (as a wine lover, I have always appreciated that aspect of Judaism). Reciting a blessing over the wine sanctifies it; that is, the blessing changes it from ordinary wine into something sacred and holy. So, too, marriage is sanctified and made holy through the recitation of blessings. The *kiddush* is a powerful prayer in the wedding ceremony; even for Jews who have not entered a synagogue for years, the blessing over the wine often remains embedded in the memory.

Traditionally, the wine is not drunk after the *kiddush* but is held until after the betrothal blessing. The *Birkat Erusin* is a more complicated blessing that focuses on placing boundaries and limits on sexuality, explaining which relationships God condones and blesses and which are forbidden. It reads:

בָּרוּךְ אַתָּה יְיָ

אֱלֹהֵינוּ מֶלֶךְ הָעוֹלָם,

אֲשֶׁר קִדְּשָׁנוּ בְּמִצְוֹתָיו וְצִוָּנוּ עַל הָעֲרָיוֹת,

וְאָסַר לָנוּ אֶת הָאֲרוּסוֹת,

וְהִתִּיר לָנוּ אֶת הַנְּשׂוּאוֹת לָנוּ עַל יְדֵי חֻפָּה וְקִדּוּשִׁין.

בָּרוּךְ אַתָּה יְיָ,

מְקַדֵּשׁ עַמּוֹ יִשְׂרָאֵל עַל יְדֵי חֻפָּה וְקִדּוּשִׁין.

Baruch atah Adonai
Elohaynu melech haOlam,
asher kidshanu b'mitzvotav v'tzivanu al haArayot,
v'asar lanu et haArusot,
v'hitir lanu et haNesuot lanu al y'day chuppah v'kiddushin.
Baruch atah Adonai
m'kadaysh amo Yisrael al y'day chuppah v'kiddushin.

Blessed are You Adonai,
Sovereign of the Universe,
who has made us holy with *mitzvot* and
commanded us concerning illicit relations,
who has forbidden to us women who are betrothed,
but permitted to us women who have been taken
according to *chuppah* and *kiddushin*.
Blessed are You, Adonai,
who sanctifies the People Israel through *chuppah* and *kiddushin*.

As you notice from reading the text, the blessing really addresses men only. Because of the sexist nature of the blessing, the Reform movement removed it from its ceremonies years ago and simply moved from the *kiddush* to the exchange of rings, which comes next. If you find the blessing problematic, you may eliminate it, too.

Another option is to work with your rabbi to modify the blessing so it includes both partners and focuses on the relationships that are blessed, rather than on those that are forbidden. You may also want to talk with your rabbi about writing your own original blessing—it could be in English—about the sanctity of your relationship.

After both blessings are recited, it's time to drink the wine. This first cup of wine, blessed under the *chuppah*, is sometimes shared by the bride and groom with all the loved ones standing with them under the *chuppah*. It can create a beautiful ritual moment to offer the *kiddush* cup to your in-laws-to-be or to best friends/siblings serving as your attendants. Remember to use white wine (there are many kosher varieties available) to avoid any concerns about staining a white wedding dress, especially if your hands tend to shake at all with nerves. Also, you may want to use a special *kiddush* cup for the blessings under the *chuppah*; ideas for creative *kiddush* cups can be found in chapter 8.

Exchange of Rings

This final part of the *erusin* ceremony is the act that legally makes the two individuals standing under the *chuppah* into a married couple. Jewish law states

Reckon You'll Bedecken? A Creative Look at the Jewish Wedding Ceremony

137

that a wedding ring must be a pure, solid band, so that its value may be easily assessed. The ring ceremony comes from the ancient custom of giving the woman something of value so that she may be legally "acquired." In a traditional ceremony, the groom places the ring on the bride's right index finger and says:

הֲרֵי אַתְּ מְקֻדֶּשֶׁת לִי בְּטַבַּעַת זוֹ כְּדַת מֹשֶׁה וְיִשְׂרָאֵל.

Haray at m'kudeshet li b'taba'at zu k'dat Moshe v'Yisrael.

Behold, you are consecrated to me with this ring,
according to the tradition of Moses and Israel.

Traditionally, the bride is not given any formal response and the ceremony continues on. In liberal circles, many different creative possibilities have been added to the traditional ring ceremony in an attempt to make it more egalitarian. One example is simply to create a double-ring ceremony so that the bride also gives the groom a ring and says that same statement as above, but with gender-appropriate changes to the Hebrew, such as:

הֲרֵי אַתָּה מְקֻדָּשׁ לִי בְּטַבַּעַת זוֹ כְּדַת מֹשֶׁה וְיִשְׂרָאֵל.

Haray atah m'kudash li b'taba'at zu k'dat Moshe v'Yisrael.

Behold, you are consecrated to me with this ring,
according to the tradition of Moses and Israel.

My husband and I chose to use this formula, and we added Miriam along with Moses to honor the role of women in the tradition of the People of Israel.

Other ways to create an egalitarian exchange of rings is to change the language of *kinyan* (acquisition) altogether and insert Jewish texts that speak to the idea of partnership and commitment. Some couples choose a line from *Shir HaShirim* (Song of Songs), such as the very popular:

אֲנִי לְדוֹדִי וְדוֹדִי לִי.

Ani l'dodi v'dodi li.

I am my beloved's and my beloved is mine.

Another choice comes from the Book of Hosea:

I will betroth you to me forever; I will betroth you to me with righteousness, justice, kindness, and mercy. I will betroth you to me with faith. (Hosea 2:21–22)

Some lesbian couples like to use this moment to pay homage to the biblical relationship of Ruth and Naomi, with Ruth's pledge to accompany her aging mother-in-law back to her homeland:

Wherever you go, I will go; wherever you stay, I will stay; your people shall be my people, and your God, my God. Where you die, I will die, and there I will be buried. (Ruth 1:16–17)

Rachel Adler, in *Engendering Judaism,* suggests that instead of the traditional ring ceremony, couples might use a lesser-known talmudic formula for establishing partnership, in which both partners pool their resources in one bag and lift the bag together. After this symbolic ritual, both partners are said to be owners of the contents of the bag. If the wedding rings are placed in the bag and then lifted, suggests Adler, then both parties are making a joint acquisition. This departure from a simple exchange of rings may require some explanation for your wedding guests, but with a simple note in your wedding program your guests can easily learn about your intentions with this innovation.

If you choose not to follow the single-ring ritual (groom to bride), take some time to talk with your rabbi about what alternative might work best for your ceremony.

Reading of the *Ketubah*

It has become customary as a way of linking the two parts of the wedding ceremony to do a public reading of the *ketubah* at this time. Especially if you have done the *ketubah* signing with only a small group of loved ones, the reading of the *ketubah* allows all your guests to hear the vows you are making to each other.

The decision to read the *ketubah* aloud or not is often based on whether you are using a traditional or an original *ketubah* text. For example, if you are using a traditional *ketubah* and many of your guests are familiar with the text, you might elect to skip a translated English reading. On the other hand, if you and your partner have worked very hard at writing an original text, you might want it to be read in English so that everyone can hear and understand it. If your original text is very long, you may also decide to read just an excerpt from the text, then showcase the *ketubah* in a prominent location during the reception so that guests who want to read the entire text may do so.

Who will read the *ketubah*? You could give this honor to one of your attendants or to another friend, preferably one with a strong speaking voice. Reading the *ketubah* could also be done by the bride and groom. Because there are no traditional vows in a Jewish ceremony in the way that there are in a Christian ceremony (the "I do" moment), it is nice to create a moment when your guests actually get to hear your voice.

When Rabbi Shai suggested that Fred and I read from our *ketubah*, I immediately balked, worrying that I would be too choked up to speak. He asked us to think about it some more; in his experience, when couples had written original commitments into their *ketubah* it was lovely to hear them pronounced. After giving the idea some more consideration, we decided to try it, with the fallback plan that our matron of honor and best man would read it for us if we felt that we couldn't get through it at the time. Rabbi Shai read the introductory and closing sections, while we read everything that was in the first person, going back and forth between our mutual promises. Although I did feel a little bit nervous reading under the *chuppah*, I felt strong speaking our pronouncements out loud, and many guests told us that it was one of their favorite parts of the ceremony.

If you and your partner haven't written any original *ketubah* text, you might think about composing some personal vows to each other and reading them at this point in the ceremony. You might write in the form of a love letter, a poem, or, if you are musically inclined, a song. Sharing something that you wrote can be one of the most meaningful moments in your ceremony.

Officiants may also interject some personal remarks to the couple at this time. Some rabbis will talk to you ahead of time and ask you whether there is anything that they should not say. If you know and trust your wedding officiant, the personal address will be a beautiful moment. If you don't know your rabbi at all, you might be in store for some generic remarks about marriage, which could be nice, but probably will not be all that meaningful to you. Again, choosing a rabbi or other officiant whom you know, or come to know, and deeply trust will certainly enhance and enrich the overall experience.

The *Nesuin* Ceremony

Now comes the ceremony of nuptials, where the focus shifts from legalities to the sacred relationship of two partners joining together in a loving commitment. Because *nesuin* is about blessing the couple, it can include blessings in many creative forms.

Sheva Brachot

Nesuin begins with the chanting of the *Sheva Brachot* (Seven Blessings). Here the language of the ceremony moves away from legal issues entirely to express such themes as joy and the power of creation, humanity as created in the Divine image, and the joy and timeless quality of two people loving each other. The blessings bring the bride and groom into a moment of universality: The *Sheva Brachot* use imagery recalling the Garden of Eden to bring to mind the everlasting and ongoing power of love. Here stands one couple but what we see are every pair of beloved companions who have ever made such a commitment to one another. The blessings also ground the couple in Jewish time and community by referring to the voice of bride and groom as "heard in the cities of Judah and within the walls of Jerusalem." The blessings also encompass the age-old yearning of the Jewish people: That soon, in Jerusalem, all that will be heard are voices of happiness—those of the bride and groom and the community rejoicing with them.

The blessings, from one to seven, increase with intensity of feeling so that they culminate in a metaphorical explosion of love and celebration. The set of blessings begins with the *kiddush*, the blessing over the wine, and, from there, each blessing enlarges the circle to include not only the couple standing under the

Reckon You'll Bedecken? A Creative Look at the Jewish Wedding Ceremony

141

chuppah but also the entire Jewish community—past, present, and future. The blessings' poetic language and imagery in the original Hebrew give rise to equally evocative English translations. Over the past thirty or so years, many different translations of the *Sheva Brachot* have appeared, some incorporating feminine God language, some honoring same-sex unions. Here are the traditional blessings and some of these variations.

בָּרוּךְ אַתָּה יְיָ אֱלֹהֵינוּ מֶלֶךְ הָעוֹלָם,
בּוֹרֵא פְּרִי הַגָּפֶן.

Baruch atah Adonai, Elohaynu melech haOlam,
boray p'ri haGafen.

Blessed are You, Adonai our God, Sovereign of the Universe,
Creator of the fruit of the vine.

בָּרוּךְ אַתָּה יְיָ אֱלֹהֵינוּ מֶלֶךְ הָעוֹלָם,
שֶׁהַכֹּל בָּרָא לִכְבוֹדוֹ.

Baruch atah Adonai, Elohaynu melech haOlam,
shehakol bara lichvodo.

Blessed are You, Adonai our God, Sovereign of the Universe,
Who created everything for Your glory.

בָּרוּךְ אַתָּה יְיָ אֱלֹהֵינוּ מֶלֶךְ הָעוֹלָם,
יוֹצֵר הָאָדָם.

Baruch atah Adonai, Elohaynu melech haOlam,
yotzayr haAdam.

Blessed are You, Adonai our God, Sovereign of the Universe,
Creator of human beings.

בָּרוּךְ אַתָּה יְיָ אֱלֹהֵינוּ מֶלֶךְ הָעוֹלָם,
אֲשֶׁר יָצַר אֶת הָאָדָם בְּצַלְמוֹ,
בְּצֶלֶם דְּמוּת תַּבְנִיתוֹ,
וְהִתְקִין לוֹ מִמֶּנּוּ בִּנְיַן עֲדֵי עַד.
בָּרוּךְ אַתָּה יְיָ, יוֹצֵר הָאָדָם.

Baruch atah Adonai, Elohaynu melech haOlam,
asher yatzar et haAdam b'tzalmo,
b'tzelem d'moot tavnito,
v'hitkin lo mimenu binyan aday ad.
Baruch atah Adonai, yotzayr haAdam.

Blessed are You, Adonai our God, Sovereign of the Universe,
Who created human beings in Your image,
according to your likeness, and has fashioned from it a lasting mold.
Blessed are You, Adonai, Creator of human beings.

שׂוֹשׂ תָּשִׂישׂ וְתָגֵל הָעֲקָרָה
בְּקִבּוּץ בָּנֶיהָ לְתוֹכָהּ בְּשִׂמְחָה.
בָּרוּךְ אַתָּה יְיָ,
מְשַׂמֵּחַ צִיּוֹן בְּבָנֶיהָ.

Sos tasis v'tagel haAkarah
b'kibbutz baneha l'tochah b'simcha.
Baruch atah Adonai,
m'samayach Tziyon b'vaneha.

Reckon You'll Bedecken? A Creative Look at the Jewish Wedding Ceremony

143

May the barren one [Jerusalem]
be joyful and glad when her children gather in her midst in happiness.
Blessed are You, Adonai,
Who causes Zion to rejoice with her children.

שַׂמֵּחַ תְּשַׂמַּח רֵעִים הָאֲהוּבִים
כְּשַׂמֵּחֲךָ יְצִירְךָ בְּגַן עֵדֶן מִקֶּדֶם.
בָּרוּךְ אַתָּה יְיָ,
מְשַׂמֵּחַ חָתָן וְכַלָּה.

Samayach t'samach rayim haAhuvim,
k'samaychacha y'tzircha b'gan ayden mikedem.
Baruch atah Adonai,
m'samayach chatan v'challah.

Cause these beloved companions to rejoice
as You caused Your creation to rejoice in the Garden of Eden.
Blessed are You, Adonai,
Who causes the groom and bride to rejoice.

בָּרוּךְ אַתָּה יְיָ,
אֱלֹהֵינוּ מֶלֶךְ הָעוֹלָם,
אֲשֶׁר בָּרָא שָׂשׂוֹן וְשִׂמְחָה,
חָתָן וְכַלָּה, גִּילָה, רִנָּה,
דִּיצָה וְחֶדְוָה, אַהֲבָה וְאַחֲוָה
וְשָׁלוֹם וְרֵעוּת.
מְהֵרָה יְיָ אֱלֹהֵינוּ
יִשָּׁמַע בְּעָרֵי יְהוּדָה וּבְחֻצוֹת יְרוּשָׁלַיִם

The Creative Jewish Wedding Book

קוֹל שָׂשׂוֹן וְקוֹל שִׂמְחָה,
קוֹל חָתָן וְקוֹל כַּלָּה,
קוֹל מִצְהֲלוֹת חֲתָנִים מֵחֻפָּתָם
וּנְעָרִים מִמִּשְׁתֵּה נְגִינָתָם.
בָּרוּךְ אַתָּה יְיָ,
מְשַׂמֵּחַ חָתָן עִם הַכַּלָּה.

Baruch atah Adonai,
Elohaynu melech haOlam,
asher bara sason v'simcha,
chatan v'challah, gilah, rinah,
ditzah, v'chedvah, ahavah, v'achavah,
shalom v'rayut.
M'hayra Adonai Elohaynu
yishama b'aray yehudah uv'chuztot Yerushalayim,
kol sason v'kol simcha,
kol chatan v'kol kallah,
kol mitzhalot chatanim maychupatam
une'arim mimishtay n'ginatam.
Baruch atah Adonai,
m'samayach chatan im haKallah.

Blessed are You, Adonai our God,
Sovereign of the Universe,
Who has created joy and gladness,
a groom and his bride, mirth and exultation,
dancing and jubilation, love and harmony,
peace and companionship.
O Adonai our God,
may there soon be heard again in the cities of Judah and in the streets of
Jerusalem
glad and joyous voices,

the voices of groom and bride,
the jubilant voices of those joined in marriage under the chuppah,
the voices of young people feasting and singing.
Blessed are You, Adonai,
Who causes the groom to rejoice with his bride.

Once the *Sheva Brachot* are recited, the couple drinks the wine from the *kiddush* cup.

Some simple changes in the English translation can capture the essence of the original Hebrew while lending more poetry to the rhythm of the blessings. Also, changing the name for God from Adonai, with its connotations of "Lord" and masculinity, to something more open-ended in its imagery may help many people embrace the blessings more fully. An example of such a version created by Rabbi Marcia Prager is included in Appendix III.

Rabbi Arthur Ocean Waskow and spiritual leader Phyllis Ocean Berman have adapted the *Sheva Brachot* in both Hebrew and English so that the language refers to the couple as "soulmate and beloved" rather than *"chatan* and *kallah* [bride and groom]," making the blessings appropriate for both same-sex or heterosexual couples. In their version, they also alternate between using masculine and feminine God language. Waskow and Berman also place the *kiddush* at the end of the blessings, as a culmination, rather than at the beginning, as an introduction. Their version also appears in Appendix III.

In addition to adapting the content of the *Sheva Brachot*, there is much room for creativity in their presentation. The blessings can be chanted in Hebrew, with their traditional melody, and then chanted or read in English. The set of blessings could be chanted by the rabbi or cantor, or divided up as an honor among seven different friends (or even fourteen if you plan to do both Hebrew and English). Some couples use the moment of the *Sheva Brachot* as an opportunity to invite seven friends or family members to offer seven original blessings, composed ahead of time, in addition to the traditional ones. At a traditional wedding, the *Sheva Brachot* are repeated as part of the *Birkat Hamazon*, the blessing after a meal, so some couples choose to have them chanted in a traditional way during the ceremony and then recited in a creative way later on at the reception (or vice versa). Some rabbis also open up the moment of blessing to include all the guests, inviting them to offer a spontaneous blessing for the couple. This can be a beautiful moment in a small group but can become overwhelming in a large crowd. If you want to include this option in your ceremony, make sure that people are seated close enough so that the spontaneous blessings can be heard by both the guests and the bride and groom.

The possibilities for creativity in interpreting the *Sheva Brachot* are limitless. When I was invited to read the translation of the *Sheva Brachot* at my dear friend Sheila Nissim's wedding, I asked her whether it would be okay if I read the translation and also a short, original interpretation of how I imagined the blessing applied to her and her groom, Michael. Sheila liked the idea and during the ceremony, her wedding officiant chanted a blessing in Hebrew, and I followed each one with my English translation and interpretation. The interpretations read as follows:

May this wine be as sweet as your life together, Sheila and Michael.

May each day of your life together be a joyous act of creation.

May you both always regard each other as sacred beings—made of flesh and blood, but reaching toward the heavens.

May the strength of your love, Michael and Sheila, spread to all you meet and give strength and courage to those in need.

May your love be laughter. May it be timeless, constant, and natural as breath.

In all the world, Sheila and Michael, in all times, may love and strength like yours today cause waves of delight and celebration! May your love shine with a radiance like no other.

As you consider the possibilities for interpreting the *Sheva Brachot*, consider a few questions:

> Do you want the blessings to convey a traditional tone?

> Do you imagine the blessings as a focused moment of chanting or as a looser, possibly longer, expanse of blessing?

Are there people you would like to honor by inviting them to lead a blessing? How many people come to mind?

With creativity and planning, the *Sheva Brachot* can be a moment of abounding blessing for you and your partner.

Pronouncement and Benediction

At this point in the ceremony, we are approaching the conclusion. In theatrical terms, we think of this moment as the dénouement: After the climax of the *Sheva Brachot*, the pronouncement and benediction are like a long, slow exhale. Because a rabbi or cantor marries a heterosexual couple with the authority of Jewish tradition and the authority of the state where the wedding is taking place, this is usually the time when he will say something such as, "By the authority given to me in the eyes of the Jewish community and the authority given to me by the state of Oklahoma, I pronounce you husband and wife."

In most American states, same-sex marriages are not recognized at this time. Yet it may feel to the couple, to the rabbi, and to the guests who are present that something is missing if a "pronouncement" of the couple's union is not made at this moment. Many officiants have come up with creative solutions. Phyllis Ocean Berman and Rabbi Arthur Ocean Waskow, for example, use the moment as a way to invest everyone present at the wedding with the power to offer a pronouncement, such as the following: "With the authority given to each of us, all present pronounce you as committed, loving companions."

In addition to making the pronouncement, the officiant will often leave the couple with a final blessing. This is also a lovely moment to invite a parent or someone else close to you to offer the final blessing. Some people choose to use the *Shehecheyanu* blessing here, rather than earlier in the ceremony, which can be recited by one person or sung as a whole community. In many weddings, the priestly blessing—the most ancient of all Hebrew blessings—is recited as the final blessing for the couple. With hands raised by the officiant over the couple, in the tradition of the high priest of biblical times, who came forward on Yom Kippur to offer a blessing for the people, the just-married loving companions are blessed with these words:

יְבָרֶכְךָ יְיָ וְיִשְׁמְרֶךָ.
יָאֵר יְיָ פָּנָיו אֵלֶיךָ וִיחֻנֶּךָּ.
יִשָּׂא יְיָ פָּנָיו אֵלֶיךָ וְיָשֵׂם לְךָ שָׁלוֹם.

Y'varech'cha Adonai v'yishm'recha.
Ya'ayr Adonai panav aylecha vichuneka.
Yisa Adonai panav aylecha v'yasaym l'cha shalom.

May God bless you and keep you.
May the light of God's presence shine upon you and be gracious to you.
May God's countenance turn toward you, and grant you wholeness and peace.

Breaking of the Glass

Now, ladies and gentlemen, the moment we've all been waiting for—the breaking of the glass! This final ritual in a Jewish wedding ceremony is probably the best known of all. Over the years, many different rationales were advanced for this ritual. Many people regard the custom as rooted in the superstitions of the Middle Ages, when shattering a glass was said to ward off evil spirits. A most common interpretation is that the shattering of a glass reminds us of the destruction of the Temple—that even in our moments of greatest joy, we remember the sadness and lack of wholeness in the world.

Many liberal Jews use this concept to bring special meaning to the end of their ceremony. Some ask for a moment of silence before stepping on the glass, a moment for their guests to pray for or reflect on anything that they feel is broken or fragmented in the world. Other couples focus this moment on the need to work toward ending an injustice in the world: helping the economically disadvantaged or protecting the environment, for example. Some couples make a short pronouncement, while others write their dedication in their wedding program.

Traditionally, the glass is broken by the groom—usually by being stepped on, although it is customary in some communities for the groom to throw the glass against a wall. Some couples choose to use two glasses and have both partners

A *Havdalah* Wedding

Some couples choose to begin their wedding with *havdalah*, the short ceremony that marks the end of Shabbat and differentiates the sacred time of Shabbat from the other six days of the week.

Because Jewish tradition prohibits weddings on Shabbat, Saturday night weddings need to begin after the sun has gone down. Very few rabbis, even in the more liberal denominations, will perform a Saturday night wedding before the official end of Shabbat.

Not only is *havdalah* a way of making that distinction, but it also allows you to draw on the ritual to create a separation in time before the wedding and after. As the beginning of a wedding ceremony, *havdalah* distinguishes between the time when a couple was not formally committed and the time just ahead—when they will stand together under the *chuppah*, making a sacred commitment to each other.

Besides, the ritual of *havdalah* is fun—wine for *kiddush* (another glass won't hurt anyone's nerves!), sweet-smelling spices, and a braided candle with multiple wicks. The ritual elements set a magical tone when they are brought together.

Havdalah traditionally takes place once three stars are seen in the sky (city dwellers can estimate or check a Jewish calendar). The *kiddush* cup, full of wine, is raised and an official recitation is said,

Reckon You'll Bedecken? A Creative Look at the Jewish Wedding Ceremony

149

followed by the *havdalah* blessings. These blessings can involve your guests; sweet-smelling spices can be passed around for everyone to sniff. The ceremony ends in a most dramatic way with the *havdalah* candle being extinguished by dipping it into what's left of the *kiddush* wine. For a wedding, the processional could begin as soon as the flame is extinguished.

Keep in mind that if your guests are strict observers of Shabbat, they would probably do *havdalah* on their own before driving to your ceremony. But, if your wedding is going to take place within walking distance of where your guests will be staying, you could safely plan your Saturday night wedding to start with a cocktail/hors d'oeuvres hour, followed immediately by *havdalah*, then your official ceremony.

There are many beautiful melodies that the *havdalah* blessings can be sung to; singer/composer Debbie Friedman's melody is especially popular and well-known (see Appendix I for online sources of Jewish music).

step on them simultaneously. Some couples use the *kiddush* cup(s) that were used in their ceremony for this ritual moment, as a way to emphasize that their ceremony was a unique and sacred moment in time, not to be repeated.

Once the glass is broken, it's the cue for everyone to shout *"Mazel tov!"* as the couple walks out from under the *chuppah* to head for *yihud* (seclusion). Make sure you have one of your attendants scoop up the pieces of glass into a little bag or container for you to have later, as they can be used to create an original work of art (see chapter 8 for creative ideas).

After the Ceremony

Aaaaahhhh, you made it! Jewish tradition is eminently wise: It builds in a moment of complete privacy for bride and groom to savor the moment and just relax a bit before going back out to party with their guests. *Yihud* was actually the time in years gone by when the newly married couple would leave the *chuppah* and consummate their marriage. As we know, times have changed, and now it's more common for couples to use *yihud* just to have some quiet time together.

Arrange in advance for a special room to go to, and make sure that one of your attendants or friends puts some snacks and drinks in the room for you. Especially if you've been fasting, you'll be ready for a bite of something. Keep in mind that you probably won't be eating much during your reception, so a good snack now will give you the energy you need to mix and mingle, dance and enjoy. Some couples choose to stay in *yihud* for eighteen minutes: Honoring the Jewish numerical equivalent for the Hebrew word *chai* (life) is considered good luck. If you want to have a receiving line, you can have parents and attendants get it going, and then you can join in right after *yihud*.

Envisioning Your Wedding Ceremony

Now that you are familiar with the structure of the Jewish wedding ceremony, it is time to start visualizing what you want your own ceremony to look like. The prayers and rituals described above are not ends in themselves; they are the means for you and your partner to share an intimate, loving journey, a journey from under the *chuppah* to a new sense of commitment and dedication to each other. Life after your wedding—even for the most wonderfully matched, loving, dedicated couple—is not easy. Marriage presents many challenges and obstacles that will surface as you grow together. But hopefully, the process of creating—and then experiencing—your wedding ceremony will help you form the deepest bond possible and emerge strong and united to face life's challenges.

Although each Jewish wedding ceremony encompasses many of the same rituals—with some variations in language and order—it is individualized and personalized by the intentions you bring to the ceremony. Understanding your intentions will help you use the rituals to evoke the kind of feelings and presence that you want to surround you under the *chuppah*.

Take some quiet time together, open up your journals, and read the following questions to each other slowly. I suggest that you take turns reading a question, then taking some time for each of you to respond. Wait until you are finished responding to all the questions to share what you have written.

> It is the hours just before your wedding ceremony. Who is with you? Is it a quiet time? A social time? A private time celebrated with a few friends? A time to laugh and joke with as many guests as possible?

> Your *ketubah* will be signed by witnesses, attesting to your commitments to each other. Whom do you see signing your *ketubah*?

> As people enter the site of your wedding ceremony, what do they see? Whom do they see? What do they hear, smell? What feelings do these visions, sounds, scents evoke in them?

You enter to take your place under the *chuppah*. Who walks with you there? Where do you enter? Who stands with you when you reach the *chuppah*?

Imagine the ways that your wedding ceremony expresses your unique Jewish connections. Listen to the words in the blessings and prayers that are being sung. Do you hear traditional God language? Feminine versions of God's name? Are the blessings recited in both Hebrew and English? Do you hear original blessings along with the traditional ones?

Look at your friends and family surrounding you. What feelings does the ceremony evoke in them? How do they get to participate, to show their love and support?

Your ceremony is nearing the end. The glass is broken. Look into your beloved's eyes. Describe what you feel . . .

As with all of these visioning exercises, listen to each other's responses with an open mind and heart. If you find that your responses differ, that's okay. Your ceremony will become even richer by incorporating and blending both of your visions.

As you and your partner learn to communicate and listen to each other's ideas without passing judgment, you will gain insight into how to design your wedding ceremony, as well as how to deal with major issues that will come up in your life together. Marriage is a process of learning how to listen and support each other, even when you don't see eye to eye. Try to keep in mind that you can use all the time and energy you are devoting to planning your wedding to strengthen your relationship and draw you and your partner closer together. Here are a few tips to help with this process:

- Listen without judgment. This is difficult for all of us. The ego part of our psyche is quick to judge. As outrageous as your partner's idea may sound to you, try to hear it out without passing judgment. Perhaps you are adamantly opposed to including your pets in your processional. Okay.

But if your partner really wants his beloved Great Dane accompanying him down the aisle, listen to his ideas without jumping down his throat. In hearing why he is passionate about this idea, you might be able to come up with a creative compromise that addresses that passion in a way that works for both of you.

- Be willing to compromise. The flip side of listening to each other without judgment is trusting that, if you really hate something your partner suggests, she will make an adjustment for you. The agreement to compromise must be made by both partners. Be willing to give in from time to time if you and your partner get stuck. What is most important after all: that you get your way or that you create a ceremony that makes you both happy?

- Take your time. Designing a wedding is a process; allow yourself time to consider important decisions about your ceremony. One month you may feel very strongly about how you want the *Sheva Brachot* to be included, but after thinking through your idea for a few more weeks, you may get an idea that you like better. Be patient and don't rush each other.

- Seek help. If you get seriously stuck, don't hold a grudge and give up. Go to your rabbi; talk it over. Again, if issues that come up while you are designing your wedding seem very serious, it might be wise to go for some couples counseling before your wedding.

- Remember the big picture. In any event, your wedding is one day, but your whole life together lies ahead of you. Keep that thought in the back of your mind, and write it on a slip of paper that you keep in your pocket. You don't have to agree on everything in the end, and you don't have to create the "perfect" wedding. Let it be real, let it be you, and let yourselves relax and have fun together along the way.

Other Considerations: Integrating Music and Readings

To make their ceremony as meaningful as possible, many couples like to integrate music, poetry, and literary passages into the wedding liturgy. In the next section, we'll look at some of the most popular styles of Jewish music for wedding ceremonies.

Many couples wonder whether it is appropriate to include a secular song or reading—one outside the Jewish literary or musical canon. They also wonder whether it's okay to include an original song, poem, or love letter that the bride and/or groom has written. The experts I spoke with—rabbis and cantors who have been leading wedding ceremonies for years—all rang out with a resounding "yes." That is, on the condition that the song or poem is sacred in its feeling and intentions. If a Beatles song feels spiritual to you, for example, and has significance to your relationship, by all means include it. If the reading or song, on the other hand, would in any way detract from the sacredness of the moment, then it is best to omit it.

But where and how do you insert a Shakespearean sonnet, a Rumi poem, or an original rock-and-roll love song seamlessly into a Jewish ceremony? The best way to figure out where music and readings fit into your ceremony is to talk it over with your wedding officiant; she or he may have some experiences that have worked well in the past. But among the rabbis and cantors I spoke with, the consensus is to insert them in one of the following two ways:

> *As the bridge:* A short poem or song could be a nice interlude between the *erusin* and the *nesuin* sections of the ceremony. A song that captures the ideas you express in your *ketubah*, for example, could be a lovely way to expand on its themes after it is read aloud.
>
> *As blessings:* After the *Sheva Brachot* are chanted, your additional poems or readings are extensions of the idea of blessing. Again, as long as the reading comes with a sacred *kavannah*

(intention), it is appropriate to include. Think about your favorite poets, authors, or passages of text that have really moved you. If you are interested in including Jewish literary sources, see chapter 2. From the wealth of love imagery in the Hebrew Bible to the sensual poetry of Israel's most beloved poet, the late Yehuda Amichai, a Jewish reading on love and commitment can intensify the spiritual feeling of your ceremony.

As you think through the readings and songs that will become part of the ceremony, try to bring your whole self to the wedding. If you are a country-music lover, include Patsy Cline. If you have a passion for Pablo Neruda, recite his poems. Being Jewish in America means that you straddle more than one civilization. Your wedding is going to be Jewish, and you are creatively exploring ways to highlight your Jewish connections. But don't be shy about integrating the other parts of yourself, your background, and your interests. Spend time talking with your partner about the tone you want to set at your wedding. Choose the readings and songs that will establish that tone. But be aware that adding too many extras can water down your ceremony. An ideal ceremony runs approximately twenty to thirty minutes. Be selective about choosing additional songs and readings. Less is more: Your guests will be able to focus more intently on one poem than on five.

Music in Your Wedding Ceremony

There is no Jewish law stating that you must have music in your ceremony to make your wedding valid in the eyes of the community. However, music has been an important part of Jewish wedding celebrations for centuries. In the Hasidic tradition, for example, music is seen as a spiritual tool, helping to elevate one's soul to a place of connection to the Holy One. As you consider how and when to integrate music into your ceremony, keep in mind that your musical choices can have a great impact on the tone and energy that you want to create.

Places for Music

There is something about music that moves right into our hearts and spirits in a different way than spoken language does. Choosing the right music for your ceremony can lift and intensify people's emotions and you and your partner's connections to each other and to God.

The good news is that there is no prescribed music that must accompany a Jewish wedding. There are certainly traditional tunes that you may want to use, and some particularly Jewish styles of music that will help infuse your *kavannah* (intention) into your ceremony. But in this category, you have a whole lot of breathing room to bring in music that you love, music that moves your spirit.

Some Jewish music falls into the category of liturgical music—music created especially for a religious context. This is the music of the cantorial tradition, some of which, if you grew up in or currently belong to a synagogue, you already know. Many traditional wedding songs fit into the liturgical category. But there is also a wide array of Jewish "secular" music—folk songs, soul music, Israeli pop—that could also enliven your ceremony. I put the word secular in quotes because I don't believe that categories like these are discrete: A folk, pop, jazz, blues, rock, or hip-hop song could have spiritual or even religious resonance for you.

Before the ceremony. Music that is played before your ceremony can set the tone for what lies ahead. You may choose to have music accompany your pre-ceremony *ketubah* signing, for example. You could open your *ketubah* signing with a simple song to center everyone's attention. Or you may wish to include the beautiful background music of a string quartet or a single musician playing softly, gently underscoring the meaning of the *ketubah* signing.

If most of your guests will not be attending pre-wedding rituals but will go directly to the ceremony site, you can use music as a way of welcoming them to the space. Pre-ceremony music—whether it's live music or a CD—invites your guests into the space and should evoke the feelings to come. If some of your guests are not familiar with the sound of Hebrew, listening to some music with Hebrew lyrics before the actual ceremony begins can help ease the transition for them. It does not have to be religious or liturgical music but rather music that connects to your spirit, music that you want to share with your guests. You can mix Jewish music with whatever other kinds of music you like; think about how the songs work together to create the mood you desire. (If you are not particularly musical, you may want to ask a musical friend or relative to help you arrange and order your pre-wedding songs.)

Processional music. Because Jewish weddings have no set processional music, you can choose whatever music you want while you and the wedding party walk to the *chuppah*. The music could be upbeat and rollicking, quiet and soulful, or something in between. It might be played by professional musicians or musical friends of yours. You might choose to walk in to a *niggun*, a wordless melody (lai, lai, lai), sung together by all your guests. Remember, it is customary in some circles to have the music change just before the bride's entrance for dramatic effect. One couple I spoke with decided to walk into their *chuppah* in total silence, as a way of honoring the seriousness and sacredness of the commitment they were making and focusing everyone's attention on the moment at hand.

Within the ceremony. There are many places where music can be inserted into the traditional ceremony for enhancement and effect. When choosing your officiant, you should ask him how comfortable he feels singing. Obviously, if you are choosing a cantor, she is going to have a trained voice and will sing beautifully, but you do not want to assume that a rabbi comes with the same skills. Although he will be confident and comfortable chanting the ceremonial blessings, his voice might not be in perfect key. If having an officiant who sings beautifully is important to you, you might prefer a cantor to a rabbi. Teams of rabbis and cantors, whose skills complement each other, often work together. Before deciding when and how much music to include in your ceremony, talk with your rabbi and/or cantor about their experiences. Some officiants like to sing most of the blessings; others prefer speaking them, but they might welcome the opportunity to include additional music. You may want to involve musical family and friends when you think about adding music to your ceremony.

If you and your partner are including *hakafot* (circling) as your first ritual, you have a decision to make: Do you want to do the circling in silence, or with music underscoring your movement? Remember, this is the first moment that bride and groom have met under the *chuppah*, and all eyes will be focused on you. Music will have just been playing for your processional to the *chuppah*. The music that you walked in to could continue to play, it could change to a new melody, or it could end and allow for a moment of silence.

If you are into the world-music scene, you may have had the opportunity to explore some of the "Jewish world music" that is out there. But if you are less familiar with Jewish music, searching for the right music for your wedding gives you an opportunity to get to know the sounds of contemporary Jewish composers and musicians. As you listen, some of the music may sound familiar to you, but some of it might sound surprisingly exotic in its rhythms and tones. Once you get a sense of the range of music available, you can figure out what kind of music to include in your ceremony.

Varieties of Jewish Music

Music is a wonderful way to get everyone involved in your ceremony and create a feeling of community among your guests. It is also a tool to deepen moments within the wedding ceremony and to underscore rituals. Take some time to explore various musical styles before making any decisions about music.

Klezmer: Klezmer, the musical tradition that comes to us from Eastern Europe, has been experiencing a major renaissance in the last decade. Bands such as the Klezmatics have brought the sounds of "klez" to the mainstream, and many klezmer musicians have been fusing this traditional Jewish soul music with jazz, bluegrass, and even funk. Rollicking klezmer is definitely great party music, but there are ways to incorporate its slower soulful strains into your ceremony as well. Imagine a solo klezmer-style clarinet accompanying your processional down the aisle to your *chuppah*, or a spirited klezmer ballad being sung as part of your ceremony.

Ladino music: Ladino, or Judeo-Spanish, the language created by the Jews of Spain and Portugal, is beautiful when set to music. In recent years, many vocal artists have been reclaiming their Sephardic or Mizrachi ancestry and singing both lost Ladino melodies and new songs based on the Ladino musical tradition. If you like Brazilian, Cuban, or Afro-pop music, you should check out some contemporary Ladino artists. Their love songs might fit beautifully into your ceremony.

Israeli folk: As people from many different cultures emigrated to Israel, they each brought gifts from their homeland to the Holy Land. As people began to mix and borrow from each other's native cultures, a new culture was born, echoing the Old World but with a distinctive Israeli sound, because the music is sung in Hebrew. The folk tradition contains love songs drawn from biblical sources and other songs inspired by the Israeli landscape. A simple folk guitar can provide a lovely background

Some couples like to include a welcoming song right after the *Mi Adir* welcome. You can find some traditional wedding songs in a resource called *Kol Dodi: Jewish Music for Weddings*, which includes a CD recording and a songbook (see Appendix I for details).

The *Sheva Brachot* are usually chanted in a traditional melody. Afterward, continuing the theme of blessing the couple, a solo could be inserted into your ceremony. This moment is approaching the end of the ceremony, so a song that would be included here needs to be somewhat climactic and capture the energy and essence of everything that has happened under the *chuppah* up to this point.

One final note: The above are suggested places to insert music. You probably do not want to include a musical piece in all those places—it would make for one very long ceremony!

Right after the ceremony. Once the glass has been shattered, it is customary for everyone to shout *"Mazel tov!"* and then usually break out into song. Check with your rabbi or cantor, but the most common tune that is sung at this moment goes:

סִימָן טוֹב וּמַזָּל טוֹב,
מַזָּל טוֹב, סִימָן טוֹב
יְהֵא לָנוּ וּלְכָל־יִשְׂרָאֵל.

Siman tov u'mazel tov, mazel tov siman tov (3X)
Y'hei lanu
Y'hei lanu, y'hei lanu, u'lichol Yisrael (2X)

It is a good and fortunate sign for us and for all Israel.

If you think that some of your guests won't know that song and tune, just put the words in your program and everyone will be able to follow along with ease. I was once at a wedding, sitting with a non-Jewish friend, and when everyone broke out into "Siman Tov," she elbowed me and asked why everyone was singing about cinnamon toast!

Of course, you could end with a different song. You just might want to cue guests with a note in your program so that everyone can joyously chime in and sing along.

Wedding Programs

A program is a welcome addition to any Jewish wedding. A program can guide your wedding guests through the different parts of your ceremony and allow them to learn about the background and significance of any of the ritual objects you will be using in your ceremony. This is helpful for both non-Jewish guests and Jewish friends and family members who may have attended many Jewish weddings but were not clear about the different parts of the ceremony. A program is also a wonderful way to honor and thank all those friends and family members who helped make your wedding possible.

A wedding program does not need to be another big expense. Using your computer, you can type up a neat, concise program and design a creative cover. Some couples like to have their wedding program covers match the design on their invitation. Another simple but effective approach is to photocopy a nice picture of you and your partner for a cover design. Choose a paper color that complements your floral design and away you go. Don't spend an inordinate amount of time creating your program—it doesn't need to be an anthology. Just write out a simple guide with information that you think would be helpful to your guests.

Be yourself in your program: If you are funny people, it's okay to be funny. If you and your wedding are on the formal side, then the language in your program should reflect that tone. Writing up your program is just another way to express who you are.

When my husband and I were writing our program, we wanted above all to make sure that our non-Jewish friends felt included and that the more traditional

sound as guests enter your space.

Contemporary American: If you grew up in a Jewish youth group, you know the names of some of America's most popular Jewish songwriters/songleaders such as Debbie Friedman, Craig Taubman, and Jeff Klepper, and probably know their tunes by heart. Among their works are many pretty, melodic songs that could enhance a wedding ceremony, including "Dodi Li" (inspired by the Song of Songs) and musical settings for the priestly blessings. If these composers' names don't ring a bell for you, checking out their music may open a new avenue into Jewish prayer. Many new Jewish recording artists, including some well-known acoustic groups, also create sacred music.

Chant: Chanting is not just for monks or Buddhists anymore; there is a movement, especially in Jewish Renewal circles, to bring chanting into Jewish sacred worship. This form of repetitive, melodic prayer might enhance and deepen different parts of your wedding, especially if you have a rabbi or cantor who is comfortable leading chants. With just a few words repeated over and over, chants will be easy for all your guests to learn and sing.

Carlebach: The late Shlomo Carlebach deserves a category all his own. This Lubavitcher-trained rabbi touched the souls

Reckon You'll Bedecken? A Creative Look at the Jewish Wedding Ceremony

159

of many religious and secular Jews with his prayerful melodies. Carlebach's tunes blend a traditional Jewish sound with a very contemporary, accessible energy. Many of his tunes are especially beautiful when sung as *niggunim*— songs without words. By singing "lai, lai, lai" or "yi, di, di," people who don't know Hebrew or who have never heard the song before are able to join in without much effort. Carlebach's tunes could make beautiful pre-wedding or processional music.

Take some time to listen to these and other Jewish music styles. You can find recordings at big music stores such as Tower Records, at specialty Judaica shops, and online at such retailers as www.jewishmusic.com. Listen, make notes, and get a sense of the kind of music that appeals to you, whether it be secular or sacred.

members of our families could understand why we altered some of the traditions. We wanted everyone to be able to follow the ceremony. We are pretty informal people, so we felt comfortable including some light touches. Our program reads:

> We are so delighted that you are here to share this sacred day with us. Your friendship through the years, and your presence today, truly makes our wedding a celebration!
>
> We have designed this program as a guide to our wedding ceremony. We know that for some of you it may be your first Jewish wedding and for many others, your first "Reconstructionist" Jewish wedding. Essentially, we have kept the forms of a traditional Jewish ceremony but, with the help of our Rabbi, Shai Gluskin, we have made the rituals within the ceremony egalitarian and expressive of our love and commitment to one another. We have also infused our wedding with music and poetry that express our deepest sentiments.
>
> Sit back, relax, and enjoy the music of Jon Kaplan (Gabrielle's brother). Shortly, we will be joining you! Rabbi Shai will lead you in singing "Pitchu Li" as we proceed down the aisle. If you don't know Hebrew, don't worry—you can follow the phonetics or just hum along.
>
> Jewish weddings take place under a *chuppah* (wedding canopy), symbolic of the couple's first home together. Our *chuppah* is very special to us: It is made of squares of material that our parents and brothers and sisters and their children decorated for us. Today is our first time seeing our *chuppah* (oh, the suspense!), so please excuse us if we're looking up a lot! We will display the *chuppah* in our home and will treasure it always. Our parents will stand with us under the *chuppah*, acknowledging that this wedding is the union of two families.
>
> When we both reach the *chuppah*, you will see us circle one another. In the traditional *hakafot*, the bride walked around the groom, accompanied by the bride's and groom's mothers. In our ceremony, we will each circle each other. The circling represents the care and protectiveness we will provide each other in our lives together.

The Creative Jewish Wedding Book

The marriage ceremony consists of two parts: *kiddushin* (holiness) and *nesuin* (marriage). We begin *kiddushin* with none other than the *kiddush*—the blessing over the wine. This blessing symbolizes celebration and joy. We are using two *kiddush* cups given to us by our families.

Next is the ring ceremony. Traditionally, only the groom presented a ring to the bride. We will be exchanging rings—simple metal bands symbolizing the wholeness of marriage and the hope of an unbroken union.

Next comes the reading of our *ketubah* (writing). With the help of Rabbi Shai, we used the beautiful literary forms found in a traditional *ketubah* but also wrote in our own original commitments to each other. We commissioned an artist to create a frame for our "Covenant of Love" that further expresses our hopes and dreams for our lives together.

Just before the wedding, our witnesses signed our *ketubah*. We welcome you to take a look at it after the wedding.

In the *nesuin* section of our marriage, you will hear the *Sheva Brachot*—Seven Blessings—which we are honored to have sung by Rabbi Burt Schuman of Temple Beth Israel.

As part of this time of blessing, we are including some very special readings: "How Do I Love Thee," by Elizabeth Barret Browning, and "On Marriage," by Kahlil Gibran.

We are also including one of our favorite songs: "Unchained Melody" by the Righteous Brothers, sung by Celia Mayer and accompanied by Jon Kaplan.

Next comes the part of the ceremony you are probably most familiar with: the breaking of the glass. Explanations regarding this tradition abound. One common interpretation suggests that the shattered glass provides a reminder that, although a wedding grants a taste of redemption, the world is still broken and requires our care. After the glass is broken, it's your cue to shout, *"Mazel Tov!"*

Right after the ceremony, we'll be heading off to *yichud*. Traditionally, this private time was when the bride and groom consummated the marriage

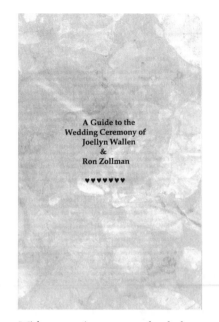

With some nice paper and a desktop printer, it's easy—and inexpensive—to create your own wedding program.

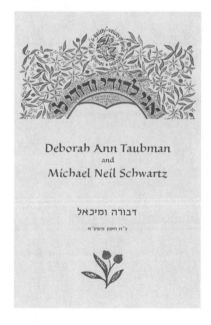

(whatever happened to foreplay?). Most likely, we'll use this eighteen minutes alone to exhale and enjoy a few moments of privacy before the party begins!

We then included our extended list of thank yous to the many people who helped make our wedding possible, from Rabbi Shai to my friend Rachel's mom, Ginnie, who sewed little fabric bags in which we put wildflower seeds as a party favor for our guests. Many people told us that our program helped make their understanding of our wedding much deeper.

Wedding programs don't need to take a lot of paper. If you are concerned about wasting paper on principle, condense your text and use recycled paper. You can let your guests know that your program was created with the Jewish value of *bal taschit*—not wasting—in mind.

Special Considerations for Interfaith Couples

If you and your partner come from different religious backgrounds, you may have read this chapter about the Jewish wedding ceremony with great interest, and also, perhaps, great confusion and even some trepidation. Depending on your commitment to Jewish practice and establishing a Jewish home, you may or may not both relate to the idea of a Jewish ceremony. Or you may like the idea of the wedding rituals and what they express but hope to create a ceremony that incorporates both your backgrounds and customs.

The bottom line is this: There is no one correct wedding ceremony for an interfaith couple. The first thing you should do is take time to answer some important questions (if you haven't done so already). What are your plans in terms of religious practice once you get married? Is conversion a possibility for either partner? How do you hope to raise your children? How strongly do you feel about your extended family's religious life and celebrations?

When you meet with a rabbi, he will ask you these kinds of questions, and it will help everyone involved if you've given them some thought beforehand. As you work with your rabbi, you may discover that a Jewish ceremony feels right for you. Or it might be that family pressures on both sides push you to choose a nonreligious ceremony led by a justice of the peace. A rabbi can help you figure out the best approach for you. Some couples opt for a civil ceremony but honor Jewish tradition by reciting the *kiddush* blessing, standing under a *chuppah*, and perhaps breaking a glass.

You and your partner may decide to have a Jewish wedding, yet you may be feeling concerned about how to honor both your families and make sure that all your guests, Jewish and non-Jewish alike, feel welcomed and included. One way to do so is to make the language in the ceremony as universal as possible. When Maurice Harris, who is Jewish, and his wife Melissa Crabbe, who was not Jewish at the time, got married, they looked for places where they could make the language in the Jewish ritual universal rather than specific to Jews only. For example, during their ring exchange, they changed the language from *"k'dat Moshe v'Yisrael* (in the tradition of Moses and Israel)" to *"lefne Mikor haAhavah* (before the Source of Love)." Another change was in the language of their *ketubah*. They changed their text to read, "May all the households in the world be blessed," rather than the original wording that appeared in the text they chose, which spoke of their home "among the households of Israel" being blessed. As subtle as these changes seem, they made the rituals feel more honest and authentic for the couple, and they hoped that they would resonate for their guests on both sides as well.

You can also use your wedding program as a guide for non-Jewish family and friends, to help them better understand the ceremony and more fully participate in it. "We really used our wedding program to put it all out there," Melissa Crabbe says. "We wrote something like 'For those of you who have never been to a Jewish wedding, this ceremony will feel very Jewish. And for those of you who have been to lots of Jewish weddings, this one may not seem as Jewish as other ones you've been to.'" Use humor and a personal touch in your program to make everyone feel at ease.

Another great way to include non-Jewish family in a Jewish wedding ceremony is to use ritual objects from the family. A *chuppah*, for example, might be created from some special heirloom fabric from the non-Jewish family. A special glass from the family could be used for the *kiddush* cup. Both members of the couple could wear something from both sides of the family—say, a handkerchief,

Reckon You'll Bedecken? A Creative Look at the Jewish Wedding Ceremony

163

a garter, a special piece of jewelry, or cuff links—and that can be noted in the wedding program as a way of making both sides feel connected and appreciated.

You might also choose to insert some elements that aren't traditionally part of a Jewish ceremony to make it feel more accessible to everyone present. For example, you can include "I do" vows and a "You may now kiss the bride" moment at the end of the ceremony. These small touches can help make the wedding feel more familiar to the whole family.

You could also think about how to include both sides of the family in special ways during your ceremony—whether that means inviting both set of parents to stand under the *chuppah* with you or asking family on both sides to share a song or an original blessing. Use music as much as possible to connect your families. Choosing Jewish music with simple lyrics (such as a chant or *niggun*) can allow everyone to participate. If there is a song that honors the background or heritage of the non-Jewish partner, find a place to include it in your ceremony.

As you plan a Jewish ceremony, be aware that friends and family on both sides may disagree with your choices and fail to support your efforts. It is hard not to take this personally, but keep supporting each other and reaching out to both sides in good faith. The way that other people react to your efforts is out of your control.

Maurice Harris and Melissa Crabbe felt that they both learned a lot—about each other and about the cultures they each came from—as a result of creating their wedding. "I think that if I had to give any advice to an interfaith couple," Melissa says, "it would be to really enjoy learning about each other's culture and not to worry so much about the religion piece. If you were dating someone from Tibet or Italy, you'd get really excited about learning about their customs and rituals. People get hung up on the religion piece, but it's only one piece of it. Embrace your partner's culture. It will give you a different perspective on the world, and you get to see your own culture reflected through your partner's eyes."

After much study and thought, some interfaith couples decide that a religious wedding—of any type—is not right for them. It may be too hard on one, or both, sides of the family, or the couple may be in the process of working through their conflicts and questions around religion. Or perhaps the couple simply doesn't feel religious at all.

That was the case for Julianne Bernstein Theodoropulos and Christos Theodoropulos. Julianne comes from a Jewish family; Chris was born and raised in Greece in the Greek Orthodox tradition. The couple knew that neither of them wanted to convert to each other's religion and that they wanted to create a wedding that would reflect their mutual love of poetry, theater, and philosophy. When they discovered that Quaker weddings were legal in Pennsylvania, they decided to use the Quaker format to create a wedding that would honor both their traditions.

Julianne and Chris asked a close friend to serve as Master of Ceremonies, and on their wedding invitations they asked their guests to let them know whether they would like to offer a blessing for them. They suggested that people could create an original blessing or borrow from a poem or literary passage.

"What we created was totally spontaneous and organic," Julianne recalls. "People offered prayers from their cultures. People spoke in Greek and their prayers were translated. My father gave us the priestly blessing. Chris read words from the New Testament and I read a poem by Marge Piercy." One of the most extraordinary moments during their ceremony was the reading of Julianne's great-grandfather's *ketubah*, signed in Dubzyn, Poland, in 1889.

Because both families had wanted either a Jewish or a Greek wedding, Julianne and Chris's solution stayed respectful of both cultures. Neither one of them is religious, and they didn't want to take on traditions that didn't feel honest or right to either of them.

At the party, music was used as great way to honor both cultures: Their jazz band played Jewish and Greek favorites, and everyone got up and danced together. Julianne and Chris saw the commonalties in both their backgrounds emerge— the emphasis on family, celebration, music, and food.

Family and friends agreed that it was a unique wedding for a unique couple. Guests felt welcomed, and the bride and groom felt elated. Parents on both sides *kvelled* (beamed with pride). Julianne offers her experience as one option for a ceremony that can blend the best of two worlds.

Reckon You'll Bedecken? A Creative Look at the Jewish Wedding Ceremony

165

Incorporating Other Spiritual Traditions into Jewish Ceremonies

Many contemporary Jews identify themselves as "culturally Jewish" while looking to other faiths for spiritual guidance. For example, so many Jews find themselves drawn to Buddhism that there is a name for them: Ju-Bus. For many such Ju-Bus (including my husband), Buddhism is a complementary and compatible faith with Judaism and has helped its devotees better reconnect to Judaism. Some Jewish people are experiencing a similar phenomenon as they explore other spiritual traditions.

Bringing elements of those faith traditions to a Jewish wedding ceremony is certainly possible, but a couple seeking to do so needs to find a rabbi who is understanding and accepting of this concept. This blending of faiths is harder for some people to comprehend than interfaith issues, which appear on the surface to be more black and white. Talk openly and honestly with your rabbi about your spiritual practice and what the exploration of other traditions means to you.

There are a number of places within a Jewish wedding ceremony in which you might honor those facets of your practice. The beginning of your ceremony is all about sharing your *kavannah* with your guests. If you practice meditation, you might ask wedding guests to come into the space and sit in silent meditation (ask ushers to let your guests know about this, and put a note in your program). You could use music as well. Imagine starting your wedding with a Native American wedding song, for example.

Within the Jewish ceremony structure, the time of blessing following the *Sheva Brachot* is another opportunity to include a meaningful reading, poem, or song that could honor your spiritual path. You might choose a friend who comes from the community you practice in or who shares your beliefs to do the reading.

Another place where different faith traditions might fit into your ceremony is during the breaking of the glass. As described earlier, many people use this point in the ceremony to offer a dedication relating to some cause that is especially important to them. If you're interested in earth-centered spirituality, you might expand the ritual of breaking the glass into a message that everyone present should remember that we must work together to protect the environment.

My husband offered a dedication to the memory of a Buddhist leader he greatly respected, whose life work was about repairing the world.

Depending on your community, integrating other cultures' traditions into a Jewish ceremony may be commonplace or quite shocking. If you think that this is the first time most of your guests will experience this kind of blending, write helpful notes of explanation in your program. But don't feel that you have to go overboard or apologize for what you are doing: Some people will appreciate it and others may not. Again, make sure that your *kavannah* is clear and strong; that is what matters.

Special Considerations for Gay and Lesbian Couples

In many ways, gay and lesbian couples have a great advantage when they start planning their Jewish wedding ceremonies. Because gay unions have no analogue in Jewish tradition, creating new rituals gives the couple a certain freedom to fashion a meaningful, personalized ceremony. Some gay and lesbian couples prefer to model their wedding ceremonies on the traditional Jewish ceremony and make changes only in language when it feels appropriate to do so (such as during the exchange of rings and the *Sheva Brachot*). They understand the power of traditional ritual and strive to adapt those rituals in an inclusive way.

Some same-sex couples use a traditional Jewish ceremony and work for a place within the tradition alongside heterosexual couples. In secular terms, they may use the words "wedding," "marriage," and "engagement" to show that their commitment is just as legitimate as a union between a man and a woman. Other gay and lesbian couples, however, view this approach as "assimilationist," arguing that, indeed, gay and lesbian unions are different and should be celebrated for their difference. They seek to transform Judaism beyond a few liturgical changes and argue that gay and lesbian relationships can be models for straight couples as well. Gay and lesbian couples locate themselves at various points along this spectrum of thought. Within a couple, moreover, the partners may hold differing perspectives. Open communication is crucial so that solutions are found to honor both people.

Reckon You'll Bedecken? A Creative Look at the Jewish Wedding Ceremony

167

As a gay or lesbian couple, you must find a rabbi who can help you examine the ceremony and determine which aspects to maintain and where to make changes. It is critical to find a member of the clergy who can help you create a meaningful ceremony and be there to support and guide you through the often troubling dynamics surrounding your union. It should be your special day—not a day when you have to deal with anyone else's anxiety or negative energy. Take a look at some of the new gay and lesbian rituals that are cataloged on a most helpful website, www.ritualwell.org, and talk with your rabbi about any interesting ritual ideas that you find there.

When Jonathan Krasner and Frank Tipton were planning their wedding, they knew that they wanted a ceremony that was rooted in Jewish tradition but was clearly original in its application to a gay male union. They selected a *ketubah* with gender-neutral language and omitted parts of the traditional wedding liturgy that did not fit their relationship. For the exchange of rings, they recited the verses from Hosea, "I will betroth you to me forever. . . . " They also adapted the language for the *Sheva Brachot*, using Marcia Falk's adaptation from her *Book of Blessings*, along with two original blessings created by some friends. They did so because they felt that any references to Eden, feminine fertility, and heterosexual unions were not appropriate for their ceremony.

Jonathan and Frank also spent time composing an original blessing that felt especially fitting to their marriage, which their rabbi used to bless them after the *kiddush:*

Be who you are—and may you be blessed in all that you are.

If you and your partner are planning a gay wedding, it is most likely that for many of your guests, including your family, this will be the first gay wedding that they attend. This reality can put enormous pressure on you as a couple—not only are you creating the ceremony that you want, but you are also carrying the burden of teaching your guests about what a gay or lesbian ceremony looks and feels like. In addition to that pressure, a wedding or commitment ceremony is very often a "coming out" event for the couple. Many extended family members may not have known or openly acknowledged your being gay prior to this event.

Jonathan and Frank were aware that their wedding was the first gay wedding that many of their guests had attended, and you and your partner should also keep that in mind. Creating a wedding program that explains something about gay marriage and any changes in traditional Jewish wedding rituals will be especially helpful, so that everyone can participate and understand more about the *kavannah* inspiring any ceremonial or language changes.

When Alex Volin and Sheila Campbell chose to marry, they decided to follow Rachel Adler's ceremonial format (found in her book *Engendering Judaism*), which replaces the traditional *erusin* section of the wedding ceremony with a new section called *brit ahuvim* ("covenant of love," the same name as the document that Adler suggests could replace a *ketubah*). Adler's ceremony made the most sense to them in terms of creating a feminist aesthetic, honest to their ideals of love and partnership. Alex and Sheila's wedding was a unique blend of traditional Jewish ritual and feminist innovation, created with time, care, and the guidance of two trusted rabbis, both experienced in officiating at lesbian weddings.

Remember: You and your partner have control over the guest list. If it feels better to invite supportive friends and go easy on the family members, that is just fine. If your day is going to be happier and easier if you don't have to come out to your mother's fourth cousins, whom you haven't talked to in years, then don't feel that you have to send them an invitation. Some couples make up their guest list and just wait to see who RSVPs, figuring that anyone who makes the effort to come is at least trying to be supportive.

When possible, figure out who among your family will be your real allies and root for you all the way. If you know that your sister will be there to deal with your parents' anxiety, ask her to be pro-active and handle any tense issues that arise. Knowing that you have a few point people to depend on can take much of the burden off your shoulders.

Many parents of gays and lesbians are thrilled that their children have found someone to love, but there is sadness that their child's wedding day is not what they had imagined. Furthermore, they may be supportive of the couple but feel uneasy about making the celebration so public. They may not be "out" to their own friends. This can create a very difficult family dynamic. Be sure to talk about it, and seek counseling from your rabbi or other supportive people. In the end, you are making a most powerful statement about your love and commitment, and you deserve to create a loving, supportive environment for your ceremony.

Reckon You'll Bedecken? A Creative Look at the Jewish Wedding Ceremony

169

In addition to working with spiritual issues, as the above-cited couples did, gay and lesbian partners planning a wedding need to think about legal issues. Because a gay or lesbian wedding does not, unfortunately, make you legal partners in the United States, gay and lesbian couples need to meet with a lawyer to hammer out the legal rights and responsibilities involved in this domestic partnership, which are automatically granted to heterosexual couples (see Appendix I).

Gay and Lesbian Marriage

Since the publication of the first edition of this book in 2004, there is now one state in the United States where gay and lesbian marriage is legal, Massachusetts and more states that honor civil unions: Vermont, New Hampshire, Connecticut and New Jersey. There is ongoing controversy in California whether or not to legalize gay and lesbian marriage. Domestic partnership is honored by the states of Oregon, Washington, and the District of Columbia. New York recognizes the gay marriages of couples who were married out of the state. Canada as a country recognizes gay marriage, and Mexico recognizes civil unions. Depending on the state and country of residence, gay and lesbian couples may have the option of planning a full marriage, civil union, domestic partnership, or commitment ceremony. Generally, your rabbi will work with you on the religious part of your ceremony and a lawyer can be helpful regarding the civil questions connected to your marriage.

Family Dynamics and Your Wedding Ceremony

A wedding is a loaded occasion. As much as people are gathered to celebrate you and your beloved, they bring with them their own feelings and associations about marriage itself, which may be positive or negative. The ideal guest recognizes those feelings and is able to put them aside, if they are less than positive, to focus on your celebration. However, as we all know, not all your guests are "ideal," and some of the guests carrying the most baggage may be your immediate family members.

The wedding of a child is also a major life-cycle event for parents, marking a real moment of letting go. No doubt some of the *meshugas* (craziness) that surrounds weddings comes from the unspoken anxieties about this transition that parents are feeling. Even when children have been out of the house for years and have started creating their own lives, separate from their parents, these primal issues of letting go may still surface. Rabbi Marcia Prager likes to use this energy in a ritual moment as part of *kabbalat panim,* as described earlier. An open and honest conversation in the months or weeks leading up to the wedding can also do wonders to ease tensions between parents and kids. Plenty of issues can surface among siblings, too, especially when some aren't married yet or are going through a divorce or don't believe in marriage—whatever the case may be. Let your family know how much you need their support right now. And don't be afraid to set limits if people are acting irrational or obsessive. Let them know (kindly) what you need and what you expect. My hope is that engaging your family in creative projects—whether it's writing an original blessing or designing a piece of your *chuppah*—will help them feel valued by you and invested in helping you create the loveliest wedding possible.

All life-cycle occasions bring unresolved family issues to a head. If people in your family are open to it, the time leading up to your wedding is ideal for seeking therapy so that you have a safe place, either individually or together, to acknowledge and work on resolving old issues. That way, you can all move forward carrying less old psychic baggage.

Divorce

When there has been a divorce on one or both sides of the family, tensions may run high. Depending on how recent and acrimonious the divorce was, bringing both parents together (along with their new partners, if applicable) can open up wounds for everyone. As the person getting married, you have the right to let your parents know how important it is to you for everyone to try their best to get along at the wedding. You aren't expecting anything major—just courtesy and politeness.

You may want to talk with your rabbi about the best way to involve divorced parents without having to engage them together. For example, if you feel closer to your mom, you may want her to walk you down the aisle. There could be another way to honor your dad, such as having him read your *ketubah* during the ceremony. Depending on their current relationship, you can determine how safe it is to have them together as opposed to keeping them separated.

You may find yourself in the position of making some tough choices; for example, you may decide it is best not to have any of your parents stand with you under the *chuppah*. If your parents are divorced but your partner's parents are not, they may have a hard time understanding why they can't be up there under the *chuppah* with you and may be feeling a degree of resentment as a result. Ask your partner to talk with them about how much you appreciate their support, and ask them to try to understand the difficulty of the situation. Ultimately, you need to create the safest, most loving space for both of you to enter for your ceremony, and that may mean making decisions that will not please everyone.

If your parents had an especially brutal divorce, brought on by an ongoing issue such as alcoholism or drug abuse, and you have not been in touch with one of them, you may be wondering about whether to invite that parent to the wedding. Talk with your rabbi about this issue; don't make a decision too quickly. Weddings can be a wonderful opportunity for healing. At the same time, as painful as it sounds, there are situations when it is best not to invite someone whose presence at your ceremony could be toxic. If you do decide to invite someone who has a drug or alcohol problem or issues with explosive anger, you may want to ask a friend or relative to be on duty, staying close to that person to make sure he remains under control and doesn't do anything to undermine the sanctity of the occasion.

Many couples with divorced parents are amazed at how courteous and well their parents get along at their wedding; no doubt, many parents are so delighted and hopeful for their children that they are able to set aside their own feelings for the moment.

When a Parent Has Died

One of the most difficult aspects of celebrating happy occasions is dealing with feelings of grief and loss. If one of your parents has died, whether recently or some time ago, you may be experiencing feelings of sadness even as you plan your celebration, and you may be struggling with those feelings. There are many ways for you to acknowledge those feelings and create rituals as part of your wedding ceremony that will honor the memory of the loved ones you have lost.

When Jane Berman and Adam Diamond got engaged, Jane was still mourning the loss of her mother, who had died a year before. Jane, in her early twenties at the time, had also lost her father a few years earlier. "Planning our wedding was exciting, but also terribly sad for me," Jane recalls. "I wanted to find a way to bring my parents' spirit to our wedding."

Jane and Adam came up with a few creative ways to acknowledge Jane's loss and to celebrate her parents' spirit as part of the ceremony. Jane had found the *tallit* that her father had become a bar mitzvah in, so their rabbi wrapped that *tallit* around Jane and Adam during their wedding ceremony, enveloping them in his presence. Jane also wears her mother's engagement ring and used her wedding ring in their ceremony.

Jane was appreciative that her mother-in-law was so supportive and helpful during the wedding planning. She also leaned on her two sisters, who walked her down the aisle to the *chuppah*.

"I think it was harder to imagine getting married without my parents being there than it was actually to do it," Jane says. "We didn't want their absence to be the focus of the wedding, and it wasn't. We made sure to feel their presence there, and we did. It was the beautiful day that we imagined."

Jane's advice to other couples in her position is to work with your rabbi to figure out the best way to incorporate your parent's (or other loved one's) presence into the ceremony, without the loss becoming the focus of the ceremony itself. Some couples choose to leave an empty seat in the first row or to write a loving acknowledgment in their wedding program.

Rabbi Yohanna Kinberg, who had lost her father several years before her wedding, wanted to honor the memory of her father and his absence on her special day. The night before her wedding ceremony, Yohanna and her partner Seth created a ceremony in the tradition of *Yizkor*, the worship service on the High Holy Days and Jewish festivals to remember those who have died. Yohanna lit a *yahrzeit* candle for her father and everyone joined in reciting psalms that she had chosen. Yohanna spoke about moving from sadness to joy; she felt that the formal ritual helped her acknowledge her loss, then move to a place of celebration. She brought the lit *yahzreit* candle under the *chuppah* to feel her father's presence during her wedding ceremony the next day.

Nancy Zerner Broderick got married only six weeks after her father died, which was very hard. Because the thirty days of mourning that come after a loved one's death had passed, and the wedding had been planned before her father's passing, Nancy's rabbi urged her to go ahead with the wedding as scheduled. During the processional, her two sisters walked down the aisle holding a lit candle. When they reached the *chuppah*, they used that candle to light a larger one in memory of their father. Nancy's twin brother walked her down the aisle, and the rabbi, who had known her father well, spoke briefly about his legacy at the beginning of the ceremony. While Nancy and her partner were in *yihud*, a minyan of family members gathered to say *kaddish* for her father.

Jewish tradition offers many opportunities to acknowledge feelings of sadness and mourning for loved ones we have lost, and as much as your wedding celebration is about joy and gladness, there is nothing wrong with being open about any loss you are feeling. Emotions are not simple and easy to compartmentalize: You may feel joy and sadness at the same time. Moments of great joy can trigger deep pain, too; it is in the opening of your heart that many bottled-up emotions can pour out. Consider the examples above, and talk with your rabbi about what might work best for you.

When Religious Observance Differs among Families

Today's Jewish families are complex for many reasons. One of those reasons includes the diversity of religious practice among American Jews today. Gone are the days when people joined the synagogue closest to their neighborhood and that was that; in most major metropolitan areas across the United States, Jews can choose from among a wide variety of congregations. So what happens when someone who grew up in a Reform family meets and falls in love with someone from a modern Orthodox background? Or if someone from an active Jewish Renewal family plans to marry someone from a family who is culturally Jewish but has no religious practice to speak of? Or when a secular Israeli is engaged to someone from a very observant Conservative home?

You get the idea. These connections happen all the time. People meet in college or graduate school, through Jewish singles events or mutual friends. Families may be thrilled, initially, to hear that their son or daughter has found a Jewish boyfriend or girlfriend. But once couples become engaged and start planning their wedding, questions and issues involving observance may shatter the illusion that finding a Jewish partner will make everything smooth sailing.

For example, if one family strictly follows *kashrut* (Jewish dietary observance), they may insist on having kosher caterers for the wedding. If the other side of the family thinks that *kashrut* is ridiculous, they may not be pleased to pay the (generally) higher price for a kosher caterer. As another example, consider the case of a couple with one partner from a Reform background and the other from a Conservative or Orthodox background. Say this couple chooses to get married in a Reform synagogue, by a Reform rabbi. The Conservative or Orthodox family may be concerned about how much of the ceremony will be in English, what kind of dress code will be established (are men required to wear *kippot*?), and the like. Their concerns, if not framed delicately, can seem extremely rude and patronizing to the Reform family.

What is a couple to do when such cross-Jewish-cultural dynamics surface? The first thing to do is to take a deep breath and simply acknowledge and accept that there are many different ways to be Jewish in the world today. The second thing is to try to share kindly this observation to your own parents. Try to explain that although the Cohen family may do things a bit differently than the Goldsteins, we are all Jews, and differences can be a healthy thing. Try to negotiate issues whenever possible: Explain to the nonkosher side how important *kashrut* is to the other side. Ask Conservative parents to attend a Reform ceremony in advance of the wedding so they can become familiar and more comfortable with the setting. Point out that you both respect each other's backgrounds and would appreciate your parents making an effort to do so as well.

Your extended families may encompass a range of Jewish practices and observances. It is not your job to create a ceremony that will please all of them, but rather to create a ceremony that reflects your spirits and captures your love. You can take steps to make your guests feel included and welcome, such as creating a program with clear explanations, but it is ultimately up to them to accept and respond to the ceremony you create.

When Shoshanah Feher Sternlieb and Geoff Sternlieb were planning their wedding, they were concerned about how relatives from very different backgrounds would interact, and they voiced some concerns to relatives from both sides of the observance spectrum. "Our wedding was held in the summer, so we knew that some women might wear sleeveless dresses and we were concerned that would offend our very observant guests, so we asked people to please not wear sleeveless dresses," Shoshanah recalls. "On the other side, we knew that if our observant relatives didn't shake hands with our secular guests, those guests might not understand and would think they were being rude. We asked them to shake hands if someone offered his or her hand, so as not to embarrass that person." Shoshanah and Geoff made their requests known—and you can, too. Guests do not have to listen to you, of course, but at least they will hear your concerns and hopefully be more sensitive when in a mixed crowd.

Sometimes the couple getting married is more religiously observant than their own parents. Many young people today, who grew up in secular or barely observant homes, have forged a strong connection to Judaism in a religious community. This return to tradition may seem strange and even unsettling for parents, who may interpret this embrace of religious tradition as a personal rejection. If you find yourself in this situation, try to be sensitive to your parents' discomfort. Give them some background reading so they can understand the parts and traditions of a Jewish wedding. Try not to judge them or preach to them, but let them know that their participation means a lot to you, and you are more than happy to help explain the religious rituals that you are planning. They most likely want to be very involved in this major event in your life, and including them in your wedding planning can open up a new dialogue about religion, spirituality, personal choice, and community. That dialogue will hopefully continue for some time to come.

chapter seven

Party On!
Thinking Creatively about Jewish Food and Other Reception Choices

After the sanctity of the ceremony comes the party. It is Jewish law, after all, to celebrate with the bride and groom. Wedding receptions should be continuations of the ceremony—expressions of the couple's love and friendship, with involvement and excitement from the community of guests. Jewish wedding receptions encompass a number of meaningful traditions and hold many possibilities for creativity. Although the focus is on fun, a Jewish wedding reception offers opportunities for you to connect with your family and friends, to express yourselves Jewishly, and also to offer blessings. With a clear *kavannah*, you might think about your wedding reception as a time for "divine partying."

In planning your wedding reception, think about what would make it especially fun and meaningful for you. Maybe your guests come in costume; maybe your reception is a retro-'80s party. Maybe it's a family-friendly event full of kids of all ages; maybe it's a formal black-tie dinner. Your reception doesn't need to look like anyone else's in the world, and the way you create your entertainment can be as unique as you are. We are part of a great tradition that truly celebrates the bride and groom, and your creative ideas can only enhance your celebration.

Wedding Delicacies

As a culture, Jews love food! A generalization, yes, but one that rings true for most of us. In the Jewish tradition, food is warmth; food is love; food is security. In days gone by, special foods were prepared each week for the Sabbath, and our holidays and festivals are marked by distinctive culinary delicacies. Remember the classic one-liner used to sum up so many Jewish holidays, "They tried to kill us; we won; let's eat." In all seriousness, a Jewish wedding was traditionally another occasion to indulge in out-of-the-ordinary cuisine—to splurge on delicacies and lavish delights in honor of the "royal couple"—and still today, a wedding is just not a wedding without sumptuous food.

If you or your partner savors good food (and who among us doesn't?), your wedding can be an opportunity to explore the vast terrain of Jewish cuisine. Not just limited to the old standards of brisket and matzoh balls, Jewish cooking is a global phenomenon. Just like Jewish music, Jewish cuisine borrows from the myriad cultures where Jewish communities sprang up, and adds its own unique twists to common recipes and dishes. There are Jewish specialty dishes from Morocco, Italy, Spain, India—all with their own flavors and spices.

Creating your Jewish wedding may mean incorporating Jewish global cuisine into your menu. As you consider the kind of menu that you want at your wedding party—and start looking for the right kind of caterer—you might want to explore these international Jewish foods. For starters, pick up a global Jewish cookbook, such as Claudia Roden's *The Book of Jewish Food: An Odyssey from Samarkand to New York*. Roden takes her readers on a culinary journey through Jewish time and space, describing dishes—from soups to main courses, and, of course, special desserts—made for weddings by Jewish communities all over the world. Try some of the recipes, invite friends over to taste the dishes, and see which flavors and styles of Jewish cooking you really enjoy.

Of course, Jewish food is also affected by the *mitzvah* of *kashrut*—the Jewish dietary laws. Derived from biblical prohibitions regarding what kinds of food are and are not permitted to be eaten, keeping kosher is the Jewish way of adding spiritual significance to what we take into our bodies for nourishment. *Kashrut* is about sanctifying what we eat—making it holy by limiting which animals are permitted to be consumed, preparing it in special ways, separating milk and meat, and using a relatively painless manner of ritual slaughter for animals. *Kashrut* is about respecting the sanctity of all life, both animal and human. Deciding to have a kosher wedding will definitely have an impact on your food choices, so you may first want to figure out where you and your partner fall on the kosher spectrum:

- You both currently keep a kosher home.

- Your family does not keep kosher, but you do.

- You keep kosher, but most of your friends and family members do not.

- You keep a kosher home, but you don't observe *kashrut* outside the home.

- You follow eco-*kashrut* (see sidebar on following page).

- You grew up keeping kosher, but you don't keep kosher as an adult.

- You don't keep kosher, but you have many friends and family members who do.

- One of you keeps kosher, and the other partner more or less follows along.

- You don't keep kosher and neither do most of your friends and family members.

Even if you have decided together not to keep a kosher home, you may still opt for kosher food at your wedding—or a kosher presentation—to honor those who are more observant. Fortunately, there are many compromises that can make everyone happy (well, almost everyone, and maybe not happy, but at least willing to eat something). One easy compromise is to offer a completely vegetarian menu at your wedding. If this solution does not please your more observant family members and friends, ask your caterer to try to locate and provide special kosher meals for them. This takes a little more work and coordination, but it may be worth it to honor their needs.

What Is Eco-*Kashrut*?

Over the past twenty years or so, there has been a movement in liberal Jewish circles to take on the *mitzvah* of eco-*kashrut*. This movement views the Jewish dietary laws not only as a commandment that must be observed but also as an opportunity to make choices around food that support a healthy environment, treat animals with kindness and respect, and lead to better health for people and the planet. If traditional *kashrut* laws were created to sanctify the act of eating, eco-*kashrut* principles extend that idea to make us consider the economic, environmental, ethical, and physiological effects of what kind of food we purchase, where we shop, and the way we eat. It is about making responsible choices, leading to healthier lives and a healthier planet.

For example, an eco-*kashrut* wedding meal would probably be vegetarian, or it might consist of free-range and organic chicken, rather than traditionally slaughtered, cage-raised poultry. Produce would be purchased from local growers whenever possible. Leftovers might be saved and boxed up for delivery to a nearby homeless shelter.

If the idea of eco-*kashrut* interests you, you can find out more about it at www.biggreenjewish.org.

Some couples who do not normally keep kosher feel that it is important to acknowledge the Jewish dietary laws at a major life-cycle moment and will make decisions not to serve milk and meat together and to avoid shellfish and any pork products. Choosing a main course such as salmon (which is considered *parve*, a neutral food item) is also another way to ensure that most of your guests will feel comfortable eating at your party.

Of course, if you, your families, and most of your guests keep kosher, then it makes sense to seek out a kosher caterer and reception site. Fortunately, in most metropolitan areas, kosher caterers offer a broad range of menu options. There are kosher caterers who specialize in everything from macrobiotic cooking to ethnic food choices (such as Pan-Asian and Indian). Look in your local Jewish directory to find the right caterer for you.

If you live or are holding your wedding in an area with limited Jewish resources but want to have strictly kosher food at your wedding, consider making your own food or hiring a friend who also keeps kosher to help you make the food and freeze it. This is a good option only for folks who really love to cook and who have a couple of friends who can help. Food should be made ahead of time and frozen: No bride or groom should ever be rolling meatballs the week before the wedding! Take into account the number of guests at your wedding: For a smaller wedding reception (fifty guests or fewer), catering by yourself and/or a friend is a much more feasible option.

Creating a Potluck Reception

Catering costs got you down? No worries: You can create a truly original and delicious reception by throwing a potluck buffet. Guests will become part of the party and will also have a chance to sample all kinds of fantastic food. These kinds of receptions are becoming more in vogue and socially acceptable. To avoid any sense of tackiness, make sure you are gracious hosts and express proper gratitude for guests' willingness to cook or purchase food.

Organization is the key to carrying off a successful potluck. Follow these simple tips to ensure success:

Divide food items into categories: To guarantee the proper balance of courses, divide up your guest list alphabetically and assign equal numbers of folks to bring salads, main dishes, side dishes/vegetables, and desserts. Make sure you let guests know that all food items should be able to sit out for an hour or so and should not need to be refrigerated or baked before the reception.

Encourage people to bring regional/ethnic food: Your potluck will be most interesting if people bring specialty items. If you have an Indian friend who loves to cook Indian food, ask her to make samosas. If you have a friend from New Orleans, encourage him to whip up some fresh pralines. There will be something there that everyone likes and your mix of food will get people mingling and exchanging recipes and stories!

Assuage the fears of out-of-towners: Encourage them to bring something nonperishable (candy or nuts) or give them a short list of local groceries/shops so they can purchase something in town. If they are determined to bring a homemade dish in a cooler, ask the hotel whether they can refrigerate it overnight. After all, it's for a special occasion!

Think vegetarian: If you are concerned about issues of *kashrut* (or eco-*kashrut*), consider making your potluck vegetarian. Let your guests know that using dairy products is okay, but they should avoid anything containing meat.

Provide the basics: As host and hostess, you provide silverware, plates, napkins, cups, ice, and drinks. If your potluck is being held outdoors, make it one step easier and buy pretty paper goods. Make sure that there are adequate tables for all the food, as well as plenty of tables and chairs for guests to sit and eat.

Let them eat cake: A potluck saves you considerable money, so don't skimp on your wedding cake. Even if you have guests bring other desserts, what's a wedding without a really great cake?

Hire a food supervisor (or two): Find some responsible teenagers or college students who want to make a few bucks, and have them on hand to take the food from your guests upon their arrival, arrange the buffet, and help clear garbage.

By following these suggestions, you can make a potluck party enjoyable for everyone. Again, be sure to thank your guests both in person and in your thank you notes for being so gracious and bringing a special dish.

Wedding Cake Options

Today's wedding cakes come in every flavor, color, size, shape, and design imaginable. No longer must the prescribed bride-and-groom cake topper grace your cake; instead, couples can choose anything from calla lillies to personal monograms to crown their wedding confection.

Think about making your wedding cake fit into the style and approach of your wedding and party. Cakes can be made in whimsical designs, decorated with polka dots, or made to reflect a zenlike style, with simple shapes adorned with a flower or two. Cakes no longer have to be iced in white; your icing can complement your party décor.

Some couples choose to go retro and make their cakes as white and fluffy as possible, complete with a vintage cake topper. If you like this idea, check with grandparents or great-aunts to see whether any of them held on to their own cake topper. A fun twist for gay and lesbian couples is to use same-sex toppers (see Appendix I for ordering information).

Cake flavors also run the gamut of palate pleasers, from exotic spices such as ginger and tamarind to rich delicacies, including triple chocolate mousse. Think about how your cake can complement the wedding cuisine that preceded it.

If you are keeping kosher at your reception, you'll want to find a kosher bakery to create your cake. Look in your local Jewish directory or ask your rabbi for any recommendations.

Wedding Menus

Below are samples of menu ideas for different kinds of Jewish weddings. If you hope to plan a traditional kosher menu, you will have to decide whether the menu is dairy or meat. Customarily, chicken and fish are served as entrees at a Jewish wedding because they symbolize fertility. Since fish is considered to be *parve*—neither dairy or meat—it is an easy entrée choice to work with.

Sephardic weddings often begin with a first course called Sutlach—a sweet rice pudding featuring coconut milk, honey and almonds, all symbols of sweetness and prosperity. In a Sephardic menu, couscous or rice are prominently featured, while a traditional Ashkenazic meal features potatoes.

If you and your partner are vegetarians or vegan, you can create a menu full of dishes that come from Jewish tradition—including falafel, grape leaves and buckwheat kasha. Many couples who are not vegetarian but who follow eco-*kashrut* principles prefer serving grass-fed beef or free-range chicken. There are now a number of sources available for kosher grass-fed beef and kosher free-range chicken.

Traditional Kosher Menu

Appetizers
> Potato and Sweet Potato Latkes
> Smoked Salmon Canapes
> Crudite of Vegetables

First Course
> Mixed Green Salad

Entree
> Chicken Jerusalem, Julienne Peppers and Capers
> Roasted Potatoes

Jewish International

Appetizers

> Spanikopita
> Mediterranean Spreads of Hummus, Olivada, Caponata with
> Pita Chips and Toasted Lavash
> Grilled Marinated Vegetables

First Course

> Sutlach (Sweet Rice Pudding)

Entrée

> Encrusted Salmon
> Israeli Couscous
> Fresh Vegetable Medley

Eco-*Kashrut*/Vegan

Appetizers

> Antipasto Display
> Grilled Asparagus, Artichoke Hearts, Mushrooms, Squash,
> Eggplant and Olives
> Mini-falafel pitas
> Stuffed Grape Leaves

First Course

> Seasonal Gazpacho

Entrée

> Fresh vegetable ratatouille served over kasha
> Roasted green beans

Blessings Before and After Eating

As much as we love to eat, Jewish tradition contains rituals that remind us to take a moment or two and offer appreciation for what we are about to eat or what we have just eaten. You can use these rituals to help ground and connect your guests before and after the big meal. Including the *motzi*, the Hebrew blessing for bread, and the *Birkat Hamazon*, grace after eating, are ways to infuse holiness into your reception. The traditional *motzi* reads as follows:

בָּרוּךְ אַתָּה יְיָ,
אֱלֹהֵינוּ מֶלֶךְ הָעוֹלָם,
הַמּוֹצִיא לֶחֶם מִן הָאָרֶץ.

Baruch atah Adonai
Elohaynu melech haOlam,
haMotzi lechem min haArtez.

Blessed are You, Adonai,
Ruler of the world,
Who brings forth bread from the earth.

Because the *motzi* is so familiar, it allows your guests to reconnect through a moment of blessing before eating. A song could be included with the *motzi* to enhance this moment—a simple *niggun*, maybe one used in your ceremony, that will now have a lovely resonance for your guests. It is an honor to invite someone to lead the *motzi* at your reception, so this could be a great place to involve a family member or friend with a lovely singing voice.

After eating comes another occasion for blessing—the *Birkat Hamazon*, or grace after a meal. This is the time that the *Sheva Brachot* are traditionally sung once again as part of the blessing. Traditional Jews will expect *benching* (singing the *Birkat Hamazon*) to be included as part of the wedding meal. You and your partner can decide whether this ritual feels important to you to include. What is especially nice about *benching* at a wedding is that you do get to hear the *Sheva*

Brachot sung again, either in their standard form, or performed as seven creative blessings. Taking time to sing the *Birkat Hamazon* could extend to include performances of songs—either impromptu or rehearsed—by family and friends.

When singing the *Sheva Brachot* at this point in the ceremony, three *kiddush* cups (or any wine glasses) are needed. The leader of the *Birkat Hamazon* sings the first blessing of the *Birkat Hamazon*, holding one full cup of wine. That cup is then held—but not sampled—by the other people, who then recite the next six blessings of the *Sheva Brachot*. The leader then sings the final blessing over the wine, holding a second full cup. She then takes the two cups and pours from them together, filling an empty cup to the brim with wine. The bride and groom drink from this cup together. Although this ritual seems a bit complicated, it symbolizes the joining together of two people, with hope that their unified life may be one full of overflowing blessings.

If you plan to include this traditional *benching*, you will need to have copies of the *Birkat Hamazon* handy so all your guests can follow along. Some couples like to order personalized *benchers* that contain the blessing, along with numerous songs and prayers, as a souvenir for the guests to take home. If your wedding is going to take place at a synagogue, ask whether they already have photocopies of the *Birkat Hamazon* that you can use.

If you would like to honor the tradition of blessing after a meal but do not necessarily want to do a traditional *benching*, you might think about using one of the contemporary versions of the *Birkat Hamazon*. Composer and musician Shefa Gold has created several popular alternatives to traditional *benching*. You could use one of her selections, then follow the song with seven guests each delivering a short creative blessing, song, or poem for you as a couple. Her work is available on her website: www.rabbishefagold.com. One of her contemporary *Birkat Hamazon* versions set to music goes:

> You are the source of everything,
> It is because of you we sing,
> You nourish the world with goodness and sustain it with grace,
> We find you in the dust and in the vastness of space,
> We taste you in the food we eat and see you in our friends

You strengthen our rejoicing with a love that never ends.
Baruch atah Adonai Elohaynu melech haOlam
Yay da day . . .
Hazan et hakol.

Taking a few moments for blessing during your reception reminds everyone of the holiness of the occasion. It also gives you one more opportunity to extend honors to friends and family. Inviting seven people close to you to share a personal blessing draws on their creative energy, which will keep enlivening your festivities.

Music for Your Wedding Party

What's a party without music? The sounds of a Jewish wedding party should be festive and joyous, full of celebration. You have many creative options when it comes to music for your reception. Hiring professional musicians is one way to go; other alternatives can save you money, and infuse your wedding with personal flair.

One issue for every couple to address is "how Jewish" they want their party music to be. For some couples, it's an easy decision—they love klezmer music and want to have a party with lots of circle dancing. For others, it's not as clear: They may want some Jewish dancing, but they want to make sure that non-Jewish friends enjoy the music as well.

When Mark and Jill Goldberg were planning their wedding, they knew that they wanted a klezmer band to play at their party. Mark and Jill love how easy it is for everyone to dance to klezmer music. "You don't have to be coordinated, you don't have to worry about being cool, you don't have to worry if you don't have a dance partner, you just get up there and join in," Jill says. They listened to demos from a few klezmer bands (they live in northern New Jersey, where a wide range of klezmer bands was accessible to them), and chose one that was funky and upbeat and was happy to drop in some of the couple's favorite swing and Motown tunes.

Still, even with a bit of non-Jewish music mixed in, Jill and Mark worried that their non-Jewish guests might not get into the music. "Most of our guests were Jewish," Mark says. "But we both had a number of friends from graduate school and people we worked with coming to the wedding, and I was hoping that the klezmer music would be okay for them." In retrospect, Mark and Jill needn't have worried: It was their non-Jewish friends even more than their Jewish friends and relatives who wouldn't get off the dance floor! "One of my closest friends is a Japanese woman, who is Lutheran, and since our wedding, she is a bigger klezmer fan than I am," Jill says.

Not every wedding party needs a rocking band to be a success. Some couples choose quiet background music to play during their wedding reception, rather than dance music. If you are planning a smaller wedding, keep in mind that not all your guests will necessarily want to dance. If you have only five or six people out on the dance floor, it can be hard to keep the energy going. Also, some wedding receptions have been ruined by DJs or bands who play music so loud that no one can have a conversation without shouting. When deciding on your reception music, be sure to tell your band or DJ how loud you want the music to be and how many breaks for mellow music you want.

Whatever music you decide on, remember that the tradition of putting the bride and groom up on chairs and dancing with or at least carrying them is a classic moment, even at the most nontraditional Jewish weddings. When else in your life is someone going to bounce you up and down on a chair? Remember, in Jewish tradition, the bride and groom are queen and king for the day, and lifting them up above the crowd on chairs is one way to express that metaphor.

Musical Options

Your musical choices will have a great impact on the feeling you create at your wedding reception. As you think through the ways to bring music to your party, consider the following options:

> *Musical friends:* If you are fortunate enough to have family
> members and/or friends who are musicians, you may want to

invite them to use their musical gifts as part of your wedding celebration. Your friend(s) could play during the ceremony or lead a song or blessing at your reception. When inviting a friend to perform, be considerate of how much time and energy he or she will need to put in to create the music you want. For example, if you have a friend who is a professional musician but is not familiar with Jewish music at all, give plenty of time for that person to learn the songs you want played (preferably three to six months). Don't ask a friend who is a professional to play all your music unless you intend to pay for his or her services.

Musical family members and friends will most likely be honored to play a special solo at your party or to sing some pre-ceremony music, if you provide them with the music and lyrics in plenty of time and then let them do their thing. Keep in mind that they may assume you will be paying them to play the music, unless you specify otherwise. If you have family members or friends who are not professional musicians but who are musically talented, they probably wouldn't make this kind of assumption. Again, it's wonderful to involve your talented friends; just be careful not to cross the line and put too much pressure on them.

Hiring the right musicians: If you are planning to hire professional musicians to accompany your ceremony and/or to play at your reception, take some time in selecting them. Start with word of mouth: Talk to friends and family members about musicians they recommend. Most bands—especially wedding bands—have CDs so you can get a sense of their sound. Talk with the band leader about your vision for your wedding music and how much you would like to mix Jewish and secular music. Make sure that you trust the musicians you are hiring, and that the musicians listen to (and write down!) your individual requests.

Multiple musicians: If you have the resources, you may even consider hiring different kinds of musical groups for different parts of your wedding. You might use some musical friends to play pre-processional music, and then hire a band for the party music. If you are thinking about having some rollicking klezmer music for part of your party, you could hire a klezmer ensemble to play during your cocktail hour. If hiring a band for more than an hour or two puts you over your budget, think about hiring some musicians for the cocktail hour, then switch to a DJ. Whatever musical options you choose, just make sure that you know what kind of music you want. The clearer you are in your musical vision, the greater the chance that you and your musicians will be in harmony.

Finding a DJ: If your friends and family members are not musically inclined, and you choose not to hire professional musicians, look into hiring a disc jockey for your ceremony and/or reception. Although recorded music is not the same as live music, using the services of a DJ does have some major advantages. For example, if you live in an area that lacks musical groups specializing in Jewish music and you really want to have a klezmer-focused reception, you can set up your DJ with the exact CDs and recordings that you want her to play. If you have special pre-wedding music and music that you want your guests to hear as they are leaving your wedding site, a DJ can do a great job here. Make sure you hire a DJ with excellent references and take the time to sit down with her or him and explain exactly what songs you want her or him to play, in exactly which order. You can even include your song list as part of your contract for the services, just to emphasize how important your song choices are. With today's computer technology, some couples are even choosing to let a friend with a laptop and plenty of MP3s act as their DJ. Using a DJ can help you bring a range of wonderful music to your ceremony and reception and save you significant costs when compared to hiring live musicians.

Beyond Music: The *Mitzvah* of Making Merry

Remember, in Jewish tradition the bride and groom are viewed as a royal couple, a queen and king (for the day, anyway!). As was appropriate for a queen and king, wedding guests would perform all sorts of tricks, songs, acrobatics, and charades for their enjoyment. The master of ceremonies at a wedding—called the *badchan* (Yiddish for "joker")—was at the helm of all of the crazy fun.

Whether you choose a DJ or live music, your guests will love the opportunity to dance in your honor!

We all experience joy in different ways, so think about what kind of festivities would be the most fun for you. Some folks love to be toasted and roasted, while others can think of nothing less appealing. Some people want to get down and dance, while others prefer quiet conversation with a table full of close friends. There is no one right way to make merry—just focus on finding the right path for you and your partner.

Ways to Get Your Guests Involved

- *Ask a friend to be your master/mistress of ceremonies.* Do you have an especially outgoing girlfriend who loves to speak in front of a crowd? Invite her to be your modern *badchan*, punctuating your wedding reception with moments of jokes, funny toasts, and roasts. Depending on how formal your reception is, she could solicit some open-mike entertainment by your other guests, or she could plan in advance to call on others to perform special songs, magic tricks, or whatever talents your guests bring with them.

The royal couple sits on their throne, with friends leading the celebration.

Just make sure you spell out the limits you want to impose on this entertainment. For example, you may want guests to avoid raunchy jokes that would be inappropriate if you were having young nieces and nephews present; just let the emcee know to keep it family-friendly. If you want to make sure that guests have plenty of time to dance and mingle (unplanned open mikes can seem to go on forever), then let her know that the jokes, toasts, and roasts should take no more than forty-five minutes. If one of you is shy and doesn't want to be involved in any "participatory" jokes or stories, make that clear, too.

- *Get a good karaoke machine.* Considered tacky by some and a brilliant invention by others, a good karaoke machine can get all your guests out there entertaining you. After a good amount of dancing and mingling, guests may want to sit back and enjoy the wild entertainment when friends and family perform karaoke. If your guests span the generations, from very young children to great-grandparents, karaoke is a great way to get everyone into the act. Make sure your karaoke machine includes the old standards, from swing to Motown, as well as more contemporary tunes.

- *Music jam.* If you're friends with a number of musicians, invite them to bring their instruments to the party, and open up the floor to a potluck music jam for a limited time. Most musicians love meeting other musicians, and their sense of excitement will fill the room.

The Creative Jewish Wedding Book

Even if this jam session isn't something you'd necessarily choose to listen to at another time, they will have contributed some fun and entertainment to your ceremony. Be sure to give them a time limit, unless, of course, you strike some musical gold and want them to keep playing.

- *Dance, dance, dance.* Since the release of the film *Simply Ballroom*, and the ballroom and swing dance craze that followed, more couples have incorporated choreographed dance numbers into their weddings. Reversing the notion of the guests entertaining you, you and your partner performing a special dance number is a chance to show guests all your favorite moves. Whether or not you are going to "perform" a dance at your wedding, it is a good idea for any couple to sign up for a dance class or two before the wedding. It doesn't have to be anything fancy or formal: Most JCCs and neighborhood community centers offer basic swing, ballroom, or Latin dance classes. Unfortunately, we don't get as many opportunities to dance together as generations past. By taking a class or two together prior to the wedding, you will likely feel that much more comfortable getting out on the dance floor at your own party. If you and your partner are already good dancers, or your dance classes inspire you, think about performing an original dance number for your guests. In fact, this new trend is spawning an industry of professionals who specialize in working with couples to choreograph dances for their weddings.

  If you have friends or family members who are into formal dancing, invite them to be "royal entertainers" and perform a special number for you and your guests. There are also a number of traditional Jewish wedding dances that you might want to include. The *mazinke tanz* is an Ashkenazi tradition celebrating the marriage of the parents' last child to be married. The parents are seated on chairs while the children crown them with garlands of flowers and dance around them in a circle. With more people waiting until later in life to get married, and some parents wondering whether their

Making a Throne for the King and Queen

This craft project is not for the bride and groom but for a good friend, attendant, sibling, or anyone else who wants to treat the newlyweds like royalty. Have fun with this project: It can be as simple or elaborate as you choose.

To create an original royal throne, scout around at used furniture stores (or ask your friends) for two inexpensive wooden chairs with armrests. If you find chairs with some ornate detail, all the better.

Get some shiny spray paint—royal purple or maroon is best—and spray-paint the chairs completely. From there, use your creativity. You can paint more details, such as the words "King" and "Queen" on the seat or the back of the chairs, or, if you have the skill, paint a little caricature of the bride and groom on each throne.

Use a hot-glue gun to glue some fake jewels around the edges of the chair. Depending on how kitschy and over-the-top you want to go, you could even cover the armrests with velvet, glitter, or fake fur. These are for the king and queen, after all.

Don't forget to stop by a costume or Halloween shop to pick up a couple of super tacky crowns. And make sure you take plenty of photographs once the royal couple has been seated!

children will ever get married at all, you can really play up this dance and have fun with it.

- *Fun with photos.* Buy disposable cameras for each table with a note inviting guests to take silly photos. It's amazing what people will do when given full permission! You might even be able to create a funny wedding photo album to go along with your "serious" one.

Envisioning Your Wedding Party

Display your original *chuppah* at your reception so guests can take a closer look.

Because Jewish tradition considers celebrating with the bride and groom a holy task, don't feel that the energy you put into planning your party is in any way unimportant. Problems occur when couples put all their energy into party planning and none into thinking about their ceremony. If you have been thinking seriously about choices associated with the rituals and ritual objects that you use in your wedding, then creating a rich, vibrant reception should feel like a continuation of that process. The party that you create should carry on the *kavannah*—the sacred intention—that you put into your ceremony. The party is your time to let go, savor all the love coming your way from your friends and family, eat and dance, sing, exhale, and relax.

Your party is yours to create. It does not need to be a cookie-cutter copy of what anyone expects a wedding party to be. The following visualization exercise can help you think about the best way for you and your partner to create your authentic celebration. Sit back, take out your journals, and read the following questions to each other. As with all of the visualization exercises, take as much time as you need to respond, and wait until you've both finished answering all the questions to share your answers.

> You enter your wedding party as two beloved companions, committed to each other. What music do you hear welcoming and celebrating you?

Surrounding you are the most important people in your life—family and friends, both old and new. How and where are they sitting? In open formations? At long or round tables? Whom do you sit with?

Your loved ones want to honor you with toasts and blessings. Whom do you imagine offering toasts to your marriage?

Amazing aromas of sumptuous food waft through the air. What special food is being served at your party?

Music is playing as people begin to eat. As they finish, chairs are pushed away and people begin dancing. What kind of music do you hear?

Look around the room at your wedding party. What touches, what details, make the party room or outdoor area warm and inviting and uniquely expressive of who you are?

It is the middle of your party; your guests are having a fantastic time. Feel the energy in the room. How would you describe the feeling?

Listen to each other's ideas and see what you come up with. Remember that your party should reflect both of your needs, both of your visions.

Set up your reception in any number of ways: with beautiful centerpieces on the tables, extra *kippot* for your guests, and your *ketubah* available for everyone to read.

Family Dynamics and Your Wedding Party

Nothing can drain the fun out of your wedding party faster than guests who are unhappy with the seating arrangements. Especially at large weddings, where feuding family members may be encountering one another for the first time in years, there is tremendous pressure for the bride and groom to come up with the perfect seating assignments for their wedding reception. Even when family members get along, they can still act petty and complain to you about not getting seated at a "high-status" table.

One way to avoid this kind of nonsense is to do away with seating cards altogether and simply create open seating. This allows your guests to self-select who they want to sit with and it leaves you with fewer headaches. Long tables with chairs on both sides work best for this kind of seating arrangement. Your guests can sit at one end for dinner and then move to another location for coffee and cake. Your guests will fall into natural clusters and probably will meet and mingle with more folks than they would have otherwise.

As you think about your reception, also be sure to consider ways of including both of your families in giving toasts, participating in dances, and other honorary roles. It can be a delicate balance for some couples when one partner has a larger family or when one family is more gregarious than the other one. Talk to your family up front and find out what their comfort level is. If one or both of your parents is really nervous about speaking in front of a crowd, there is no reason you can't invite a brother or sister to give a toast instead.

The more your families have had the opportunity to get to know each other before the wedding, the easier it should be for everyone to relax and mingle at the reception. But if your families prefer to keep to themselves, that should not be your concern. We don't choose our families, and all of us have some eccentric relatives. If Uncle Harry has a few too many cocktails or cousin Sarah refuses to be in family photos, let it go; their behavior is outside your control and is not your responsibility. Create the party you want and include opportunities for your families to participate and celebrate. When the time for your reception comes, let go and enjoy the moment.

chapter eight

Something Oldish, Something Newish, Something Borrowed, Something Jewish

More Ritual Objects, Décor, and Clothing Ideas for Your Wedding

We've gone over all of the bigger issues you need to consider in designing your creative Jewish wedding. But beyond the big stuff, paying attention to some of the smaller details can help you create a more personal, meaningful wedding. The careful thought that you put into the *kippot* for your guests, the *kiddush* cups that you drink from under the *chuppah*, and other such decisions will all contribute to creating the wedding you desire.

This chapter also looks at one of the most important Jewish *mitzvot* connected to any major life-cycle event—performing acts of *tzedakah* (charity)—and illustrates a number of ways to make *tzedakah* an organic part of your wedding experience.

The chapter title comes from the idea that these extra touches will make your wedding that much more special. You may go digging around for a family heirloom—that's something old. You might come up with an innovative way to decorate your *kippot*—that's something new. You may choose to wear a piece of clothing or jewelry from a relative, living or deceased—that's something borrowed. And all your decisions related to your wedding planning can be influenced by your Jewish connections.

Enhance Your Wedding with Surprising Finds

As you plan your wedding, keep your eyes and mind open to small things that might add great meaning to your nuptials. When I was home visiting my parents one weekend and doing some wedding preparation with my mother (my wedding was held in my hometown), she brought out something I had never seen before: the small, faded, black, leather-bound Hebrew Bible that she carried on her wedding day. My mom brought over her wedding photo and pointed out how her bridal bouquet rested on top of it. The Bible, she told me, had been a gift that she received from her rabbi upon her confirmation. "You can have it if you want," she said offhandedly.

I picked it up and held it. I looked at her picture and felt a new connection to her. My mother and I look a lot alike; I look now almost exactly the way she did in her wedding picture. It was a little bit eerie to look at her and recognize so clearly how time passes. "I would love to carry your Bible, Mom," I said, and we put it away so we could take it along to show the florist the next day.

Later the next day, when we returned home from the florist, my father poked his nose into my bedroom with another small, faded, black leather-bound book. I opened it up and looked at the Hebrew letters. It was a *siddur* (prayer book) that had belonged to his father, and his father before that. My middle name, Shulamit, was chosen in memory of that great-grandfather, Solomon. "This is beautiful," I said, looking at my Dad's smiling face. Who knew my parents had all these little holy books tucked away all over the house? I decided to carry both my great-grandfather's *siddur* and my mother's Bible under my flowers as I walked down the aisle to the *chuppah* to meet my husband.

It turned out to be a wonderful decision. Holding those two little books in my hands helped me feel grounded during the ceremony and connected to my parents in a way that no one but us knew about. When I originally thought about my bouquet, I never would have thought of it resting on anything, let alone those books.

Wonderful treasures may be all around you, waiting for you to notice them. Those treasures may enhance your wedding experience in surprising ways.

Ritual Objects Associated with the Ceremony

In Jewish tradition, material objects are transformed into sacred objects when created with *hiddur mitzvah* in mind. For example, a *kippah*, when used for a ritual purpose, is no longer a piece of fabric but is transformed into an object of holiness. Have fun adding your own creative flourishes to these objects as a way to enhance your wedding ceremony.

Tennaim Plate

The ritual of making *tennaim* (agreements) is traditionally sealed with the breaking of a plate. The ritual can take place well in advance of the wedding or on the wedding day, just before the ceremony. Even though the plate that you use will be smashed on the floor, it could hold special significance. Some couples make a plate together at a "paint your own pottery" shop to use as their ritual *tennaim* plate. You can save the broken pieces (most likely it won't smash into shards) and keep them in a bag in your china closet or some other special place where you can dig them up from time to time and think about your agreements. You might also think about using them to create a mosaic.

Kippot

At most Jewish weddings, *kippot* (also commonly known by their Yiddish name, *yarmulkes*) are provided for guests to wear. In traditional communities only men cover their heads with a *kippah*, while lace doilies are often provided for women to wear. Wearing a *kippah* is a way of showing humility and respect for God. In Conservative and Orthodox synagogues, men are required to wear *kippot*, while most Reform and Reconstructionist congregations make *kippah* wearing optional. In many egalitarian communities, both men and women may elect to wear *kippot*. For an occasion such as a wedding, it is common to mass-order satin *kippot*, usually in a color to match flowers or other wedding colors, and have them imprinted with the couple's name and wedding date.

An original women's *kippah*

If you are interested in doing something unusual with your *kipppot*, here are a few ideas:

- *Crocheting:* Although this project could be way too time-consuming for the novice, it may be a breeze for someone experienced in crocheting. For example, if you have an aunt who loves to crochet and wants to help you with your wedding, here is a wonderful job for her. Pick out yarn in colors you like and determine approximately how many *kippot* you need (depending on whether women will be wearing them too). I know one couple who made crocheting wedding *kippot* into a special family project: Both mothers pitched in, and the couple, who had never crocheted before, did too. They would crochet in the evenings, while watching TV, and had a nice batch done before they knew it.

- *Fabric paints and markers:* Here's another fun project for a creative friend. Buy a nice assortment of fabric paints and markers and add some color flourishes to the normally solid satin or cotton *kippot*. For my wedding, my friend Maxine, a fantastic artist, used a Jackson Pollack–style approach and dropped paint in assorted colors onto our *kippot*. The result was amazing: The lavender, purple, yellow, and blue paint spatters on the *kippot* looked like a floral crown over our guests' heads.

- *Stamps and stencils:* If you want a specifically Jewish design or symbol on your *kippot*, use a rubber stamp or stencil to achieve that effect. Jewish stamps and stencils are available from specialty Judaica craft stores.

Kiddush Cups

The *kiddush* is one of the most central blessings in Jewish tradition, and it holds a prominent place in the Jewish wedding ceremony. Once the blessing is recited over a raised glass of wine, the bride and groom take a drink from it. In Jewish tradition, the *kiddush* cup has been an object of great adornment and craftsmanship. *Kiddush* cups are one of the most common pieces of Judaica found in a Jewish home; even families who consider themselves to be secular may have a *kiddush* cup or two tucked away in their cupboard. Any basic *kiddush* cup will do for your wedding ceremony, but with a little thought—and some digging—you can plan to use a cup or cups with special meaning.

Many couples like to have *kiddush* cups from both sides of the family under the *chuppah*, one to be used for each time the blessing is recited. It is another symbolic way of acknowledging the wedding as a joining of two families as well as two individuals. As you're deciding which *kiddush* cups to use, consider the following questions:

Beautiful silver heirloom *kiddush* cups on the table under the *chuppah*

> Do your parents still have the *kiddush* cup they used at their wedding? What about your grandparents?
>
> Is there a *kiddush* cup that was regularly used by a beloved family member who has passed away? Would placing that *kiddush* cup with you under the *chuppah* help invoke their presence?
>
> Do you have a *kiddush* cup that has been significant in your life—one that was given to you as a bar or bat mitzvah present, for example?
>
> Have you received any special *kiddush* cups as engagement or early wedding presents?
>
> If you and your partner observe Shabbat, is there a regular *kiddush* cup that reminds you of your Shabbat rituals together?

You may want to have a *kiddush* cup engraved with your names and wedding date in advance of the wedding or go to a "paint your own pottery" shop and make a special *kiddush* cup together for your wedding ceremony.

Broken Glass

A lovely custom has evolved into part of Jewish wedding culture over the past years: saving the pieces of the wine glass that is broken in your ceremony and incorporating the broken pieces into a new piece of Judaica, such as a *mezuzah*, a *kiddush* cup, or candlesticks. See Appendix I for places that will help you do this with your broken glass.

If you are feeling creative, you might come up with your own design for your glass pieces. Think about working them into a mosaic, a picture frame design, or something else.

Tablecloths/Coverlets

As noted in chapter 4 on *chuppot*, some couples are choosing to create a matching or complementary coverlet for the small table under the *chuppah* where the *kiddush* cups, wine, and other items for the ceremony are usually placed. The coverlet could be a piece of fabric complementing the color of the *chuppah*, or it could feature its own unique design elements. It might be embroidered with the names of the couple and the date of the wedding or be pieced together from heirloom fabric from both sides of the family. If someone close to you (and handy) asks to make something special for your ceremony, but your *chuppah* is already taken care of, you might give them the honor of making a coverlet for the table.

Infusing Other Wedding Items with Jewish Meaning

There are a number of objects and customs associated with contemporary weddings (ceremony, party, and beyond) that are not necessarily Jewish in origin or tradition. Nonetheless, with a little thought and planning they can be infused with Jewish significance.

Welcome Bags

It is customary to welcome out-of-town guests to a wedding with a small welcome bag that will greet them when they arrive at their hotel room. Welcome bags usually include a short note from the bride and groom and/or their parents (photocopying the note is just fine!) listing the schedule of events for the weekend and any other information that out-of-town guests might need: where to grab a bite to eat, local tourist attractions, and so on. Besides the note, it's nice to include a small welcome gift—maybe a food item or two native to the area, some fresh fruit, a map, or small craft items made locally.

If your out-of-town guests will be arriving on a Friday afternoon, you might want to make a little Shabbat kit for your Jewish guests: provide them with a small bottle of grape juice (or kosher wine), a small challah, a pair of candlesticks, candles, and matches. At most synagogue gift shops and Judaica shops, you can find little silver foil candleholders that work just fine in a hotel room. Your guests who observe Shabbat will feel especially welcomed, and those who are not observant may feel encouraged to light the candles and say some blessings!

Remember: If your guests keep kosher, make sure that any packaged food item you choose for your welcome bags contains a kosher symbol and that any baked goods come from a kosher bakery. Fruit and vegetables are fine as they are.

Gifts for Parents

It is customary to give both sets of parents a special gift as a way of thanking them for helping you plan or host your wedding. Especially thoughtful might be a gift of Judaica that they don't have and would enjoy. Look at the sophisticated range of work by Judaica artists today and think about what they might appreciate: a colorful Seder plate, a new *mezuzah*, or a beautiful lithograph by a Jewish artist. Your parents will be touched by your gesture. Make a special time before the craziness of the wedding festivities begin to give them your gift, along with a personal note of thanks and reflection.

Centerpieces and Decorations

As you plan the centerpieces and decorations for your wedding reception, you might consider how the timing of your wedding fits into the Jewish yearly cycle of holidays and festivals. If your wedding falls close to a holiday, think about how your decorative choices could bring out the holiday theme. For example, when friends of ours got married during Hanukkah, they placed a beautiful *hanukiah* (the *menorah* used during Hanukkah) in the center of each table. Around each *hanukiah* were eight small bowls of floating roses representing the eight days of Hanukkah. It was a beautiful touch, and functional, too: During the reception, the lights were dimmed and we sang the Hanukkah blessings. Then someone from each table lit their *hanukiah* and the room was filled with marvelous candlelight.

Here is a list of the major Jewish holidays and some ideas to tie your décor to a holiday theme. Note: Holidays such as Rosh Hashanah and Yom Kippur, when Jewish weddings are prohibited, are not included.

> *Sukkot (weddings allowed on the intermediate days):* Sukkot is the Jewish celebration of harvest and thanksgiving, a time to be grateful and joyous for autumn's abundance. It generally falls around the secular month of October. If your wedding is taking place during this time of celebration, there are lots of easy ways to bring out its themes in your décor. Think grape vines, palm leaves, centerpieces incorporating colored leaves, and cornucopias. Bowls of fresh seasonal fruit, including pomegranates and pears, as well as autumn objects, such as dried gourds and miniature pumpkins, will enhance the effects. Rich autumn colors for your tablecloths and other linens—purples, reds, greens, and gold—add a lovely seasonal accent. If your wedding reception is being held indoors, try to bring the experience and atmosphere of eating outside in a *sukkah* inside. During the holiday it is a *mitzvah* to eat in the *sukkah*, a small hut with an open roof covered with leaves or

branches. People decorate their Sukkot with all kinds of hanging fruit and gourds, colorful tapestries, and hanging lights. For your party, think about stringing lights or hanging lanterns indoors for an added effect.

Hanukkah: If your wedding takes place during Hanukkah (which falls during December), make lighting a highlight of your décor. Spiritual light—as symbolized by the story of the oil to light the Temple *menorah*, which lasted for eight days—is a central theme of the holiday and a powerful, resounding theme throughout Jewish tradition. While *hanukiyot* make beautiful centerpieces you could also use them in other ways. Why not invite your guests to bring their own *hanukiyot* to the reception and create a table (lined with aluminum foil, of course) where they can be displayed and lit? The colors usually associated with Hanukkah are blue and white; playing with some variations could give you a broader palette to choose from. Consider mixing in silver or gold linens with different shades of blue. Include a *latke* bar at your reception, where your guests can taste traditional potato pancakes along with a variety of innovative *latkes*, such as sweet potato or carrot-zucchini *latkes*.

Tu B'Shvat: Falling in January or February, this "Jewish Arbor Day," the New Year of the Trees, has taken on special significance in every generation. Tu B'Shvat is viewed by many contemporary Jews as a sort of Jewish Earth Day, a time to focus on Jewish teachings about ecology and the environment. If your wedding falls close to Tu B'Shvat, you can easily incorporate connections to Israel, trees, or nature in general into your décor and design. Each table might have a small tree as a centerpiece—think diminutive bonsai trees. Place on the tables small glass bowls containing some of the common foods associated with Tu B'Shvat—carob, almonds, raisins, figs, dates, olives—as little noshes before the meal is served. Your place cards could be printed on recycled or handmade paper in honor of trees.

Purim: What more fun time to get married than on or near Purim (in late February or March)? Although a minor Jewish holiday, Purim holds a special place in the hearts of young and old alike. A time of masks, masquerades, and magic, Purim offers all sorts of imaginative tie-ins for wedding décor. Imagine your guests finding their seating assignment tucked into a plastic mask or *gragger* (noisemaker)? Picture a bowl of *hamentaschen*—the traditional Purim pastry—surrounded by colorful flowers and candles as your table centerpieces. You could invite your guests to come in costume and host a costume parade during the merrymaking part of your reception. This is a time when a *badchan* can go all out, toasting and roasting the couple (and their guests). Jugglers and musicians could hop from table to table, entertaining your guests.

Lag B'Omer: Generally in May, this is one of the few days when weddings are allowed to take place during the counting of the Omer between Passover and Shavuot. Lag B'Omer is a joyous day, celebrated with bonfires, archery matches, and other outdoor activities. Falling during a popular time for weddings, Lag B'Omer would be an auspicious wedding date if you were planning an outdoor ceremony and/or reception. Think picnics, barbecues, horseshoes, croquet, archery, Frisbee, softball, or other outdoor activities that your guests might enjoy.

Yom Ha'atzmaut (Note: Some rabbis allow weddings to take place on this day, while others do not): A wedding on or near Israeli Independence Day (generally falling in May) naturally lends itself to a celebration of Israeli culture. You could make Israeli products an integral part of your reception. Each table could have bottles of Israeli wine, inscribed with your names and the wedding date. Bowls of Israeli chocolates and nuts could grace your tables. Bring in an Israeli dance teacher to instruct your guests in some dance moves. Israeli dance is not just folk dancing anymore; it also incorporates funk and hip-hop moves.

Rosh Hodesh: If your wedding is taking place on or close to this monthly celebration of the New Moon, you might want to include images of the moon in your décor. Think silver shimmers—sparkling tablecloths and confetti and bowls of water filled with floating silver candles. Create place cards with a moon design and include a blessing for the New Moon on each table. Make up a poster for your guests to sign, asking them to predict where the two of you will be at the next New Moon and the other New Moons that will fall during your first married year.

Take-Home Favors

What wedding is complete without a little something for your guests to take home to remember your special day? Common favors include small boxes of chocolates or other sweets, miniature bottles of wine, or handmade crafts. When you are thinking about your wedding favors, consider purchasing products from Israel. The current intifada has had far-reaching effects on the Israeli economy, and purchasing Israeli products helps fill the gap that lagging tourism has created. Whatever your politics, a healthy Israeli economy will help all the people there. Purchasing Israeli products in conjunction with your wedding is a way of showing support for the Jewish community there.

Another idea for wedding favors dovetails with the previous section about tying your wedding to the closest Jewish year-cycle event: Imagine sending guests home with beautiful, hand-painted *graggers* for a Purim wedding, a bag of wildflower seeds to plant for a Tu B'Shvat wedding, or a *havdalah* candle for a

Showering Your Wedding Party with Gifts

It's traditional to give the folks in your wedding party a gift of some sort as a thank you for their participation in your wedding. However, these gifts can add up to another large expense if you have selected a large number of attendants.

You might want to think about creating a unique handmade gift for your attendants. Even if you're not a super artsy-craftsy person, these ideas are easy enough to allow everyone to create a special gift that will be much appreciated:

- *Create a photo frame.* You can buy unfinished picture frames at any craft store. Add jewels, paint, ribbon, or other accessories to create an original frame. Send your attendants a wedding picture to add to the frame so they can always remember being part of your big day.

- *Paint some pottery.* Don't consider yourself an artist? No problem. Most metropolitan areas, and plenty of small towns, now feature "paint your own pottery" studios, where you can buy all sorts of ceramic items from jewelry boxes to coffee mugs, flower vases to water pitchers, and paint to your liking. It's pretty hard to mess up here, and your friends will appreciate your effort and unique contribution.

- *Use your talents.* Why do gifts have to be traditional? Give your friends "gift certificates" redeemable for a special service that utilizes your unique skills. Computer help, landscaping, making a gourmet meal—anything goes!

- *Select a fine book.* Make a list of your friends' interests and take a trip to a rare or antique book collector's shop, where you can often find costly books at bargain prices. Choose something that would be especially meaningful to each member of your wedding party, and inscribe the book with a personal thank you. Because you took the time to find a book that would not necessarily be on the shelves of Borders or Barnes & Noble, this gesture will be appreciated.

Saturday night wedding that included a *havdalah* ceremony. Research the customs and ceremonial objects associated with the closest holiday and see what you come up with. Your non-Jewish guests will enjoy these unusual items, too.

One of the best wedding favors that I ever heard of was created by Yohanna Kinberg and Seth Goldstein, who made *tzedakah* boxes for their guests to take home. *Tzedakah* boxes are containers, traditional in a Jewish home, in which the family regularly puts coins to go toward a charity of their choosing. Many Jewish families put coins in their *tzedakah* boxes just before lighting Shabbat candles.

Seth and Yohanna bought plain aluminum cans that could be used for kids' banks with a slit in the top for coins. They printed up labels with their name and wedding date and pasted them onto the cans. Seth and Yohanna asked their guests to collect coins in their *tzedakah* boxes until they were full, and then make a donation in their honor (they specified a few of their favorite charities). Seth and Yohanna said it was really nice to see the *tzedakah* boxes prominently displayed—and obviously being used—when they would visit friends and family. If you like this idea, consider making beautiful labels or decorating your *tzedakah* boxes in a festive way, reminiscent of your wedding.

The Ritual of Wedding Dress

Think of choosing your wedding clothes as part of the sacred ritual of creating your wedding. Just as you put careful thought into such matters as what you will say during your ceremony and what your guests will eat, bring a focused awareness to the process of selecting your clothing. As you browse and shop, keep in mind that what you choose to wear should be an external reflection of your inner beauty. Your wedding outfit can be as unique as you are. Don't let the wedding industry bully you into thinking that you have to look a certain way to be a gorgeous bride or a handsome groom. Open your mind, and let yourself find the right wedding clothes to bring out the royal you.

Coming from a theater background, I love the ritual of dressing up for special occasions. Just as putting on a costume can help an actor get into character, the act of putting on a particular kind of clothing can help you make the mental shift to taking on a certain role. Changing into a sharp-looking suit before a job interview, for example, can give you a sense of confidence and poise.

As you think about how you want to dress for your wedding, remember the Jewish image of royalty: this is your day to play king and queen (or queen and queen, as the case may be!). You want to choose a dress or suit that makes you feel spectacular. In American culture today, there is a nice range of wedding dress styles and colors and many choices for men in terms of suit selection. Although white is still the most common choice for a bridal gown, plenty of women are stepping out and choosing dresses (and even pantsuits) in other colors.

In Jewish tradition, white is more a symbol of spiritual purity than it is of virginity. One important wedding dress custom to consider is that of wearing a *kittel*. A *kittel* is a simple white robe that traditional Jews also wear on Yom Kippur, considered to be the holiest day of the year. It is the garment that Jews for generations have been buried in. Its simplicity represents the soul's purity and a letting go of earthly matters. The wedding day has certain parallels to Yom Kippur: fasting is a traditional ritual on both days to help focus one's thoughts on spiritual rather than physical matters. On Yom Kippur, we are said to stand before God and seek atonement for our wrongdoings. On our wedding day, it is said that we stand under the *chuppah* and have direct access to God, to share all our hopes and dreams. Because a Jewish wedding is about making a covenant and commitment with a life partner before God and community, the tradition of wearing a *kittel* for the ceremony can help you fully absorb the seriousness of the moment.

Traditionally, a *kittel* was worn only by men, but in some egalitarian circles today, brides also choose to don a *kittel* for the wedding ceremony. Because it is only worn during the ceremony, guests still get to see your dress or suit during all the other festivities. In deciding whether or not to wear a *kittel*, consider whether it is going to help you feel more spiritually pure and connected when you stand under the *chuppah*.

One word of warning: make sure you know which *kittel* belongs to each of you. When Jane Berman and Adam Diamond got married, they both chose to wear a *kittel*. Unfortunately, their *kittels* got mixed up just before the ceremony, so Jane was swimming in Adam's *kittel*, while Adam was squeezed into Jane's much

This bride and groom chose to wear *kittels* over their clothes for their wedding ceremony.

smaller *kittel*. To avoid such a problem, you might want to put your initials inside your *kittel* in an unobtrusive place.

Traditional Jews also consider the value of *tzniut*—modesty—when thinking about dress. Orthodox brides wear dresses that cover the neckline, and possibly the wrists and ankles. Fortunately, there are many designers today creating great-looking dresses that fall within these guidelines.

As you are thinking about your wedding dress, you also need to consider what kind of head covering to wear. For women, a wedding veil was not only customary but also an important ritual item used in the *bedecken*. Your wedding day is probably the only time in your life that you will have the opportunity to wear a veil. For some feminists, a veil has negative connotations of patriarchy and control of women. But many other women are reclaiming the veil as a woman's symbol of privacy and beauty. If you are not interested in wearing a traditional veil, there are lots of possibilities for alternative-style *bedecken* rituals (see chapter 6). You may want to try on some wedding veils in a dress shop or borrow one from your mother, sister, or friend before you make your final decision.

Women who do not choose to wear a veil might consider wearing a beautiful *kippah* as a symbol of holiness. There are lots of styles of *kippot* today that are specifically designed for women (see Appendix I for ordering information).

Men do not have to be relegated to the standard satin *kippah* so commonly found in American synagogues. Not only do contemporary *kippot* come in a range of fabrics, from suede to velvet, but they also come in a range of styles. The *kippot* created and worn by Bukharan Jews, for example, stand upright like a beenie rather than flat and come in a range of bright colors.

Women from Sephardic backgrounds might want to wear a wedding dress representative of their heritage. When Yohanna Kinberg was planning her wedding, she researched Moroccan wedding clothing and was pleased to discover that white wedding dresses were not part of the tradition. "In Morocco, white is considered to be a symbol of death," she explains. "Moroccan brides wear more vibrant colors, like reds and golds." Not finding a wedding dress that captured the Moroccan flair, Yohanna ended up having a bridal outfit made for her: a red dress with a matching brocade coat. "It felt really important to me to wear something that felt authentic," she said.

Consider the way that your wedding apparel fits into the overall style and approach of your wedding. A dress for an outdoor picnic wedding would be different than what you might wear for a more formal affair. And although you and your partner may choose not to see each other's outfits before the big day, you could talk to each other in generalities about overall style so that you are both thinking along the same lines.

Kippot are available in many different styles, colors, and fabrics.

Incorporating *Tzedakah* into Your Wedding

One of the loveliest aspects of Jewish tradition is that even at our most joyous moments—the happiest times in our lives—we are asked to look beyond ourselves and think about our relationship to humanity and the larger world. Giving *tzedakah* (which literally means "justice") is one way of performing *tikkun olam*, repair of the world. In years gone by, weddings would naturally be an occasion to help the poor—wedding feasts were open to the entire community and it was customary to make sure that the poor were given a seat and able to enjoy the food and festivities. Today, it takes more conscious effort to incorporate the Jewish *mitzvah* to help the poor and the stranger in our midst.

In your wedding planning, think about the charitable organizations that are most meaningful to you and brainstorm ways you could use your wedding as an occasion to help their good works. A few suggestions:

> *Creative centerpieces:* Instead of spending money on floral arrangements, you could use beautiful potted plants and baskets that could then be donated to a women's shelter, nursing home, or hospital. You could also eliminate centerpieces altogether and write up a small card in the center of your tables letting your guests know that the money that would

have been spent on flower arrangements was instead donated to the charity of your choice.

Collect canned goods: Suppose you were having two hundred wedding guests and each of them brought two cans of food to your wedding? That amounts to a healthy donation to a local food pantry. Canned foods are neat enough and easy enough to carry, even to a formal occasion; just place clearly marked drop-off boxes near where guests will enter. Let out-of-town guests know where the market or convenience store closest to their hotel is. Even if only half your guests bring the canned goods you request, you still will have a nice donation. Arrange for a friend to take the food from your wedding site to a food bank so that you and your partner don't need to deal with it on your big day.

Donate leftovers: The likelihood is that you will have huge amounts of food left over from your wedding reception. Many cities have agencies that will pick up leftover food to take to homeless shelters. Call a local shelter in advance and see whether they know who to contact. Again, select a friend to be a point person so you don't have to worry about that detail after your reception.

Let your guests know that a contribution is just fine: Many couples, especially if they have been previously married and already have a well-stocked kitchen, lovely china, and a household full of precious items, prefer to have their guests make a contribution to charity in lieu of a traditional wedding gift. You can make note of this preference in a small line on your invitation, on your wedding website (see Appendix II), or on any other mailing that your guests will receive. Many people will still bring you gifts, but some will bring a small gift and make a donation as well. Younger couples, who often need the "stuff" of wedding gifts (and rightly so), can still create a page on their website letting guests know which are their favorite charities. That way, people who choose to make a contribution in your honor will know which organizations would be most meaningful to you. You can write a short sentence or two explaining your choices, for example:

We would be most honored if you choose to make a donation in our names in honor of the *simcha* of our marriage. Some charities that are important to us include:

The American Cancer Society, www.cancer.org, P.O. Box 22718, Oklahoma City, OK 73123-1718. As you know, David's grandmother died of ovarian cancer last year. A contribution to the American Cancer Society would honor us—and honor her memory.

Mazon, www.mazon.org, 1990 S. Bundy Drive, Ste. 260, Los Angeles, CA 90025-5232. We will be contributing three percent of what we spend on our wedding costs to Mazon, a Jewish organization fighting hunger. We would be honored if you joined us in this important effort.

The ASPCA, www.aspca.org, 424 E. 92nd Street, New York, NY 10128-6804. We are both huge animal lovers (we will have a total of five cats when we combine households!), and the ASPCA is a very important charity to us.

See—nothing fancy, just the basics and a little note about the significance of the charity. Some guests do not like to give donations because they feel these kinds of gifts are impersonal, but if they understand your connection to the organization, they are more likely to make a charitable donation because it means something to you.

A donation in honor of your rabbi and/or synagogue: If you belong to a synagogue and the rabbi from your congregation will be marrying you, it is usually meaningful to the rabbi if you and your partner make a contribution to the synagogue's *tzedakah* fund. Because you are not paying the rabbi for his time,

Contributing to Mazon

Since 1985, Mazon has done incredible work in the world, bringing together people from all walks of the Jewish community to help in the efforts to fight hunger. Mazon provides hunger relief to agencies in the United States, Israel, and in poor countries worldwide, helping people of all backgrounds, faiths, and races. Mazon's efforts—rooted in the Jewish *mitzvah* to feed the hungry—create a bridge between the Jewish community and the rest of the world.

One of the ways that Mazon earns a percentage of its funding is through their *simcha* program, in which people are encouraged to contribute three percent of the food costs for their happy event—bar/bat mitzvah, naming ceremony, graduation party, or wedding—to Mazon.

Giving money for people in need is not only an important *mitzvah*, but it can also give added depth and meaning to your wedding celebration. Mazon provides place cards that explain the donation being made so all your guests can learn more about this important organization.

If you plan the contribution ahead of time, it won't take you by surprise later on. Compare that three percent to the amount of money you are spending on other wedding-related items—flowers, dresses, music, and so on.

Although the amount may not be significant when compared to your entire wedding budget, it is significant when you consider how many hungry people can be helped when everyone gets in the habit of giving that three percent.

For more information on Mazon, contact the organization at:

www.mazon.org
(310) 442–0020
1990 S. Bundy Drive
Suite 260
Los Angeles, CA 90025-5232

a donation to the synagogue (whatever size you feel is appropriate) is a wonderful way to show your gratitude for his work. You could give a monetary donation or buy something that you know the synagogue needs (some prayer books, for example). If your rabbi is not affiliated with a synagogue, you might ask her whether she has particular charities that are meaningful to her, and then surprise her with a donation in her honor.

Visit elderly or infirm relatives who cannot attend your ceremony: This act falls more into the category of *gemilut Chasidim,* acts of lovingkindness. One or both partners may have a grandparent, great-grandparent, or other dear relative in a nursing home who is unable to attend your ceremony. Go to the nursing home dressed in your wedding clothes so that she can see you. It certainly doesn't need to be on your wedding day: It could be in the weeks (or months) before or after. Just seeing you in your wedding clothes will make her feel part of your wedding celebration.

Sign up for the I Do Foundation: By signing up with this organization, you can create a wedding gift registry that will donate up to 10 percent of any item that is purchased on the registry to your favorite charity. Also, if you book honeymoon travel plans through I Do, 3 percent of your travel expenses will be donated to charity as well. For more information, check out www.idofoundation.org.

chapter nine

Have It Your Way

Final Advice for Creating the Wedding You Desire

You've read. You've studied. You've discussed, disagreed, visualized, and contemplated. Creating your wedding is a lot of work, but if you stay connected and grounded, and keep in mind the reasons that you are putting energy into this effort, the work can be most rewarding.

Here are a few more ideas to help you create the wedding of your dreams and deepen your commitment as a couple in the process.

Wedding-Planning Goals

As you plan your wedding, it is easy to slip into the "Must get things done!" frame of mind and lose sight of why you are creating a wedding in the first place. To keep yourself focused, I urge you to set aside some time alone, at the beginning of the wedding-planning process, to write up a checklist of your goals—how you hope to grow and what you want to learn from creating your wedding. In making this checklist, think about your goals in terms of how you relate to your partner, parents, siblings, and future in-laws. Think about how you relate to being Jewish, how you relate or do not relate to God. This spiritual checklist—jotted down in your wedding journal—should be able to put you back on track in moments of stress or doubt.

Write the items on your spiritual checklist in informal, clear language that makes sense to you. Some examples might include:

- I am going to be patient when dealing with my sisters.

- I promise to make sure my sweetie and I talk about things other than wedding plans and do something fun, such as go to a movie or a club, when we get too obsessed with planning our wedding.

- I will read at least one new book about Judaism, so I can understand my history and traditions a little bit more.

- I want to be as relaxed as possible on my wedding day and will connect with as many people there as I can.

You might find yourself adding new items or crossing out old ones as your wedding planning goes along. Remember that with all your "to-dos," you need to set aside time to relax and replenish yourself. Stressing out over details is not going to get anything done more quickly or easily.

When you are attuned to your goals on a spiritual level, you are creating more than a wedding—you are setting the groundwork for a calm, loving, sacred home and relationship. Your wedding marks the beginning; each day thereafter continues the journey.

Visualization

Use the visualization exercises in this book time and again to help you envision your ideal wedding. The clearer the picture you can create in your mind's eye, the better you will be able to articulate your wishes to everyone—your partner, rabbi, musicians, floral designer, and caterer. Don't hold back in your visions: See everything as vividly and concretely as you can. Smell the scents; listen to the sounds. Visualization is about bringing out your intuitive side. Sometimes we tend to let our practical side intimidate our intuitive side. We believe, for example, that if we are on a fixed budget, we can only visualize "so big." Nonsense! Dream big and then journal what you see. Holding a picture in your mind's eye can help you make your vision a reality. Someone may just show up and offer you a gift that will ease your budgetary concerns. You may suddenly discover the kind of musician you were dreaming about. A friend might sketch just the right design for your invitation or wedding program cover.

Affirmations

Creating an affirmation to repeat to yourself is a wonderful way to start thinking positively about anything that is potentially stressful. Creating a wedding, while full of joy, learning, and growth, can trigger plenty of stress as well. Write an affirmation, in the present tense, that you can repeat over and over when stress starts to surface. Soon you will internalize your affirmation.

Sample Affirmations

- We create our wedding in just the right way for us.

- The resources we need to create our wedding are here and available to us.

- Only love comes to my beloved and me.

Play around with your affirmation language. It can be personal and private, and it doesn't need to be shared with anyone else. This is your wedding—create it well!

Final Thoughts

Jewish tradition offers you a wealth of ways to express the nuances of your relationship through both wedding rituals and the important objects used in those rituals. Even if you feel alienated from Judaism, your wedding is a fresh opportunity to reconnect. When you decide to create a meaningful Jewish wedding, you are opening yourself up to the possibility of connecting Jewishly in a new way. By considering the words in your *ketubah*, the art of your *chuppah*, the music in your ceremony, and other such creative choices depicted in this book, you are bringing a sacred awareness and *kavannah* to your wedding.

I have no doubt that the efforts you put in now as you plan your wedding will pay off a millionfold when you stand under the *chuppah* with your beloved partner. To be fully present, to be able to take in the love around you, and to bask in the rewards of opening yourself up to the treasures and wisdom of your rich heritage—these are all great gifts. Each creative Jewish wedding adds depth and meaning to Judaism's understanding of what a wedding signifies and what it can be. From a larger perspective, Judaism needs all our creative energy not only to survive but also to thrive. Each couple who infuses tradition with personal meaning helps make our religion healthier and more viable for all Jews.

As you read these suggestions and advice, remember that you should take on only the projects that feel right to you. Be gentle and patient with yourself, with your partner, and with your families. For all the work that you put in, your wedding will be over in a snap. My hope for you is that the very process of creating your wedding will help you and your partner connect more deeply to each other, to your family and friends, to your Jewish heritage and community, and to your own spirituality.

The process of growing to love and understand each other more deeply will continue every single day for the rest of your life. The process of learning to negotiate your differences and to disagree respectfully will likewise take a lifetime. And what an amazing blessing that you have found a partner who will stick by you for that journey, someone who is making a commitment to love you each day, as you learn better and better how to love and support each other.

Appendix I
Books and Online Resources

Whether you are planning your wedding from a large city or a small town, you can use resources in books and on the Internet to help in your efforts. The Internet offers fantastic resources for Jewish wedding planning. The following guide can help you find the resources you need to create the wedding of your dreams.

Websites

Jewish Weddings, General

www.ritualwell.org: This inspiring website provides resources for creating innovative, contemporary Jewish rituals, for weddings as well as for all kinds of life-cycle rituals and holidays. Highly recommended!

www.jewishweddingfindit.com: A national directory of Jewish vendors.

www.jewishcelebrations.com: A Jewish wedding gift shop and helpful resources.

www.myjewishlearning.com: A helpful overview of Jewish wedding history and contemporary issues in the lifecycle and marriage section.

http://judaism.about.com/od/weddings/ss/wedding_how_2.htm: Customs and photographs detailing a traditional Jewish wedding.

www.do-it-yourself-weddings.com: Craft projects and more from a do-it-yourself perspective.

Weddings, General

www.theknot.com: This helpful site contains articles about wedding traditions, innovative ideas, and stories from recently married couples.

www.foreverwed.com: This site links to wedding vendors across the country.

www.weddings-online.com: A general showcase of wedding-related products.

www.consciousweddings.com: Offers helpful ways for brides and their families to deal with the many emotions that arise during wedding planning and helps them manage their anxiety and tension.

www.indiebride.com: A great site for the independent-minded bride (grooms may appreciate it, too!).

www.weddings.ivillage.com: Daily tips, message boards and helpful articles for wedding planning.

www.budgetdreamweddings.com: Wedding planning with an eye towards saving.

www.realsimple.com/realsimple/package/0,21861,1737779,00.html: Excellent wedding planner from *Real Simple* magazine.

Green Weddings

www.greatgreenwedding.com: Excellent ideas and resources to
   make your wedding green.

www.treehugger.com/files/2007/02/going_to_the_gr.php: Featuring
   how-to and also important statistics about why to go green.

www.greeneleganceweddings.com/apparel.htm: More helpful ideas
   and links for green weddings.

Invitations

Many online paper companies can print Jewish wedding invitations with Hebrew
text. Some popular choices include:

www.crane.com: An excellent selection of paper choices.

www.invitations4less.com: Great selection, good savings.

If you are interested in making your own invitations and want to find unusual
paper, check out:

www.createforless.com: Great prices, awesome selection.

www.paper-source.com: Inspiring papers, envelopes, and ideas!

www.miracle-envelope.com: A creative assortment of envelope
   choices.

If you want more information about papermaking, browse through craft websites,
including:

www.fiber-images.com: Excellent overviews and ideas.

www.craftgoods.com: Papermaking recipes and resources.

If you plan to type out your text on a computer and need Hebrew software,
click onto:

www.davka.com: The home page of Davka software.

www.jewishsoftware.com: A resource for all the Jewish software on the market.

Invitations, Green and Recycled

www.sealandsend.net: Lots of recycled paper choices, no envelope needed.

www.twigandfig.com/home.html: Organic cotton paper with extremely elegant aesthetics.

www.foreverfiances.com/Unique_wedding_invitations_s/Eco_frien dly_wedding_invitations_s/36.htm: Plantable invitations, 100 percent recycled paper embedded with wildflower seeds.

www.foreverfiances.com/Unique_wedding_invitations_s/Eco_frien dly_wedding_invitations_s/36.htm: Unique, recycled paper invites for under $1.

Invitations, Hebrew text

www.invitations123.com: Lots of choices in colors and fonts.

www.irasperipheralvisions.com/jewish_wedding_invitations.htm: Good prices for custom and personalized invitations.

Ketubah Artists

At many websites that feature the work of contemporary *ketubah* artists, you can purchase lithographs or find an artist to commission for an original *ketubah*. Check out these popular sites:

www.nmajh.org

www.artketubah.com

www.ketubahtree.com

www.ketubah.com

www.ketubahworks.com

www.kolbo.com

www.modernketubah.com

www.agoodcompany.com: For interfaith couples.

www.creativity-portal.com/howto/writing/calligraphy.html: How-to resource for learning calligraphy.

www.shopketubah.com/about_ketubah_personalizing.php

www.jewishbride.com/store/ketubah.html

www.ketubahartists.com

www.ketubah-gallery.com

www.mpartworks.com

www.micahparkerartworks.com

www.ketubahcolors.com

www.pearleditions.com/ketubah_prints.html

www.ketubahstore.com

www.shabsaisart.com/ketubot/

Jewish Art

As you create your wedding, you may want to look at paintings by Jewish artists for inspiration for a *ketubah* or invitation design. You may want to purchase a print by a Jewish artist as a gift for your parents, your rabbi, or some other important person. The following resources can help you find and learn more about Jewish art:

www.jewishart.org: The American Guild of Judaic Artists home page.

www.jewish-art.org: Helpful explanations of Jewish ritual objects.

www.jewishartshop.com: Purchase prints, lithographs, Judaica,
and more.

Chuppah Artists

You may be inspired to work with a professional fabric artist specializing in Judaica to create an original *chuppah*. Some popular *chuppah* artists include:

Elsa Wachs, www.elsawachs.com

Marjorie and Eli Langner: www.originaldesignhuppah.com

Annica, www.artcreationsunlimited.com/anicca/anicca_home.html

Tasya Sherman, www.mychuppah.com/about.html

Marilyn, The Tallit Maven
http://levyjudaica.homestead.com/chuppah.html

Anita Rabinoff-Goldman, www.pomegranatejudaica.com

Corinne Soikin Strauss, www.chuppah.com

Carol Attia, www.underthechuppahonline.com

Also, pre-made *chuppot* are available at www.e-chuppah.com

Other Resources for Creating Your *Chuppah*

Embroidery

www.kolot.com: The site features basic information about Jewish embroidery, such as how to work with fabric and how to make various kinds of stitches.

Quilting

www.quiltknit.com: Features Elizabeth Rosenberg's Jewish holiday patterns, which could be easily adapted for wedding tableaus.

Tie-dye

www.ritdye.com: Helpful information on the art of tie-dyeing.

www.dharmatrading.com: More tie-dye information.

Tallitot

www.judaicartkits.com: You can purchase a kit to make your own *tallit* that could be used for your *chuppah*; comes with *tzitzit* (fringes).

Kippot

www.judaicadirect.com: This Israeli supplier brings you discounted products from Israel. Features Yemenite-style *kippot*, as well as *kippot* made out of suede, satin, and velvet.

www.a-zara.com: Another Israeli distributor; features hand-crocheted and women's *kippot*.

www.kippot.com: Custom-made *kippot* for women; handcrafted filigree with multicolored glass beads or pearls.

www.theshofarman.com: Features a nice selection of Bukharan-style *kippot*.

www.yarmulke.com: *Kippot* in many different fabrics, including moire, satin, cotton, suede, velvet, brocade, and more.

www.judaicaemb.com: This emporium of Jewish embroidery features *kippot* and other embroidered wedding products, such as *chuppot* and *tallitot*.

www.kippahking.com/philanthropic-gift.html:10 percent of profits go to Israeli charities.

www.mayaworks.org: Fair Trade Judaica objects (including *kippot*) created by Mayan artisans.

www.kulanuboutique.com/servlet/Detail?no=4: Proceeds benefit the Abayudaya community of Uganda.

Ordering Jewish Products

With a click of your mouse, you can easily order any kind of Judaica or Jewish product that you might need for your wedding—from Hebrew software to bulk-ordered *kippot*. Just search "Judaica" online.

To turn your broken wedding glass pieces into Judaica, check out:

www.judaism.com

www.judaicaspecialties.com

Jewish Music

If you are looking for a Jewish band, consult your city's local Jewish directory. But if you do not live near a Jewish music scene, you might check out these links and think about bringing in a popular Jewish wedding band.

www.klezmershack.com: This all-encompassing website for the klezmer music enthusiast includes a worldwide listing of klezmer bands.

www.Jewishweddingfindit.com: This site helps you locate a range of wedding vendors in your area, including musicians and DJ services.

www.jmwc.org: The Jewish Music Web Center offers articles, music reviews, and links to other Jewish music sites of interest.

www.jmi.org.uk: This site for Jewish Music International provides a wealth of listening and learning opportunities.

www.613.org/music/niggun.html: This website is dedicated to *niggunim* and focuses on the music of Shlomo Carlebach.

www.zamir.org: The home page for the Zamir Chorale of Boston includes excellent information and links about Jewish music.

For purchasing Jewish music, check out:

www.jewishmusic.com: Includes an online audio library, a great assortment of Jewish CDs and tapes, and a wealth of books of sheet music. Go to the weddings link under music books and you will find any music that your musicians might need.

www.etranscon.com: The website for Transcontinental Music includes musical selections from a variety of contemporary and classical Jewish recording artists. Among the best finds on this website are Transcontinental Music's sheet music and a CD for *Kol Dodi: Jewish Music for Weddings*. This collection includes Ladino love songs as well as traditional melodies.

www.hatikva.com: This website specializes in both American and Israeli recording artists. From cantorial music to Ladino and klezmer, you'll find whatever resources you need here.

Food/Wine/*Kashrut*

As you plan your wedding, you may want to research Jewish wedding food and learn more about the laws of *kashrut*. These links can also help you find kosher restaurants and caterers in your area.

www.kashrut.com: An up-to-date resource about the basics of keeping kosher, as well as a guide to kosher products.

www.kosher.co.il: An online database that includes thousands of kosher restaurants worldwide.

You may want to check out some popular kosher wineries to select wine for your wedding. From California to Israel, kosher wine is no longer limited to sweet, sticky stuff. It is now a major industry. Kosher Israeli wines include:

> www.golanwines.co.il: Home page for Golan Heights wine.

> www.carmelwines.co.il: Home page for Carmel wines.

Kosher American wines include:

> www.ganeden.com: Home page for Gan Eden wines (California-based).

> www.hagafen.com: Home page for Hagafen wines (California-based).

> www.kosher-wine.com: Home page for Abarbanel wines (New York-based).

To learn more about eco-*kashrut*:

> www.ecojew.com: This website helps explain eco-*kashrut* and other ways of integrating Judaism and ecological living.

> www.shalomctr.org: The home page for the Shalom Center includes an informative article about eco-*kashrut* by Rabbi Arthur Waskow.

Rabbis

If you and your partner do not belong to a synagogue or have a particular rabbi in mind to marry you, you might consider contacting a rabbinical school and hiring a student rabbi to officiate at your wedding:

> Hebrew Union College–Jewish Institute of Religion (Reform)
> www.huc.edu

Reconstructionist Rabbinical College (Reconstructionist)
www.rrc.edu

Jewish Theological Seminary (Conservative)
www.jtsa.edu

American Jewish University (Conservative)
www.ajula.edu

College or graduate students may be able to find a rabbi through their local Hillel or by contacting Hillel at www.hillel.org.

If you are interested in a wedding that takes place in the wilderness, contact:

"Adventure Rabbi" Jamie Korngold,
www.adventurerabbi.com

"Torah Trek" Rabbi Mike Comins,
www.torahtrek.com/weddings.htm

Jewish Movements

As you plan your wedding, you may find yourself becoming interested in "synagogue shopping"—finding a congregation that matches you and your partner's needs. If you are curious about the differences between the major Jewish movements, you can begin by checking out their websites:

www.ou.org: Orthodox

www.youngisrael.org: Orthodox

www.aleph.org: Jewish Renewal

www.shj.org: Society for Humanistic Judaism

www.jrf.org: Reconstructionist

www.uscj.org: Conservative

www.rj.org: Reform

Gay/Lesbian Resources

www.glbtjews.org: The website for the World Congress of Gay, Lesbian, Bisexual and Transgender Jews.

www.gayweddings.com: This helpful site also delves into the enjoyable side of the wedding-planning process.

www.gaywedding.ca: This site helps couples plan weddings in Canada, where gay weddings are legal.

www.vermontgaytravel.com: This site helps couples who choose to marry in Vermont find wedding sites, officiants, and the like.

www.glaad.org: The Gay and Lesbian Alliance Against Defamation website provides helpful information for couples dealing with legal issues.

www.twobrides.com: Not just for ladies! This site helps gay, lesbian, bisexual, and transgender couples with everything from finding same-sex cake toppers to choosing a wedding site.

www.gayweddingplanners.com: Wedding consultants specializing in same-sex unions.

www.rainbowweddingnetwork.com: Featuring gay friendly wedding vendors.

www.gaymarriageworld.com: Featuring wedding vendors and stories.

www.gayrites.net: Financial and legal advice and wedding vendors.

Interfaith Resources

www.rcrconline.org: The Rabbinic Center for Research and Counseling helps interfaith couples find a rabbi to officiate at their wedding.

www.joi.org: The Jewish Outreach Institute also helps interfaith couples find a rabbi. The institute's website features a helpful question and answer page about interfaith marriage.

www.interfaithfamily.com: Many helpful articles, including some about marriage.

www.dovetailinstitute.org: Publisher specializing in articles and books about interfaith issues, including marriage.

Israeli Products

By purchasing Israeli products for your wedding—from *kippot* to kosher wines—you are helping to support Israel's sagging economy. A few helpful sites from Israel include:

www.rotem.net: This website features silver Judaica arts and crafts, such as *kiddush* cups and *mezuzot* by Israeli artists.

www.israeliproducts.com: This full-service site includes everything from books and music, to Judaica made in Israel, to popular beauty items, all shipped from Israel.

www.shopinisrael.com: This site supports the Israeli economy and includes flowers, wine, and business services by Israelis.

www.judaicaheaven.com: This Israeli site features lots of wedding-related products, including *ketubot* and *kippot*.

Tzedakah

These links can help you learn more about the Jewish *mitzvah* of *tzedakah*, as well as link you to organizations that you might want to give *tzedakah* to.

www.just-tzedakah.org: This fantastic site profiles Jewish charitable organizations and provides easy ways to give *tzedakah* online.

www.socialaction.com: This site includes a wealth of ideas about how to get involved in social-action projects and networks.

www.ziv.org: Gives great suggestions for incorporating *tzedakah* into your life and also profiles many interesting *tzedakah* projects.

www.ajritz.com: This website includes resources and links to other sites concerning *tzedakah*.

www.mazon.org: The website for the Jewish organization leading the fight against hunger in the United States, Israel, and around the world.

www.Idofoundation.org: When you sign up for a gift registry at this site, eight percent of the purchases will be donated to charity.

Jewish Learning

The following websites offer general information about the basics of Judaism.

www.myJewishlearning.com: Articles, recipes, and dialogues for folks new to Judaism as well as those with more Jewish knowledge.

www.jewfaq.org: Basic questions and terms and an online encyclopedia of Jewish facts.

www.ujc.org: The United Jewish Communities (Federation) home page offers news, a Jewish calendar, and information about topics ranging from Israel to social action.

www.shamash.org: The home page for the Jewish Internet network offers great links, discussion boards, and Jewish chat rooms.

Craft Supplies

The ideas in this book have hopefully inspired you to take on a creative project for your wedding. From stenciling a design for your *chuppah* to painting your *kippot*, the possibilities are only limited by your imagination. Fortunately, the Internet is a wonderful resource for excellent craft suppliers. A few of my favorites include two great art supply stores, now available online:

www.pearlpaint.com

www.utrechtart.com

For people planning to do some kind of fabric art, check out:

www.joann.com

www.handknitting.com

www.fiberartshop.com

For a discount art and craft supplier, check out:

www.factorydirectcraft.com

Eco-*kashrut*

www.jcarrot.org/category/eco-kashrut: The Jew and the Carrot web
site explores Judaism, food and sustainability.

Matchmakers/Singles Organizations

Since finishing the job of creating the world, it is said that God has been keeping
busy by making matches. In Jewish tradition, the matchmaker has always held an
honored position. Just because you are getting hitched, don't forget about your
single friends. Some helpful resources for Jewish dating online include:

www.jdate.com

www.jqs.com (Jewish Quality Singles)

www.thejewishpeople.org (Jewish Singles Connection)

Books

Judaism

Adler, Rachel. *Engendering Judaism: An Inclusive Theology and Ethics.* Boston: Beacon Press, 1999.

Bloch, Ariel, and Chana Bloch. *The Song of Songs: A New Translation with an Introduction and Commentary.* New York: Random House, 1995.

Diamant, Anita. *The New Jewish Wedding: Revised and Updated.* New York: Simon & Schuster, 2001.

Dobrinsky, Herbert C. *A Treasury of Sephardic Laws and Customs: The Ritual Practices of Syrian, Moroccan, Judeo-Spanish and Spanish and Portuguese Jews of North America.* New York: Yeshiva University Press, 1986.

Falk, Marcia. *Song of Songs: A New Translation.* San Francisco: HarperSanFrancisco, 1993.

Feld, Merle. *A Spiritual Life: A Jewish Feminist Journey.* Albany: State University of New York Press, 2000.

Fuchs-Kreimer, Nancy, and Nancy H. Wiener. *Judaism for Two: A Spiritual Guide for Strengthening and Celebrating Your Loving Relationship.* Woodstock, VT: Jewish Lights, 2005.

Gross, David C., ed. *Treasury of Jewish Love: Poems, Quotations and Proverbs in Hebrew, Yiddish, Ladino and English.* New York: Hippocrene Books, 1994.

Kaplan, Aryeh. *Made in Heaven: A Jewish Wedding Guide.* New York: Moznaim Publishing Corporation, 1983.

Kula, Irwin, and Vanessa L. Ochs. *The Book of Jewish Sacred Practices: CLAL's Guide to Everyday & Holiday Rituals & Blessings.* Woodstock, VT: Jewish Lights, 2001.

Matlins, Stuart M. *The Jewish Lights Spirituality Handbook: A Guide to Understanding, Exploring & Living a Spiritual Life.* Woodstock, VT: Jewish Lights, 2001.

Meszler, Joseph B. *A Man's Responsibility: A Jewish Guide to Being a Son, a Partner in Marriage, a Father and a Community Leader.* Woodstock, VT: Jewish Lights, 2008.

Milgram, Goldie. *Living Jewish Life Cycle: How to Create Meaningful Jewish Rites of Passage at Every Stage of Life*. Woodstock, VT: Jewish Lights, 2009.

Mitchell, Stephen. *A Book of Psalms: Selected and Adapted from the Hebrew*. New York: HarperCollins, 1994.

Olitzky, Kerry M., and Daniel Judson, eds. *The Rituals & Practices of a Jewish Life: A Handbook for Personal Spiritual Renewal*. Woodstock, VT: Jewish Lights, 2002.

Piercy, Marge. *The Art of Blessing the Day: Poems with a Jewish Theme*. New York: Knopf, 1999.

Rosenberg, David. *Blues of the Sky: Interpreted from the Original Hebrew Book of Psalms*. New York: Harper & Row, 1976.

Strassfeld, Michael. *A Book of Life: Embracing Judaism as a Spiritual Practice*. Woodstock, VT: Jewish Lights, 2006.

Syme, Daniel B. *The Jewish Wedding Book*. New York: Pharos Books, 1991.

Wiener, Nancy H. *Beyond Breaking the Glass: A Spiritual Guide to Your Jewish Wedding*. New York: CCAR Press, 2001.

Gay/Lesbian

Ayers, Tess, and Paul Brown. *The Essential Guide to Lesbian and Gay Weddings*. San Francisco: HarperSanFrancisco, 1999.

Butler, Becky, ed. *Ceremonies of the Heart: Celebrating Lesbian Unions*. 2nd Ed. Seattle: Seal Press, 1997.

Curry, Hayden, Denis Clifford, and Frederick Hertz. *A Legal Guide for Gay and Lesbian Couples*. 14th Ed. Berkeley, CA: Nolo Press, 2007.

David, K.C., *The Complete Guide to Gay and Lesbian Weddings*, New York: St. Martin's Griffin, 2005.

Feinsinger, Mary. *Kol Dodi: Jewish Music for Weddings*. New York: Transcontinental Music Publications, 2002.

Ochs, Vanessa. *Inventing Jewish Ritual*. Philadelphia: Jewish Publication Society, 2007.

Interfaith

Friedland, Ronnie, and Edmund Case, eds. *The Guide to Jewish Interfaith Family Life: An InterfaithFamily.com Handbook.* Woodstock, VT: Jewish Lights, 2001.

Lerner, Devon A. *Celebrating Interfaith Marriages: Creating Your Jewish/Chrisitan Ceremony.* New York: Henry Holt, 1999.

Olitzky, Kerry M. *Introducing My Faith and My Community: The Jewish Outreach Institute Guide for the Christian in a Jewish Interfaith Relationship.* Woodstock, VT: Jewish Lights, 2004.

——. *Making a Successful Jewish Interfaith Marriage: The Jewish Outreach Institute Guide to Opportunities, Challenges and Resolutions.* Woodstock, VT: Jewish Lights, 2003.

Petsonk, Judy, and Jim Remsen. *The Intermarriage Handbook: A Guide for Jews and Christians.* New York: HarperCollins Publishers, 1991.

Alternative/Creative

Claro, Danielle. *How to Have the Wedding You Want (Not the One Everybody Else Wants You to Have).* New York: Berkeley Publishing Group, 1995.

Cotner, June. *Wedding Blessings: Prayers and Poems Celebrating Love, Marriage and Anniversaries.* New York: Broadway, 2003.

Paffrath, April, and Laura McFadden. *The Artful Bride: Simple, Handmade Wedding Projects.* Gloucester, MA: Rockport Publishing, 2003.

Paul, Sheryl. *The Conscious Bride: Real Women Unveil Their Emotions about Getting Hitched.* Oakland, CA: New Harbinger Publications, 2000.

Ross-McDonald, Jane. *Alternative Weddings: An Essential Guide for Creating Your Own Ceremonies.* Dallas: Taylor Publishing, 1997.

Stallings, Ariel Meadow. *The Offbeat Bride: Taffeta-Free Alternatives for Independent Brides.* Berkeley, CA: Seal Press, 2006.

Jewish Art Books

Grossman, Grace Cohen, and Jacobo Furman. *Treasures of Jewish Art.* Santa Monica, CA: Beaux Arts Editions, 1997.

Shadur, Joseph, and Yehudit Shadur. *Traditional Jewish Papercuts: An Inner World of Art and Symbol.* Hanover, NH: University Press of New England, 2002.

Calligraphy

Kastin, Judy. *100 Keys to Great Calligraphy.* Cincinnati: North Light Books, 1996.

Shepherd, Margaret. *Learn Calligraphy: The Complete Book of Lettering and Design.* New York: Broadway Books, 2001.

Siegal, Richard, and Michael Strassfeld, eds. *The First Jewish Catalog: A Do-It-Yourself Kit.* Philadelphia: Jewish Publication Society, 1973.

Ketubah

Frankel, Ellen, and Betsy Platkin Teutsch. *The Encyclopedia of Jewish Symbols.* Lanham, MD: Rowman & Littlefield Publishers, 1996.

Nahson, Claudia J. *Ketubbot: Marriage Contracts from the Jewish Museum.* San Francisco: Pomegranate Press, 1998.

Sabar, Shalom. *Ketubbah: The Art of the Jewish Marriage Contract.* New York: Rizzoli International Publications, 2001.

———. *Ketubbah: Jewish Marriage Contracts of the Hebrew Union College Skirball Museum and Klau Library.* Philadelphia: Jewish Publication Society, 1990.

Judaism and Ecology Books

Benstein, Jeremy. *The Way Into Judaism and the Environment.* Woodstock, VT: Jewish Lights, 2008.

Bernstein, Ellen, ed. *Ecology and the Jewish Spirit: Where Nature and the Sacred Meet.* Woodstock, VT: Jewish Lights, 1998.

Isaacs, Ronald H., ed. *Jewish Sourcebook on the Environment and Ecology.* Northvale, N.J.: Jason Aronson, 1998.

Waskow, Arthur, ed. *Torah of the Earth: Exploring 4,000 Years of Ecology in Jewish Thought.* Vol. 1: Biblical/Rabbinic; Vol. 2: Zionism/Eco-Judaism. Woodstock, VT: Jewish Lights, 2000.

Appendix II
Wedding Planning

Timeline

These days, many couples have a long engagement for a variety of reasons—they're in college or graduate school, relocating, or working out how to combine families from previous marriages. One advantage of a long engagement is that it gives you the opportunity to create your wedding gradually, without the stress of rushing.

Here is a general timeline for wedding preparations based on a year-long engagement. If your engagement is going to be longer or shorter, you can adjust these guidelines according to your needs and work from there.

One Year in Advance

Jewish Issues

- Consult a Jewish calendar and select a wedding date.

- Clear the wedding date with the synagogue (if the wedding will take place there).

- Begin the process of finding an officiant.

- Read the *ketubah* chapter of this book and start browsing through art books and looking at lithographs.

Creative Planning

- Purchase a special wedding journal for your visualization exercises and other notes.

- Make a list of your creative friends and relatives and how they might help in your wedding planning.

- Let yourself daydream and "see" the wedding you hope to create.

Practical Concerns

- Talk about the size wedding you want.

- If you and your partner's families haven't met yet, plan an occasion for them to do so.

- Create a realistic budget and have a straightforward conversation with parents about who is paying for what.

- Visit caterers and reception sites.

- Talk to friends and get references for various wedding vendors: florists, photographers, musicians, and so on.

Nine Months in Advance

Jewish Issues

- Select your rabbi/cantor and set up appointments with him for premarital counseling and ceremony planning.

- Start reading and talking about the elements and rituals connected to the Jewish wedding ceremony.

- Interfaith couples (and other couples wanting to expand their Jewish education) may want to sign up for an introduction to Judaism class at a local synagogue or community center.

Creative Planning

- Determine whether or not you will commission an original *ketubah* design; if so, choose an artist and contact her as soon as possible (you may want to talk with several artists about their methods and prices before selecting one).

- Decide which kind of *chuppah* you would like. Are you going to make it or involve family/friends in making it? This is the time to ask for help and make arrangements for its construction.

- Draft sample wording for invitations. Think about invitation design, color, and paper.

- Listen to some Jewish music and get a sense of which styles/genres of music you prefer.

Practical Concerns

- Finalize arrangements for your reception site, synagogue (if the wedding is taking place there), caterer, photographer, and videographer.

- Talk to friends whom you wish to be attendants and/or help out with your wedding in any way.

- Contact a local hotel and reserve a block of rooms for your out-of-town guests.

- Start thinking about any honeymoon/travel plans.

- Gay and lesbian couples should hire a lawyer to deal with legal issues, including power-of-attorney, wills, and health care directives.

Six Months in Advance

Jewish Issues

- Set aside time in your schedule each week to talk with your partner about ideas for your ceremony.

- Read Jewish poetry, listen to Jewish music, and immerse yourselves in other Jewish arts that might enrich your ceremony.

- Make a list of questions related to Jewish wedding customs, rituals, or traditions and ask your rabbi/cantor for answers.

- Think about ways you might incorporate *tzedakah* (sacred giving) into your wedding.

Creative Planning

- If you are planning to write your own *ketubah* text or other personal vows, start working on it.

- Start putting together a wedding website (if you desire).

- Finalize plans for your invitations: start making them or place your order.

- Check in on the progress of your *ketubah* and/or *chuppah*.

Practical Concerns

- Hire musicians and/or DJ.

- Create a gift registry (if you desire).

- Make up your guest list and ask parents to do so as well (if applicable); enter names into a database.

- Start shopping for wedding clothes and rings.

- Make firm travel plans for your honeymoon.

- Make arrangements with a florist, cake maker, and any other professionals you may need.

- If you are hosting a rehearsal dinner, reserve a space and choose a menu. If parents are hosting the dinner, hand all related tasks over to them.

Three Months in Advance

Jewish Issues

- Select ritual objects for use in the ceremony (*kiddush* cups, *kippot*, and so on).

- Decide which pre-wedding rituals you want, such as visiting a *mikvah* and holding an *aufruf*.

- If you would like to do an *aufruf*, check with your rabbi about arrangements. It is customary for the couple to host a *kiddush* lunch after the service.

Creative Planning

- Launch your wedding website and let guests know about it through e-mail.

- Sit down with your musicians and/or DJ and go through all your music requests (be sure to give them a written copy).

- Check on *ketubah* and/or *chuppah* progress.

- Think about any other creative "details" you might want to incorporate, from centerpieces to decorated *kippot*.

- Start drafting the wedding program text.

Practical Concerns

- Get dresses, suits, and headpieces to a seamstress for any alterations.

- Check in with the hotel to make sure that room blocks are set for your guests.

- Address invitations and determine when to mail them (they should go out six to eight weeks in advance of the wedding).

- Purchase or order rings.

One Month in Advance

Jewish Issues

- If you are participating in an *aufruf,* make sure that you know the *aliyah* blessing.

- Go through the ceremony's outline with the wedding officiant.

- Make arrangements for any other Jewish rituals—contact a local *mikvah,* for example. Talk about whether or not you are going to fast on the day of your wedding.

Creative Planning

- Write up the wedding program and add design elements as you choose.

- Review your *ketubah* text to make sure that everything is correct.

- Check in on any other creative projects that friends are handling.

Practical Concerns

- Find out from local officials when you need to get your marriage license.

- Make transportation arrangements for you and your partner for the wedding day (limo? friends? arrive separately/together?).

- Make doctors' appointments for blood work if your state mandates it.

- Tally RSVPs and ask someone (such as an attendant or your mom) to contact any slackers.

- Create table seating arrangements (unless you prefer open seating).

- Purchase (or make) gifts for attendants, helpers, parents, and the rabbi.

- Make hair and makeup appointments. (Tip: If you can schedule a massage for as close to your wedding date as possible, it will really be worth it!)

- Confirm all plans with your professionals—make sure the photographers/videographers, in particular, know what your wishes are.

- Pick up your wedding clothes from the seamstress.

One Week in Advance

Jewish Issues

- Make time for daily prayer, meditation, walking, or another personal ritual that keeps you spiritually grounded and calm.

- Contact the wedding officiant with any last-minute questions or concerns.

Creative Planning

- Arrange for wedding programs to be picked up and brought to the ceremony.

- Check in to make sure that anyone who is doing a song, a reading, or a prayer for your wedding is all set (and is bringing his or her own copy of sheet music, for example).

- Arrange for the *chuppah* to be set up and taken down, as needed.

Practical Concerns

- Take care of the marriage license and rings.

- Pack for the honeymoon.

- Eat, get some sleep, and don't let any "well-meaning" advice-givers get you down!

- Make some time to connect with each other, even if it means shutting a door and letting the telephone ring. It's okay!

Wedding Task Checklist

In addition to the timeline above, the following task checklist can help you feel on top of things just before and on your wedding day, so that you can relax and trust that everything will fall beautifully into place. Traditionally, particular wedding-related tasks—such as keeping track of the wedding rings—belong to the best man and maid/matron of honor. If you have assembled a wedding *havurah* of your friends, you may want to divide up these tasks among the group. Delegate what you can; it's a lot of stuff to think about and you want to avoid getting so exhausted before your wedding day that you won't be able to be really present.

Before the Wedding

- Pick up out-of-town guests at the train station/airport.
- Drop off welcome bags at the hotel.
- Photocopy the wedding programs and/or pick them up at the printers.
- Make sure candy is ready for an *aufruf*.
- Check in with all vendors: flowers, cake, band, photographer, videographer, hairdressers, and caterers.
- Pick up wedding clothes from seamstress/dry cleaner and get them to the bride and groom.
- Make sure the rabbi/cantor is clear on directions and time.
- Pick up rings from the jeweler/engraver and bring them to the ceremony.
- Arrange for transportation from the wedding to the reception for the bride and groom if you are in two different locations.

On the Wedding Day

- Transport and set up the *chuppah* canopy and poles at the wedding site.
- Take the *ketubah* to the wedding site and supply pens for signing it.

- Bring glass(es) for breaking to the ceremony. (Be sure to assign one attendant to pick up the glass and save it in a small bag for later.)

- Bring *kiddush* cups and kosher wine to the wedding site; pour wine ahead of time.

- Stand outside the *yihud* space to keep it private for the couple.

- Pack up wedding presents and drop them off at the bride and groom's home or hotel.

- Collect wedding gifts in check or cash form.

Don't let the details get you down! Creating a *kavannah* (sacred intention) will help you remember the sacredness in talking with your vendors, asking friends for help, and giving careful thought to family and financial decisions that will affect the kind of wedding you hope to create. Hold on to your big vision, even as you work on the little stuff. Let your vision guide you, and know that each small step you take will contribute to helping your wedding dream come to be.

Creating a Wedding Website

The Internet has, indeed, revolutionized the way we communicate. This wonderful tool can help you immensely when planning your wedding. Not only is creating a wedding website lots of fun, but it is also an inexpensive way for you to let your guests know the basics about your wedding, including directions and hotels. By not having to photocopy and mail out hard copies of maps and hotel and tourist information, you will save a significant amount on postage. Your wedding website is also a great way to get people excited about your big event months in advance. When people finally come together for the big day, they'll feel thoroughly prepared for the wedding and affiliated events.

If you are going to have guests from a range of backgrounds and cultures, you can share some basic information about Jewish weddings on your site and even include some links to Jewish-related websites, so that everyone can learn a bit about the customs and rituals they will experience. Having a "refresher" will also help Jewish friends and relatives who have not had much Jewish education appreciate the time and thought you have put into your ceremony.

You don't need to spend a lot of money—or any money at all—on buying a domain name for your website. Most e-mail servers, such as Yahoo and Juno, have free or very cheap ways for members to create a web page. If you already have a website for a business or hobby, think about creating a separate page on that existing site for your wedding website. Friends and relatives may also have site domains and might be more than happy to host your site for a few months. If these options don't work out for you, check out www.theknot.com.

Important information to include on your wedding website:

- Directions (include links such as www.expedia.com, www.mapquest.com, and www.amtrak.com)

- Transportation: the closest airport, train station, and bus terminal to the wedding

- Basic information about Jewish weddings

- Schedule of events (include times and locations for the *aufruf*, rehearsal dinner, *ketubah* signing, and other events)

- Registry links

- Fun stuff (pictures, family bios)

- Basic information on the town/city where the wedding is being held, such as hotels and any special rates, restaurant recommendations, and points of interest

Appendix III
Alternative Sheva Brachot

Praised are You, Source of Creation, creator of wine, drink of joy.

Praised are You, Source of Creation, all of creation reflects your Glory!

Praised are You, Source of Creation, giving life to each human being.

Praised are You, Source of Creation, You made us in Your image, to live, love and perpetuate life.

Praised are You, Source of all Blessings, You give life to every being.

We hope that there will come a day when you will walk together in the land of Israel, and that it will be a land of peace, not a barren land, that will open its arms to receive you. Holy One of blessing, You make Zion rejoice with her children!

May these cherished friends rejoice with each other, as did the first man and the first woman in the Garden of Eden. Holy One of blessing, You radiate joy for *chatan* and *kallah*.

Praised are You, Creator of joy and gladness, bride and groom, mirth and song, delight and rejoicing. May there always be heard in our streets and our cities, voices of joy and gladness, voices of bride and groom; the jubilant voices of those joined in marriage, under the *chuppah*, the voices of young people feasting and singing!

Praised are You Adonai, Who causes the *chatan* to rejoice with the *kallah*.
—translated by Rabbi Marcia Prager

Baruch ata Yah, Elohaynu ruach haOlam, shehakol bara lichvodo.
Blessed are You, Yah, our God, Breathing Spirit of the world, Who infuses Radiance into all being.

Brucha at Yah, Elohaynu ruach haOlam, yotzeret haAdam.
Blessed are You, Yah, our God, Breathing Spirit of the world, Who shapes in earthiness the human spirit.

Baruch ata Yah, Elohaynu ruach haOlam, asher yatzar et haAdam b'tzalmo, b'tzelem d'mut tavnito, v'hitkin lo mimenu binyan aday ad. Brucha at Yah, yotzeret haAdam.
Blessed are You, Yah, our God, Breathing Spirit of the world, Who shapes humanity in your image and likeness and enables us to renew creation by nurturing generations to come. Blessed are You, Yah, Who shapes in earthiness the human spirit.

Sos tasis v'tagel haAkarah b'kibbutz baneha l'tochah b'simcha. Brucha at Yah, m'samachat Tziyon b'vaneha.
May all who are deeply rooted rejoice, for those they nourish will spring up to flower and be fruitful. Blessed are You, Yah, Who gladdens Zion with her offspring.

Samayach t'samach rayim haAhuvim, k'samaychacha y'tzircha b'gan ayden mikedem. Brucha at Yah, m'samachat dodim b'ahavatam.

May these loving companions rejoice as did God's first companions in the Garden of Edenic Delight. Blessed are You, Yah, Who enables lovers to rejoice in their love.

Baruch atah Yah, Elohaynu ruach haOlam, asher bara sason v'simcha, y'didah v'ahuvah, gilah, rinah, ditzah, v'chedvah, ahavah, v'achavah, shalom v'rayut. M'hayra yishama b'aray Yehudah uv'chutzot Yerushalayim: kol sason v'kol simcha, kol ahuvah v'kol y'dida, kol mitzhalot ahuvim maychupatam, v'shirei shalom mimishtay n'ginatam. Brucha at Yah, m'samachat dodim b'ahavatam.

Blessed are You, Yah, our God, Breathing Spirit of the World, creator of joy and gladness, of soulmate and beloved, of merriment, song, dance and delight, of love and harmony, of peace and companionship. May all soon hear in the cities of Judah and in the courtyards of Jerusalem, the voices of joy and rejoicing, the voices of lover and beloved, the sound of lovers' jubilation from their *chuppah*, the celebratory songs of peace. Blessed are You, Yah, Who enables lovers to rejoice in their love.

Brucha at Yah, Elohaynu ruach haOlam, boreyt p'ri hagafen.

Blessed are You, Yah, Our God, Breathing Spirit of the world, Creator of the fruit of the vine.

—Hebrew and English by Rabbi Arthur Ocean Waskow
and Phyllis Ocean Berman

Index

for same-sex couples, 50–51
students making, 44
symbols on, 52–53
thank you notes and, 58
visualizing, 42
wording options for, 44–48
Yiddish poetry on, 51
Israeli folk music, 158–159
Israeli products, 231

Credits

Every effort has been made to trace and acknowledge copyright holders of all material used in this book. The publisher apologizes for any errors or omissions that may remain, and asks that any omissions be brought to their attention so they may be corrected in future editions.

Cover Images

Ketubah (front and spine): "Allen/Volin Ketubah," 2003, by Anna Fine Foer (www.annafineart.com). See p. 79 for more about her work.

Ketubot (back cover): "The Kiss" by Nishima; used by permission of the artist. "A Good Company" interfaith *ketubah*; used by permission of A Good Company.

Interior Images

Page 43: © Jonathan Kremer. All rights reserved

Page 49: © Jonathan Kremer. All rights reserved

Page 52: © Susan Leviton, Levworks 1996. Contact: Levworks, 3417 N. 4th St., Harrisburg, PA 17110; (717) 236-0231; gorelev@aol.com

Page 53: © Jonathan Kremer. All rights reserved

Page 80: © Jonathan Kremer. All rights reserved

Page 82: © Marc Barag; (215) 848-6391

Page 85: Courtesy of Nishima; used by permission of the artist

Page 89: Courtesy of Nishima; used by permission of the artist

Page 97: Courtesy of Elsa Wachs; used by permission of the artist

Page 103: Courtesy of Elsa Wachs; used by permission of the artist

Page 109: Courtesy of Joellyn Wallen Zollman; used by permission

Page 127: Courtesy Charles Gehret Photography; used by permission

Page 128: Photograph by Merlin Detroff Photography, courtesy of Rebecca Rund; used by permission of Rebecca Rund

Page 161: Wallen/Zollman program courtesy of Joellyn Wallen Zollman; used by permission. Taubman/Schwartz program © Jonathan Kremer. All rights reserved.

Page 191: Photograph by Elizabeth Reade, courtesy of Eva Sari Schweber; used by permission of Eva Sari Schweber

Page 194: Chuppah designed and sewn by Natalie Schriger; used by permission of Shoshanah Feher Sternlieb, PhD

Page 195: Photograph by Elizabeth Reade, courtesy of Eva Sari Schweber; used by permission of Eva Sari Schweber

Page 199: Photograph by Elizabeth Reade, courtesy of Eva Sari Schweber; used by permission of Eva Sari Schweber

Page 201: Photograph by Merlin Detroff Photography, courtesy of Rebecca Rund; used by permission of Rebecca Rund

Page 210: Courtesy of Jane Berman; used by permission

Meditation

The Handbook of Jewish Meditation Practices: A Guide for Enriching the Sabbath and Other Days of Your Life   *By Rabbi David A. Cooper* Easy-to-learn meditation techniques.
6 x 9, 208 pp, Quality PB, 978-1-58023-102-2 **$16.95**

Discovering Jewish Meditation: Instruction & Guidance for Learning an Ancient Spiritual Practice
By Nan Fink Gefen Helps readers on any level of understanding learn the ancient practice of Jewish meditation on their own.   6 x 9, 208 pp, Quality PB, 978-1-58023-067-4 **$16.95**

A Heart of Stillness: A Complete Guide to Learning the Art of Meditation   *By David A. Cooper*
5½ x 8½, 272 pp, Quality PB, 978-1-893361-03-4 **$16.95**   *(A book from SkyLight Paths, Jewish Lights' sister imprint)*

Jewish Meditation Practices for Everyday Life: Awakening Your Heart, Connecting with God
By Rabbi Jeff Roth Offers a fresh take on meditation that draws on life experience and living life with great clarity rather than the traditional method of rigorous study.   6 x 9, 224 pp, Quality PB Original, 978-1-58023-397-2 **$18.99**

Meditation from the Heart of Judaism: Today's Teachers Share Their Practices, Techniques, and Faith
Edited by Avram Davis 6 x 9, 256 pp, Quality PB, 978-1-58023-049-0 **$16.95**

Silence, Simplicity & Solitude: A Complete Guide to Spiritual Retreat at Home   *By David A. Cooper*
5½ x 8½, 336 pp, Quality PB, 978-1-893361-04-1 **$16.95**   *(A book from SkyLight Paths, Jewish Lights' sister imprint)*

Ritual/Sacred Practice

The Jewish Dream Book: The Key to Opening the Inner Meaning of Your Dreams
By Vanessa L. Ochs with Elizabeth Ochs; Full-color illus. by Kristina Swarner
Instructions for how modern people can perform ancient Jewish dream practices and dream interpretations drawn from the Jewish wisdom tradition.   8 x 8, 128 pp, Full-color illus., Deluxe PB w/flaps, 978-1-58023-132-9 **$16.95**

God in Your Body: Kabbalah, Mindfulness and Embodied Spiritual Practice   *By Jay Michaelson*
The first comprehensive treatment of the body in Jewish spiritual practice and an essential guide to the sacred.
6 x 9, 288 pp, Quality PB, 978-1-58023-304-0 **$18.99**

The Book of Jewish Sacred Practices: CLAL's Guide to Everyday & Holiday Rituals & Blessings
Edited by Rabbi Irwin Kula and Vanessa L. Ochs, PhD 6 x 9, 368 pp, Quality PB, 978-1-58023-152-7 **$18.95**

Jewish Ritual: A Brief Introduction for Christians
By Rabbi Kerry M. Olitzky and Rabbi Daniel Judson 5½ x 8½, 144 pp, Quality PB, 978-1-58023-210-4 **$14.99**

The Rituals & Practices of a Jewish Life: A Handbook for Personal Spiritual Renewal
Edited by Rabbi Kerry M. Olitzky and Rabbi Daniel Judson Each chapter explores a different ritual or practice in depth and explains the why, what, and how to do it.   6 x 9, 272 pp, illus., Quality PB, 978-1-58023-169-5 **$18.95**

The Sacred Art of Lovingkindness: Preparing to Practice   *By Rabbi Rami Shapiro*
5½ x 8½, 176 pp, Quality PB, 978-1-59473-151-8 **$16.99**   *(A book from SkyLight Paths, Jewish Lights' sister imprint)*

Or phone, fax, mail or e-mail to: **JEWISH LIGHTS** Publishing
Sunset Farm Offices, Route 4 • P.O. Box 237 • Woodstock, Vermont 05091
Tel: (802) 457-4000 • Fax: (802) 457-4004 • www.jewishlights.com
Credit card orders: (800) 962-4544 (8:30AM–5:30PM ET Monday–Friday)
Generous discounts on quantity orders. SATISFACTION GUARANTEED. Prices subject to change.

Spirituality/Women's Interest

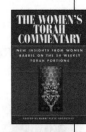

The Quotable Jewish Woman: Wisdom, Inspiration & Humor from the Mind & Heart *Edited and compiled by Elaine Bernstein Partnow* More than 2,000 quotes culled from over 250 Jewish women of different countries and backgrounds who share their insights on a wide range of topics.
6 x 9, 496 pp, Quality PB, 978-1-58023-236-4 **$19.99**; HC, 978-1-58023-193-0 **$29.99**

The Divine Feminine in Biblical Wisdom Literature: Selections Annotated & Explained
Translated and Annotated by Rabbi Rami Shapiro 5½ x 8½, 240 pp, Quality PB, 978-1-59473-109-9 **$16.99**
(A book from SkyLight Paths, Jewish Lights' sister imprint)

The Women's Haftarah Commentary: New Insights from Women Rabbis on the 54 Weekly Haftarah Portions, the 5 Megillot & Special Shabbatot *Edited by Rabbi Elyse Goldstein*
6 x 9, 560 pp, Quality PB, 978-1-58023-371-2 **$19.99**; HC, 978-1-58023-133-6 **$39.99**

The Women's Torah Commentary: New Insights from Women Rabbis on the 54 Weekly Torah Portions
Edited by Rabbi Elyse Goldstein 6 x 9, 496 pp, Quality PB, 978-1-58023-370-5 **$19.99**; HC, 978-1-58023-076-6 **$34.95**

The Year Mom Got Religion: One Woman's Midlife Journey into Judaism
By Lee Meyerhoff Hendler 6 x 9, 208 pp, Quality PB, 978-1-58023-070-4 **$15.95**

See Holidays for *The Women's Passover Companion: Women's Reflections on the Festival of Freedom* and *The Women's Seder Sourcebook: Rituals & Readings for Use at the Passover Seder.*

Spirituality / Crafts

(from SkyLight Paths, Jewish Lights sister imprint)

The Knitting Way: A Guide to Spiritual Self-Discovery
By Linda Skolnick and Janice MacDaniels 7 x 9, 240 pp, Quality PB, 978-1-59473-079-5 **$16.99**

The Quilting Path: A Guide to Spiritual Self-Discovery through Fabric, Thread and Kabbalah
By Louise Silk 7 x 9, 192 pp, Quality PB, 978-1-59473-206-5 **$16.99**

The Painting Path: Embodying Spiritual Discovery through Yoga, Brush and Color
By Linda Novick; Foreword by Richard Segalman Explores the divine connection you can experience through art.
7 x 9, 208 pp, 8-page full-color insert, Quality PB, 978-1-59473-226-3 **$18.99**

The Scrapbooking Journey: A Hands-On Guide to Spiritual Discovery
By Cory Richardson-Lauve; Foreword by Stacy Julian Reveals how this craft can become a practice used to deepen and shape your life. 7 x 9, 176 pp, 8-page full-color insert, b/w photos, Quality PB, 978-1-59473-216-4 **$18.99**

Travel

Israel—A Spiritual Travel Guide, 2nd Edition: A Companion for the Modern Jewish Pilgrim
By Rabbi Lawrence A. Hoffman 4¾ x 10, 256 pp, Quality PB, illus., 978-1-58023-261-6 **$18.99**
Also Available: **The Israel Mission Leader's Guide** 978-1-58023-085-8 **$4.95**

12-Step

100 Blessings Every Day: Daily Twelve Step Recovery Affirmations, Exercises for Personal Growth & Renewal Reflecting Seasons of the Jewish Year
By Rabbi Kerry M. Olitzky; Foreword by Rabbi Neil Gillman 4½ x 6½, 432 pp, Quality PB, 978-1-879045-30-9 **$16.99**

Recovery from Codependence: A Jewish Twelve Steps Guide to Healing Your Soul
By Rabbi Kerry M. Olitzky 6 x 9, 160 pp, Quality PB, 978-1-879045-32-3 **$13.95**

Twelve Jewish Steps to Recovery: A Personal Guide to Turning from Alcoholism & Other Addictions— Drugs, Food, Gambling, Sex ... *By Rabbi Kerry M. Olitzky and Stuart A. Copans, MD; Preface by Abraham J. Twerski, MD*
6 x 9, 144 pp, Quality PB, 978-1-879045-09-5 **$15.99**

Holidays/Holy Days

Rosh Hashanah Readings: Inspiration, Information and Contemplation
Yom Kippur Readings: Inspiration, Information and Contemplation
Edited by Rabbi Dov Peretz Elkins with Section Introductions from Arthur Green's These Are the Words
An extraordinary collection of readings, prayers and insights that enable the modern worshiper to enter into the spirit of the High Holy Days in a personal and powerful way, permitting the meaning of the Jewish New Year to enter the heart. RHR: 6 x 9, 400 pp, HC, 978-1-58023-239-5 **$24.99**
YKR: 6 x 9, 368 pp, HC, 978-1-58023-271-5 **$24.99**

Jewish Holidays: A Brief Introduction for Christians
By Rabbi Kerry M. Olitzky and Rabbi Daniel Judson 5½ x 8½, 144 pp, Quality PB, 978-1-58023-302-6 **$16.99**

Reclaiming Judaism as a Spiritual Practice: Holy Days and Shabbat
By Rabbi Goldie Milgram 7 x 9, 272 pp, Quality PB, 978-1-58023-205-0 **$19.99**

7th Heaven: Celebrating Shabbat with Rebbe Nachman of Breslov
By Moshe Mykoff with the Breslov Research Institute 5⅛ x 8¼, 224 pp, Deluxe PB w/flaps, 978-1-58023-175-6 **$18.95**

Shabbat, 2nd Edition: The Family Guide to Preparing for and Celebrating the Sabbath
By Dr. Ron Wolfson 7 x 9, 320 pp, illus., Quality PB, 978-1-58023-164-0 **$19.99**

Hanukkah, 2nd Edition: The Family Guide to Spiritual Celebration
By Dr. Ron Wolfson. Edited by Joel Lurie Grishaver. 7 x 9, 240 pp, illus., Quality PB, 978-1-58023-122-0 **$18.95**

The Jewish Family Fun Book, 2nd Edition: Holiday Projects, Everyday Activities, and Travel Ideas with Jewish Themes *By Danielle Dardashti and Roni Sarig. Illus. by Avi Katz.*
6 x 9, 304 pp, 70+ b/w illus. & diagrams, Quality PB, 978-1-58023-333-0 **$18.99**

The Jewish Lights Book of Fun Classroom Activities: Simple and Seasonal Projects for Teachers and Students *By Danielle Dardashti and Roni Sarig* 6 x 9, 240 pp, Quality PB, 978-1-58023-206-7 **$19.99**

Passover

My People's Passover Haggadah: Traditional Texts, Modern Commentaries
Edited by Rabbi Lawrence A. Hoffman, PhD, and David Arnow, PhD
A diverse and exciting collection of commentaries on the traditional Passover Haggadah—in two volumes!
Vol. 1: 7 x 10, 304 pp, HC, 978-1-58023-354-5 **$24.99**   Vol. 2: 7 x 10, 320 pp, HC, 978-1-58023-346-0 **$24.99**

Leading the Passover Journey: The Seder's Meaning Revealed, the Haggadah's Story Retold
By Rabbi Nathan Laufer Uncovers the hidden meaning of the Seder's rituals and customs.
6 x 9, 224 pp, Quality PB, 978-1-58023-399-6 **$18.99**; HC, 978-1-58023-211-1 **$24.99**

The Women's Passover Companion: Women's Reflections on the Festival of Freedom
Edited by Rabbi Sharon Cohen Anisfeld, Tara Mohr, and Catherine Spector Captures the voices of Jewish women—rabbis, scholars, activists, political leaders and artists—who engage in a provocative conversation about the themes of the Exodus and exile, oppression and liberation, history and memory, as they relate to contemporary women's lives. 6 x 9, 352 pp, Quality PB, 978-1-58023-231-9 **$19.99**

The Women's Seder Sourcebook: Rituals & Readings for Use at the Passover Seder
Edited by Rabbi Sharon Cohen Anisfeld, Tara Mohr, and Catherine Spector An unprecedented and powerful resource for those planning a women's seder and those seeking to infuse their Passover celebration with the creative and courageous voices of Jewish women. 6 x 9, 384 pp, Quality PB, 978-1-58023-232-6 **$19.99**

Creating Lively Passover Seders: A Sourcebook of Engaging Tales, Texts & Activities
By David Arnow, PhD 7 x 9, 416 pp, Quality PB, 978-1-58023-184-8 **$24.99**

Passover, 2nd Edition: The Family Guide to Spiritual Celebration
By Dr. Ron Wolfson with Joel Lurie Grishaver 7 x 9, 352 pp, Quality PB, 978-1-58023-174-9 **$19.95**